Android 9 Development Cookbook
Cookbook
Third Edition

Over 100 recipes and solutions to solve the most common problems faced by Android developers

Rick Boyer

BIRMINGHAM - MUMBAI

Android 9 Development Cookbook
Third Edition

Commissioning Editor: Amarabha Banerjee
Acquisition Editor: Larissa Pinto
Content Development Editor: Francis Carneiro
Technical Editor: Ralph Rosario
Copy Editor: Safis Editing
Project Coordinator: Sheejal Shah
Proofreader: Safis Editing
Indexer: Priyanka Dhadke
Graphics: Alishon Mendonsa
Production Coordinator: Nilesh Mohite

First published: July 2011
Second edition: March 2016
Third edition: October 2018

Production reference: 2091118

Published by Packt Publishing Ltd.
Livery Place
35 Livery Street
Birmingham
B3 2PB, UK.

ISBN 978-1-78899-121-6

www.packtpub.com

To my family for their patience while I focused on writing. To my mom, who is very excited about the book, even though she uses a phone from a different (unnamed) platform. And of course, to my wife Karen, for her encouragement and understanding!

`mapt.io`

Mapt is an online digital library that gives you full access to over 5,000 books and videos, as well as industry leading tools to help you plan your personal development and advance your career. For more information, please visit our website.

Why subscribe?

- Spend less time learning and more time coding with practical eBooks and Videos from over 4,000 industry professionals

- Improve your learning with Skill Plans built especially for you

- Get a free eBook or video every month

- Mapt is fully searchable

- Copy and paste, print, and bookmark content

Packt.com

Did you know that Packt offers eBook versions of every book published, with PDF and ePub files available? You can upgrade to the eBook version at `www.packt.com` and as a print book customer, you are entitled to a discount on the eBook copy. Get in touch with us at `customercare@packtpub.com` for more details.

At `www.packt.com`, you can also read a collection of free technical articles, sign up for a range of free newsletters, and receive exclusive discounts and offers on Packt books and eBooks.

Contributors

About the author

Rick Boyer has been programming professionally for over 20 years. He has written apps on Windows, created websites, and coded for various mobile devices, including Windows CE, Windows Phone, and Android. Almost eight years ago, he took the plunge and started his own software consulting business, NightSky Development, focusing exclusively on Android development.

I'd like to thank all the people at Packt Publishing for making this update to the book possible! A special thanks to the content development editor, Francis Carneiro, for his tireless efforts at keeping the book schedule. I'd also like to thank Emil Atanasov and Jason Morris for their technical review work. Your comments and corrections were much appreciated and made for a better book!

About the reviewers

Emil Atanasov is an IT consultant who has extensive experience with mobile technologies. He runs his own contracting and consulting company, serving clients from around the world: Appose Studio Inc. He is an MSc graduate of RWTH Aachen University, Germany, and Sofia University "St. Kliment Ohridski", Bulgaria. He has been a contractor for several large companies in the U.S. and U.K., serving variously as team leader, project manager, iOS developer, and Android developer. He teaches courses at Sofia University in Swift and iOS development. He is the author of *Learn Swift by Building Applications* and has served as technical reviewer and contributor on the following Packt titles: *Objective C Memory Management* and *Android High-Performance Programming*.

> *"I want to thank my wife, Elena, and my daughter, Sophia, and the rest of my family and friends for being very supportive, really patient, and super cool. Thank you for keeping me motivated through the endless working days. I know that, in your eyes, I'm a bizarre geeky person who is spending most of the time in the digital world. I appreciate your understanding. Thank you, guys!"*

Jason Morris is a multi-discipline software developer and technical author. He has been developing software for as long as he can remember. He's written software for desktop, servers, feature phones, smartphones, the web, and even microcontrollers. Jason programs in a range of programming languages, and delights in knowing how software works. When he's not writing code, spending time with his family, or playing synthesizers, he's probably dreaming up a new code challenge. In 2010 through 2011, he wrote *Android User Interface Development: A Beginner's Guide*, and in 2017, he wrote *Hands-On Android UI Development*. On the internet, Jason is often known as "lemnik."

> *Thanks again to my wife and daughter for always being there.*

Packt is searching for authors like you

If you're interested in becoming an author for Packt, please visit `authors.packtpub.com` and apply today. We have worked with thousands of developers and tech professionals, just like you, to help them share their insight with the global tech community. You can make a general application, apply for a specific hot topic that we are recruiting an author for, or submit your own idea.

Table of Contents

Preface   1

Chapter 1: Activities   7
  Introduction   7
  Declaring an activity   8
    Getting ready   8
    How to do it...   9
    How it works...   14
  Starting a new activity with an intent object   14
    Getting ready   15
    How to do it...   15
    How it works...   17
    There's more...   18
    See also   18
  Switching between activities   18
    Getting ready   18
    How to do it...   19
    How it works...   22
    See also   22
  Passing data to another activity   23
    Getting ready   23
    How to do it...   23
    How it works...   24
    There's more...   25
  Returning a result from an activity   25
    Getting ready   25
    How to do it...   25
    How it works...   26
    There's more...   27
    See also   27
  Saving an activity's state   27
    Getting ready   28
    How to do it...   29
    How it works...   30
    There's more...   30
    See also   31
  Storing persistent activity data   31
    Getting ready   31
    How to do it...   31
    How it works...   32

There's more...   32
    Using more than one preference file   32
See also   32
Understanding the activity life cycle   33
Getting ready   34
How to do it...   34
How it works...   35
There's more...   36

Chapter 2: Layouts   37
Introduction   37
Defining and inflating a layout   38
Getting ready   39
How to do it...   39
How it works...   40
There's more...   41
See also   41
Using RelativeLayout   41
Getting ready   41
How to do it...   41
How it works...   42
There's more...   43
See also   43
Using LinearLayout   44
Getting ready   44
How to do it...   44
How it works...   45
There's more...   46
See also   46
Creating tables – TableLayout and GridLayout   46
Getting ready   47
How to do it...   47
How it works...   50
There's more...   50
RecyclerView replaces ListView   51
Getting ready   52
How to do it...   52
How it works...   55
There's more...   56
Changing layout properties during runtime   56
Getting ready   57
How to do it...   57
How it works...   58

Chapter 3: Views, Widgets, and Styles   59
Introduction   59

Inserting a widget into a layout   61
  Getting ready   61
  How to do it...   62
  How it works...   65
  There's more...   66
  See also   66
Using graphics to show button state   66
  Getting ready   67
  How to do it...   67
  How it works...   68
  There's more...   69
    Using designated folders for screen-specific resources   69
  See also   69
Creating a widget at runtime   70
  Getting ready   70
  How to do it...   70
  How it works...   71
  There's more...   71
Creating a custom component   71
  Getting ready   72
  How to do it...   72
  How it works...   73
  There's more...   74
  See also   75
Applying a style to a View   75
  Getting ready   75
  How to do it...   76
  How it works...   77
  There's more...   77
  See also   78
Turning a style into a theme   78
  Getting ready   78
  How to do it...   79
  How it works...   79
  There's more...   80
Selecting a theme based on the Android version   80
  Getting ready   80
  How to do it...   81
  How it works...   83
  There's more...   84

Chapter 4: Menus and Action Mode   85
  Introduction   85
  Creating an options menu   86
    Getting ready   87

How to do it...   89
How it works...   90
There's more...   91
   Using a menu item to launch an activity   91
   Creating submenus   92
   Grouping menu items   92
See also   93
Modifying menus and menu items during runtime   93
Getting ready   93
How to do it...   94
How it works...   95
There's more...   96
Enabling Contextual Action Mode for a view   97
Creating a floating context menu   97
Getting ready   97
How to do it...   98
How it works...   100
There's more...   101
See also   101
Using Contextual Batch Mode with RecyclerView   101
Getting ready   103
How to do it...   103
How it works...   106
There's more...   107
See also   108
Creating a pop-up menu   108
Getting ready   109
How to do it...   109
How it works...   111

Chapter 5: Fragments   113
Introduction   113
Creating and using a Fragment   113
Getting ready   114
How to do it...   114
How it works...   116
There's more...   116
See also   116
Adding and removing Fragments during runtime   116
Getting ready   117
How to do it...   117
How it works...   120
There's more...   120
See also   121
Passing data between Fragments   121
Getting ready   124

How to do it... 124
How it works... 130
There's more... 132
See also 132
Handling the Fragment back stack 132
Getting ready 133
How to do it... 133
How it works... 136
There's more... 136

Chapter 6: Home Screen Widgets, Search, and the System UI 139
Introduction 139
Creating a shortcut on the Home screen 140
Getting ready 141
How to do it... 141
How it works... 142
There's more... 142
Creating a Home screen widget 142
Getting ready 146
How to do it... 147
How it works... 149
There's more... 150
See also 150
Adding Search to the Action Bar 151
Getting ready 151
How to do it... 151
How it works... 154
See also 156
Showing your app full-screen 156
Getting ready 157
How to do it... 157
How it works... 159
There's more... 159
Sticky Immersion 159
Dimming the System UI 159
Setting the Action Bar as an overlay 160
Translucent system bars 160
See also 160

Chapter 7: Data Storage 161
Introduction 161
Storing simple data 162
Getting ready 164
How to do it... 165
How it works... 166
There's more... 166

Read and write a text file to internal storage 167
Getting ready 167
How to do it... 167
How it works... 169
There's more... 169
Caching files 169
See also 170
Read and write a text file to external storage 170
Getting ready 170
How to do it... 171
How it works... 173
There's more... 174
Getting public folders 174
Checking available space 175
Deleting a file 175
Working with directories 175
Preventing files from being included in galleries 175
See also 176
Including resource files in your project 176
Getting ready 177
How to do it... 177
How it works... 181
There's more... 181
See also 182
Creating and using an SQLite database 182
Getting ready 182
How to do it... 183
How it works... 188
There's more... 189
Upgrading a database 189
See also 189
Accessing data in the background using a Loader 190
Getting ready 190
How to do it... 190
How it works... 194
There's more... 194
See also 194
Accessing external storage with scoped directories in Android N 195
Getting ready 195
How to do it... 195
How it works... 197
There's more... 197
See also 197

Chapter 8: Alerts and Notifications 199
Introduction 199

Lights, Action, and Sound – getting the user's attention!   200
Getting ready   201
How to do it...   201
How it works...   203
There's more...   204
See also   205
Creating a Toast with a custom layout   205
Getting ready   207
How to do it...   207
How it works...   209
See also   209
Displaying a message box with AlertDialog   209
Getting ready   210
How to do it...   210
How it works...   211
There's more...   211
     Add an icon   211
     Using a list   211
     Custom layout   212
Displaying a progress dialog   212
Getting ready   214
How to do it...   214
How it works...   215
There's more...   215
Lights, Action, and Sound Redux using Notifications   215
Getting ready   216
How to do it...   216
How it works...   218
There's more...   219
     Adding a button to the notification using addAction()   219
     Expanded notifications   220
     Lock screen notifications   222
See also   222
Creating a Media Player Notification   223
Getting ready   223
How to do it...   223
How it works...   226
There's more...   227
See also   227
Making a Flashlight with a Heads-Up Notification   227
Getting ready   228
How to do it...   228
How it works...   231
There's more...   232
See also   232

Notifications with Direct Reply	233
Getting ready	233
How to do it...	233
How it works...	235
See also	236
Chapter 9: Using the Touchscreen and Sensors	237
Introduction	237
Listening for click and long-press events	238
Getting ready	238
How to do it...	239
How it works...	240
There's more...	240
Recognizing tap and other common gestures	240
Getting ready	241
How to do it...	241
How it works...	242
There's more...	243
See also	243
Pinch-to-zoom with multi-touch gestures	243
Getting ready	244
How to do it...	244
How it works...	245
Swipe-to-Refresh	246
Getting ready	247
How to do it...	247
How it works...	248
There's more...	249
Getting ready	252
How to do it...	252
How it works...	253
There's more...	253
See also	253
Reading sensor data – using Android Sensor Framework events	254
Getting ready	254
How to do it...	254
How it works...	256
There's more...	256
Environment sensors	256
Position sensors	256
Motion sensors	257
See also	258
Reading device orientation	258
Getting ready	259
How to do it...	259
How it works...	260

There's more...   260
    Getting current device rotation   260
See also   261

Chapter 10: Graphics and Animation   263
  Introduction   263
  Scaling down large images to avoid Out of Memory exceptions 265
    Getting ready   266
    How to do it...   267
    How it works...   268
    There's more...   269
    See also   269
  A transition animation – defining scenes and applying a transition 270
    Getting ready   271
    How to do it...   271
    How it works...   273
    There's more...   274
    See also   274
  Creating a Compass using sensor data and RotateAnimation 275
    Getting ready   276
    How to do it...   276
    How it works...   279
    There's more...   279
    See also   280
  Creating a slideshow with ViewPager   280
    Getting ready   281
    How to do it...   281
    How it works...   284
    There's more...   284
      Creating a Setup Wizard   284
    See also   285
  Creating a Card Flip Animation with Fragments   285
    Getting ready   286
    How to do it...   286
    How it works...   291
    See also   291
  Creating a Zoom Animation with a Custom Transition   291
    Getting ready   292
    How to do it...   292
    How it works...   296
    There's more...   297
      Getting the default animation duration 297
    See also   298
  Displaying animated image (GIF/WebP) with the new ImageDecoder library 298
    Getting ready   298

How to do it...   299
How it works...   300
See also   301
Creating a circle image with the new ImageDecoder   301
Getting ready   303
How to do it...   303
How it works...   304
There's more...   305
See also   305

Chapter 11: A First Look at OpenGL ES   307
Introduction   307
Setting up the OpenGL ES environment   308
Getting ready   308
How to do it...   308
How it works...   309
    Declaring OpenGL in the Android Manifest   310
    Extending the GLSurfaceView class   310
    Creating an OpenGL rendered class   310
There's more...   311
Drawing shapes on GLSurfaceView   311
Getting ready   313
How to do it...   313
How it works...   315
There's more...   316
See also   316
Applying the projection and camera view while drawing   317
Getting ready   318
How to do it...   318
How it works...   320
There's more...   320
Moving the triangle with rotation   320
Getting ready   322
How to do it...   322
How it works...   322
There's more...   323
    The render mode   323
Rotating the triangle with user input   323
Getting ready   324
How to do it...   324
How it works...   326
There's more...   326
See also   326

Chapter 12: Multimedia   327
Introduction   327

Playing sound effects with SoundPool   328
  Getting ready   328
  How to do it...   329
  How it works...   331
  There's more...   332
  See also   332
Playing audio with MediaPlayer   332
  Getting ready   333
  How to do it...   334
  How it works...   336
  There's more...   336
    Playing music in the background   336
    Using hardware volume keys to control your app's audio volume   337
  See also   337
Responding to hardware media controls in your app   337
  Getting ready   338
  How to do it...   338
  How it works...   339
  There's more...   340
    Checking the hardware type   340
  See also   340
Taking a photo with the default camera app   341
  Getting ready   341
  How to do it...   341
  How it works...   343
  There's more...   344
    Calling the default video app   344
  See also   344
Taking a picture using the Camera2 API   345
  Getting ready   345
  How to do it...   345
  How it works...   352
    Setting up the camera preview   352
    Capturing the image   352
  There's more...   353
  See also   354

Chapter 13: Telephony, Networks, and the Web   355
  Introduction   355
  How to make a phone call   355
    Getting ready   356
    How to do it...   356
    How it works...   357
    See also   358
  Monitoring phone call events   358
    Getting ready   358

How to do it...   358
How it works...   359
There's more...   360
See also   360
How to send SMS (text) messages   360
Getting ready   361
How to do it...   361
How it works...   363
There's more...   363
Multipart messages   364
Delivery status notification   364
See also   365
Receiving SMS messages   365
Getting ready   365
How to do it...   365
How it works...   367
There's more...   368
Reading existing SMS messages   368
See also   369
Displaying a web page in your application   369
Getting ready   370
How to do it...   370
How it works...   371
There's more...   371
Controlling page navigation   371
How to enable JavaScript   372
Enable built-in zoom   372
See also   372
Checking online status and connection type   372
Getting ready   372
How to do it...   373
How it works...   374
There's more...   374
Monitoring network state changes   375
See also   375
Phone number blocking API   376
Getting ready   376
How to do it...   376
How it works...   379
There's more...   379
See also   380

Chapter 14: Location and Using Geofencing   381
Introduction   381
How to get the device location   383
Getting ready   383

How to do it...   383
How it works...   385
There's more...   386
        Mock locations   386
See also   388
Getting ready   388
How to do it...   389
How it works...   391
There's more...   392
See also   392
Creating and monitoring a Geofence   392
Getting ready   393
How to do it...   393
How it works...   396
There's more...   397
See also   398
Chapter 15: Getting Your App Ready for the Play Store   399
Introduction   399
The Android 6.0 Runtime Permission Model   400
Getting ready   400
How to do it...   401
How it works...   403
There's more...   404
See also   404
How to schedule an alarm   404
Getting ready   406
How to do it...   406
How it works...   408
There's more...   408
        Cancel the alarm   408
        Repeating alarm   409
See also   409
Receiving notification of device boot   409
Getting ready   409
How to do it...   410
How it works...   410
There's more...   411
See also   411
Using the AsyncTask for background work   412
Getting ready   412
How to do it...   413
How it works...   414
There's more...   414
        Parameter types   415
        Canceling the task   415

See also	416
Adding speech recognition to your app	416
Getting ready	416
How to do it...	416
How it works...	418
There's more...	419
See also	419
How to add Google sign-in to your app	419
Getting ready	421
How to do it...	421
How it works...	423
There's more...	424
See also	424
Chapter 16: Getting Started with Kotlin	425
Introduction	425
How to create an Android project with Kotlin	426
Getting ready	426
How to do it...	426
How it works...	427
There's more...	428
See also	428
Creating a Toast in Kotlin	429
Getting ready	430
How to do it...	430
How it works...	431
See also	431
Runtime permission in Kotlin	431
Getting ready	431
How to do it...	432
How it works...	434
See also	434
Other Books You May Enjoy	435
Index	439

Preface

Android was first released in 2007 after being acquired by Google, Inc. Initially, Android was primarily used on a handset. Android 3.0 added features to take advantage of the growing tablet market.

In 2014, Google announced Android had over 1 billion active users! With over 1 million applications available on Google Play, there's never been a more exciting time to join the Android community!

This year, 2018, marks a significant milestone for Android - 10 year anniversary since the first Android phone was released! And with that, we have a new OS version release as well - Android Pie. In this new edition of the book, we'll cover features released for the platform in several new topics across many chapters, as well as updates to existing popular topics to cover SDK changes. As usual, the Android platform is constantly changing!

Who this book is for

This book assumes basic familiarity with programming concepts and Android fundamentals. Or, if you are new to Android and learn best by jumping into the code, this book provides a wide range of the most common tasks. If you are new to Android, you can start at the beginning of the book and work your way through the topics as they build on previous knowledge.

As a cookbook, the topics are designed to be stand-along (with noted exceptions), to make it easy to jump to a particular topic and get the code working in your own application as quickly as possible.

What this book covers

Chapter 1, *Activities*, the Activity represents the fundamental building block for most applications. See examples of the most common tasks such as creating an activity, and passing control from one activity to another.

Chapter 2, *Layouts*, while Activities are fundamental to the UI, the Layout actually defines what the user sees on the screen. Learn the main layout options available and best to use cases.

Chapter 3, *Views, Widgets and Styles*, explores the basic UI object, from which all layouts are built. The chapter starts by exploring views and widgets - the basic building block of any app then goes on to styling the widgets and turning those styles into themes.

Chapter 4, *Menus and Action Mode*, teaches you how to use menus in Android. Learn how to create menus and how to control their behavior at runtime, including Action Mode.

Chapter 5, *Fragments*, shows how to create more flexible user interfaces by reusing UI components with Fragments.

Chapter 6, *Home Screen Widgets*, Search and the System UI, takes us to topics outside your app such as how to create a widget for the Home Screen, adding search functionality UI to your app and running your app in full-screen mode.

Chapter 7, *Data Storage*, compares multiple methods Android offers for persisting data, and when best to use each option.

Chapter 8, *Alerts and Notifications*, shows multiple options for displaying notifications to your users. Options range from alerts in your application, using the system notification and the "Heads Up notification".

Chapter 9, *Using the Touchscreen and Sensors*, learn the events for handling the standard user interactions, such as button clicks, long presses, and gestures. Access the device hardware sensors to determine orientation changes, device movement, and compass bearing.

Chapter 10, *Graphics and Animation*, bring your app to life with animations! Take advantage of the many options Android offers for creating animations – from simple bitmaps to custom property animations.

Chapter 11, *A first look at OpenGL ES*, when you need high-performance 2D and 3D graphics, turn to the Open Graphics Library. Android supports Open GL, a cross-platform Graphics API.

Chapter 12, *Multimedia* - Sounds and Camera, take advantage of the hardware features for playing audio. Use Android intents to call the default camera application or delve into the camera APIs to control the camera directly.

Chapter 13, *Telephony, Networks, and the Web,* use the Telephony functions to initiate a phone call and to listen for incoming phone events. See how to send and receive SMS (text) messages. Use the WebView in your application to display web pages and learn to use Volley to communicate directly with web services.

Chapter 14, *Location and using Geofencing*, shows you how to determine the user's location and the best-practices so your app doesn't drain the battery. Use the new Location APIs to receive location updates and create Geofences.

Chapter 15, *Getting your app ready for the Play Store*, as your polish your app for the Play Store, learn how to implement more advanced features such as Alarms, AsynchTask for background processing and add Google Sign-In to your app.

Chapter 16, *Getting started with Kotlin*, offers a first-look at the new Android language and several topics to get you started.

To get the most out of this book

1. You should know basic programming fundamentals. This book assumes the reader understands basic programming syntax and concepts. Language features such as `if/then`, `for next` and `try/catch` should already be familiar and understood.
2. Download and install the official Android development environment - Android Studio. Refer to the Hardware-Software List section for details.

Download the example code files

You can download the example code files for this book from your account at `www.packt.com`. If you purchased this book elsewhere, you can visit `www.packt.com/support` and register to have the files emailed directly to you.

You can download the code files by following these steps:

1. Log in or register at `www.packt.com`.
2. Select the **SUPPORT** tab.
3. Click on **Code Downloads & Errata**.
4. Enter the name of the book in the **Search** box and follow the onscreen instructions.

Once the file is downloaded, please make sure that you unzip or extract the folder using the latest version of:

- WinRAR/7-Zip for Windows
- Zipeg/iZip/UnRarX for Mac
- 7-Zip/PeaZip for Linux

The code bundle for the book is also hosted on GitHub at `https://github.com/PacktPublishing/Android-9-Development-Cookbook`. In case there's an update to the code, it will be updated on the existing GitHub repository.

We also have other code bundles from our rich catalog of books and videos available at `https://github.com/PacktPublishing/`. Check them out!

Download the color images

We also provide a PDF file that has color images of the screenshots/diagrams used in this book. You can download it here: `https://www.packtpub.com/sites/default/files/downloads/9781788991216_ColorImages.pdf`.

Conventions used

There are a number of text conventions used throughout this book.

`CodeInText`: Indicates code words in text, database table names, folder names, filenames, file extensions, pathnames, dummy URLs, user input, and Twitter handles. Here is an example: "Mount the downloaded `WebStorm-10*.dmg` disk image file as another disk in your system."

A block of code is set as follows:

```
<activity
    android:name=".MainActivity"
    android:label="@string/app_name">
    <intent-filter>
        <action android:name="android.intent.action.MAIN"/>

        <category android:name="android.intent.category.LAUNCHER"/>
    </intent-filter>
</activity>
```

Bold: Indicates a new term, an important word, or words that you see onscreen. For example, words in menus or dialog boxes appear in the text like this. Here is an example: "Select **System info** from the **Administration** panel."

 Warnings or important notes appear like this.

 Tips and tricks appear like this.

Sections

In this book, you will find several headings that appear frequently (*Getting ready*, *How to do it...*, *How it works...*, *There's more...*, and *See also*).

To give clear instructions on how to complete a recipe, use these sections as follows:

Getting ready

This section tells you what to expect in the recipe and describes how to set up any software or any preliminary settings required for the recipe.

How to do it...

This section contains the steps required to follow the recipe.

How it works...

This section usually consists of a detailed explanation of what happened in the previous section.

There's more...

This section consists of additional information about the recipe in order to make you more knowledgeable about the recipe.

See also

This section provides helpful links to other useful information for the recipe.

Get in touch

Feedback from our readers is always welcome.

General feedback: If you have questions about any aspect of this book, mention the book title in the subject of your message and email us at customercare@packtpub.com.

Errata: Although we have taken every care to ensure the accuracy of our content, mistakes do happen. If you have found a mistake in this book, we would be grateful if you would report this to us. Please visit www.packt.com/submit-errata, selecting your book, clicking on the Errata Submission Form link, and entering the details.

Piracy: If you come across any illegal copies of our works in any form on the Internet, we would be grateful if you would provide us with the location address or website name. Please contact us at copyright@packt.com with a link to the material.

If you are interested in becoming an author: If there is a topic that you have expertise in and you are interested in either writing or contributing to a book, please visit authors.packtpub.com.

Reviews

Please leave a review. Once you have read and used this book, why not leave a review on the site that you purchased it from? Potential readers can then see and use your unbiased opinion to make purchase decisions, we at Packt can understand what you think about our products, and our authors can see your feedback on their book. Thank you!

For more information about Packt, please visit packt.com.

Activities 1

This chapter covers the following recipes:

- Declaring an activity
- Starting a new activity with an intent object
- Switching between activities
- Passing data to another activity
- Returning a result from an activity
- Saving an activity's state
- Storing persistent activity data
- Understanding the activity life cycle

Introduction

The Android SDK provides a powerful tool to program mobile devices, and the best way to master such a tool is to jump right in. Although you can read this book from beginning to end, as it is a cookbook, it is specifically designed to allow you to jump to specific tasks and get the results immediately.

Activities are the fundamental building block of most Android applications as the activity class provides the interface between the application and screen. Most Android applications will have at least one activity, if not several (but they are not required). A background service application will not necessarily require an activity if there is no user interface.

This chapter explains how to *declare* and *launch* activities within an application and how to manage several activities at once by sharing data between them, requesting results from them, and calling one activity from within another.

This chapter also briefly explores the **intent** object, which is often used in conjunction with activities. Intents can be used to transfer data between activities in your own application, as well as in external applications, such as those included with the Android operating system (a common example would be to use an intent to launch the default web browser).

 To begin developing Android applications, head over to the **Android Studio** page to download the new Android Studio IDE and the **Android SDK** bundle:
http://developer.android.com/sdk/index.html.

Declaring an activity

Activities and other application components, such as **services**, are declared in the AndroidManifest.xml file. Declaring an activity node is how we tell the OS about our Activity class and how it can be requested. For example, an application will usually indicate that at least one activity should be visible as a desktop icon and serve as the main entry point to the application.

Getting ready

Android Studio, now at version 3.2, is used for all the code samples shown in this book. If you have not already installed it, visit the Android Studio website (see the link in the previous tip) to install the IDE and the SDK bundle for your platform.

How to do it...

For this first example, we'll guide you through creating a new project. Android Studio provides a **Quick Start** wizard, which makes the process extremely easy. Follow these steps to get started:

1. Launch Android Studio, which brings up the **Welcome to Android Studio** dialog:

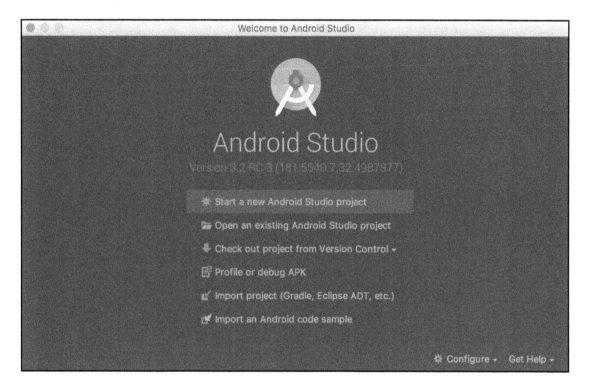

2. Click on the **Start a new Android Studio project** option.
3. Enter an application name; for this example, we used `DeclareAnActivity`. Click on **Next**:

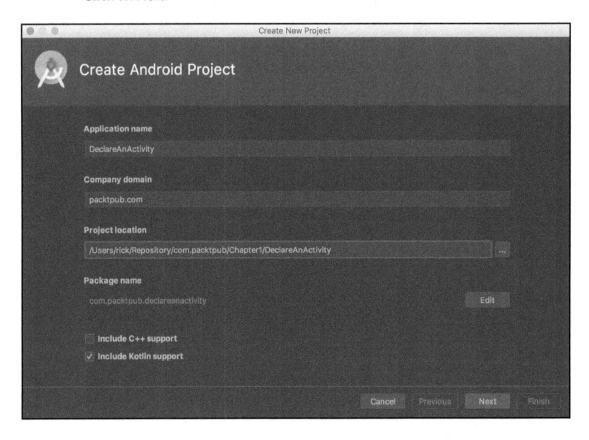

4. In the **Target Android Devices** dialog, you can leave the **Phone and Tablet** checkbox selected with the default **API 21: Android 5.0 (Lollipop)** selection for the minimum SDK (for this example, it really doesn't matter which API level you choose, as activities have existed since API level 1). Click on **Next**:

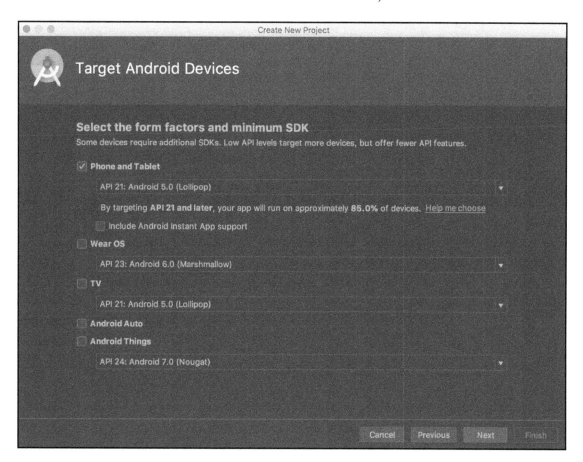

5. In the **Add an Activity to Mobile** dialog, select the **Empty Activity** option. Click on **Next**:

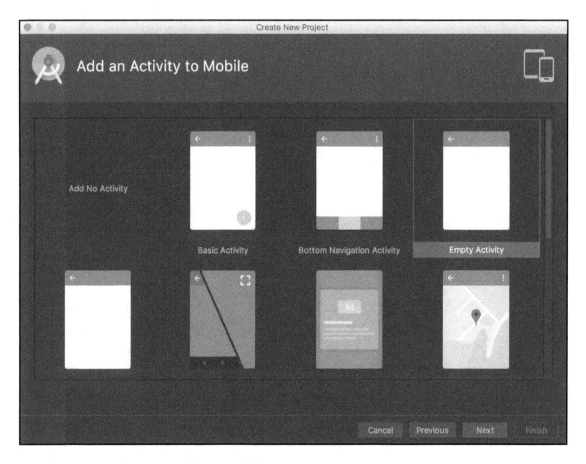

6. In the **Configure Activity** dialog, you can leave the defaults as provided, but note that the default activity name is `MainActivity`. Click on **Finish**:

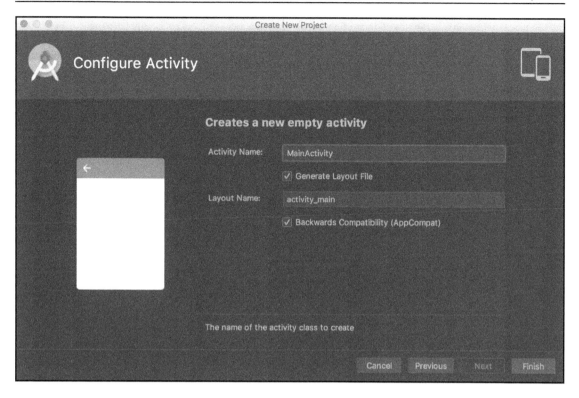

After finishing the wizard, Android Studio will create the project files. For this recipe, the two files that we will examine are `MainActivity.java` (which corresponds to the activity name mentioned in step 6) and `AndroidManifest.xml`.

If you take a look at the `MainActivity.java` file, you will realize that it's pretty basic. This is because we chose the **Empty Activity** option (in step 5). Now, look at the `AndroidManifest.xml` file. This is where we actually declare the activity. Within the `<application>` element is the `<activity>` element:

```
<activity android:name=".MainActivity" android:label="@string/app_name">
<intent-filter> <action android:name="android.intent.action.MAIN"/>
<category android:name=
 "android.intent.category.LAUNCHER"/> </intent-filter> </activity>
```

When viewing this `xml` in Android Studio, you may notice that the label element shows the actual text (`DeclareAnActivity` in this case) as defined in the `strings.xml` resource file.

How it works...

Declaring an activity is a simple matter of declaring the `<activity>` element and specifying the name of the activity class with the `android:name` attribute. By adding the `<activity>` element to the **Android Manifest**, we are specifying our intention to include this component in our application. Any activities (or any other component for that matter) that are not declared in the manifest will not be available to the application. Attempting to access or utilize an undeclared component will result in an exception being thrown at runtime.

In the preceding code, there is another attribute: `android:label`. This attribute indicates the title shown on the screen, as well as the icon if this is the Launcher activity.

For a complete list of available Activity attributes, take a look at this resource: `http://developer.android.com/guide/topics/manifest/activity-element.html`.

Starting a new activity with an intent object

The Android application model can be seen as a service-oriented one, with activities as components and intents as the messages sent between them. Here, an intent is used to start an activity that displays the user's call log, but intents can be used to do many things and we will encounter them throughout this book.

Getting ready

To keep things simple, we are going to use an intent object to start one of Android's built-in applications rather than create a new one. This only requires a very basic application, so start a new Android project with Android Studio and call it `ActivityStarter`.

How to do it...

Again, to keep the example simple so that we can focus on the task at hand, we will create a function to show an intent in action and call this function from a button on our activity.

Once your new project is created in Android Studio, follow these steps:

1. Open the `MainActivity.java` class and add the following function:

```java
public void launchIntent(View view) {
    Intent intent = new Intent(Intent.ACTION_VIEW);
    intent.setData(Uri.parse("https://www.packtpub.com/"));
    startActivity(intent);
}
```

  - While you are typing this code, Android Studio will give this warning on View and intent: **Cannot resolve symbol 'Intent'**.
  - This means that you need to add the library reference to the project. You can do this manually by entering the following code in the `import` section:

    ```java
    import android.content.Intent;
    import android.net.Uri;
    import android.support.v7.app.AppCompatActivity;
    import android.os.Bundle;
    import android.view.View;
    ```

 Alternatively, let Android Studio add the library reference for you: just click on the code highlighted with a red font and press *Alt + Enter*.

2. Open the `activity_main.xml` file and replace the `<TextView />` block with the following XML:

```xml
<Button
    android:layout_width="wrap_content"
    android:layout_height="wrap_content"
    android:text="Launch Browser"
    android:id="@+id/button"
    android:onClick="launchIntent"
    app:layout_constraintBottom_toBottomOf="parent"
    app:layout_constraintLeft_toLeftOf="parent"
    app:layout_constraintRight_toRightOf="parent"
    app:layout_constraintTop_toTopOf="parent"/>
```

3. Now, it's time to run the application and see the intent in action. You will need to either create an Android emulator (in Android Studio, go to **Tools | Android | AVDManager**) or connect a physical device to your computer.

4. When you press the **Launch Browser** button, you will see the default web browser open with the URL specified.

How it works...

Though simple, this app demonstrates much of the power behind the Android OS. An intent is a message object. Intents can be used to communicate across your application's components (such as services and broadcast receivers) as well as with other applications on the device. In this recipe, we asked the OS to start any app that could handle the data we specified with the `setData()` method. (If the user has multiple browsers installed and no default set, the OS will show a list of apps for the user to choose from.)

To test this on a physical device, you may need to install drivers for your device (the drivers are specific to the hardware manufacturer). You will also need to enable Developer Mode on your device. Enabling Developer Mode varies according to the Android OS version. If you do not see the Developer Mode option in your device settings, open the **About Phone** option and begin tapping **Build Number**. After three taps, you should see a **Toast** message telling you that you are on your way to being a developer. Four more taps will enable the option.

In this recipe, we created an intent object with the `ACTION_VIEW`. as what we want to do (our intention). You may have noticed that when you typed `Intent` and the period, Android Studio provided a pop-up list of possibilities (this is the autocomplete feature), like this:

```
public void launchIntent(View view) {
    Intent intent = new Intent(Intent.|);
    intent.setData(Uri.parse("htt    EXTRA_ASSIST_CONTEXT ( = "android.intent.extra. ... )   String
    startActivity(intent);           createChooser(Intent target, CharSequence title)          Intent
}                                     createChooser(Intent target, CharSequence title, Inte...    Intent
}                                     getIntentOld(String uri)                                    Intent
                                      getIntent(String uri)                                       Intent
                                      makeMainActivity(ComponentName mainActivity)                Intent
                                      makeMainSelectorActivity(String selectorAction, Strin...    Intent
                                      makeRestartActivityTask(ComponentName mainActivity)         Intent
                                      normalizeMimeType(String type)                              String
                                      parseIntent(Resources resources, XmlPullParser parser...    Intent
```

`ACTION_VIEW`, along with a URL in the data, indicates that the intention is to view the website, so the default browser is launched (different data could launch different apps). In this example, we just want to open a browser with the specified URL, so we call the `startActivity()` method. There are other ways to call the intent depending on our needs. In the *Returning a result from an activity* recipe, we will use the `startActivityForResult()` method.

There's more...

It's very common for Android users to download their favorite apps for web browsing, taking photos, text messaging, and so on. Using Intents, you allow your users to use their favorite apps instead of trying to reinvent all of this functionality.

See also

To start an activity from a menu selection, refer to the *Handling menu selections* recipe in `Chapter 4`, *Menus and Action Mode*.

Switching between activities

Often, we will want to activate one activity from within another activity. Although this is not a difficult task, it will require a little more setting up to be done than the previous recipes as it requires two activities. We will create two activity classes and declare them both in the manifest. We'll also create a button, as we did in the previous recipe, to switch to the activity.

Getting ready

We'll create a new project in Android Studio, just as we did in the previous recipes, and call this one `ActivitySwitcher`. Android Studio will create the first activity, `ActivityMain`, and automatically declare it in the manifest.

How to do it...

1. Since the Android Studio New Project wizard has already created the first activity, we just need to create the second activity. Open the **ActivitySwitcher** project and navigate to **File** | **New** | **Activity** | **Empty Activity**, as shown in this screenshot:

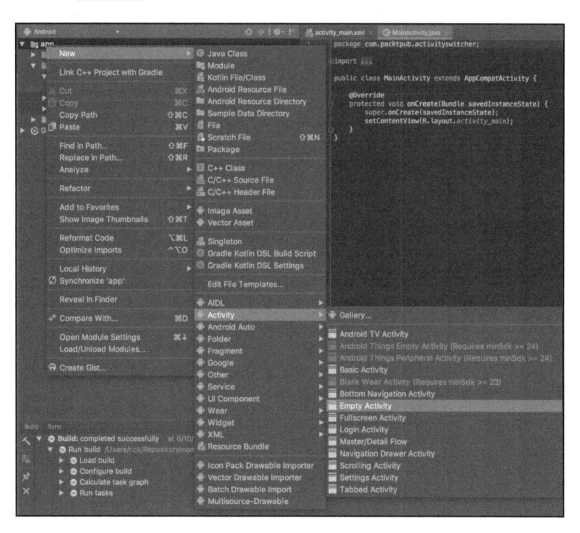

2. In the **New Android Activity** dialog, you can leave the default **Activity Name** as is, or change it to SecondActivity, as follows:

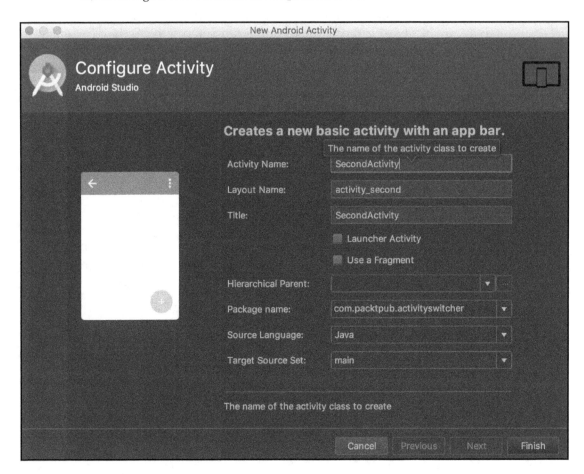

3. Open the MainActivity.java file and add the following function:

```
public void onClickSwitchActivity(View view) {
    Intent intent = new Intent(this, SecondActivity.class);
    startActivity(intent);
}
```

4. Now, open the `activity_main.xml` file located in the `res/layout` folder and replace the `<TextView />` with the following XML to create the button:

```
<Button
    android:id="@+id/button"
    android:layout_width="wrap_content"
    android:layout_height="wrap_content"
    android:layout_centerVertical="true"
    android:layout_centerHorizontal="true"
    android:text="Launch Second Activity"
    android:onClick="onClickSwitchActivity"
    app:layout_constraintBottom_toBottomOf="parent"
    app:layout_constraintLeft_toLeftOf="parent"
    app:layout_constraintRight_toRightOf="parent"
    app:layout_constraintTop_toTopOf="parent"/>
```

5. You can run the code at this point and see the second activity open. We're going to go further and add a button to `SecondActivity` to close it, which will bring us back to the first activity. Open the `SecondActivity.java` file and add this function:

```
public void onClickClose(View view) {
    finish();
}
```

6. Finally, add the **Close** button to the `SecondActivity` layout. Open the `activity_second.xml` file and add the following `<Button>` element to the auto-generated `ConstraintLayout`:

```
<Button
    android:id="@+id/buttonClose"
    android:layout_width="wrap_content"
    android:layout_height="wrap_content"
    android:text="Close"
    android:layout_centerVertical="true"
    android:layout_centerHorizontal="true"
    android:onClick="onClickClose"
    app:layout_constraintBottom_toBottomOf="parent"
    app:layout_constraintLeft_toLeftOf="parent"
    app:layout_constraintRight_toRightOf="parent"
    app:layout_constraintTop_toTopOf="parent"/>
```

7. Run the application on your device or emulator and see the buttons in action.

How it works...

The real work of this exercise is in the `onClickSwitchActivity()` method from step 3. This is where we declare the second activity for the Intent using `SecondActivity.class`. We went one step further by adding the close button to the second activity to show a common real-world situation: launching a new activity, then returning to the original calling activity. This behavior is accomplished in the `onClickClose()` function. All it does is call `finish()`, but that tells the OS that we're done with the activity. Finish doesn't actually return us to the calling activity (or any specific activity for that matter); it just closes the current activity and relies on the application's **back stack** to show the last activity. If we want a specific activity, we can again use the Intent object and specify the activity class name when creating the Intent.

This activity switching does not make a very exciting application. Our activity does nothing but demonstrates how to switch from one activity to another, which of course will form a fundamental aspect of almost any application that we develop.

If we had manually created the activities, we would need to add them to the manifest. Using the New Android Activity wizard will automatically add the necessary elements to the Android Manifest file. To see what Android Studio did for you, open the `AndroidManifest.xml` file and look at the `<application>` element:

```
<activity android:name=".MainActivity">
    <intent-filter>
        <action android:name="android.intent.action.MAIN" />

        <category android:name="android.intent.category.LAUNCHER" />
    </intent-filter>
</activity>
<activity android:name=".SecondActivity"></activity>
```

One thing to note in the preceding auto-generated code is that the second activity does not have the `<intent-filter>` element. The main activity is generally the entry point when starting the application. That's why MAIN and LAUNCHER are defined so that the system will know which activity to launch when the application starts.

See also

- To learn more about embedding widgets such as the Button, visit Chapter 2, *Views, Widgets, and Styles*

Passing data to another activity

The intent object is defined as a messaging object. As a message object, its purpose is to communicate with other components of the application. In this recipe, we'll show you how to pass information with the intent and how to get it out again.

Getting ready

This recipe will pick up from where the previous one ended. We will call this project `SendData`.

How to do it...

Since this recipe is building on the previous recipe, most of the work is already done. We'll add an `EditText` element to the main activity so that we have something to send to `SecondActivity`. We'll use the (auto-generated) `TextView` view to display the message. The following are the complete steps:

1. Open `activity_main.xml` and add the following `<EditText>` element above the button:

   ```
   <EditText
       android:id="@+id/editTextData"
       android:layout_width="match_parent"
       android:layout_height="wrap_content"
       app:layout_constraintLeft_toLeftOf="parent"
       app:layout_constraintRight_toRightOf="parent"
       app:layout_constraintTop_toTopOf="parent"
       app:layout_constraintBottom_toTopOf="@+id/button" />
   ```

   The `<Button>` element that we created in the previous recipe doesn't change.

2. Now, open the `MainActivity.java` file and change the `onClickSwitchActivity()` method as follows:

   ```
   public void onClickSwitchActivity(View view) {
       EditText editText = (EditText)findViewById(R.id.editTextData);
       String text = editText.getText().toString();
       Intent intent = new Intent(this, SecondActivity.class);
       intent.putExtra(Intent.EXTRA_TEXT,text);
       startActivity(intent);
   }
   ```

3. Next, open the `activity_second.xml` file and add the following `<TextView>` element:

```
<TextView
    android:id="@+id/textViewText"
    android:layout_width="wrap_content"
    android:layout_height="wrap_content"
    app:layout_constraintLeft_toLeftOf="parent"
    app:layout_constraintRight_toRightOf="parent"
    app:layout_constraintTop_toTopOf="parent"
    app:layout_constraintBottom_toTopOf="@id/buttonClose"/>
```

4. The last change is to edit the second activity to look for this new data and display it on the screen. Open `SecondActivity.java` and edit `onCreate()` as follows:

```
protected void onCreate(Bundle savedInstanceState) {
    super.onCreate(savedInstanceState);
    setContentView(R.layout.activity_second);
    TextView textView = (TextView) findViewById(R.id.textViewText);
    if (getIntent() != null &&
getIntent().hasExtra(Intent.EXTRA_TEXT)) {
textView.setText(getIntent().getStringExtra(Intent.EXTRA_TEXT));
    }
}
```

5. Now, run the project. Type some text in the main activity and press **Launch Second Activity** to see it send the data.

How it works...

As expected, the Intent object is doing all the work. We created an intent just as in the previous recipe and then added some extra data. Did you notice the `putExtra()` method call? In our example, we used the already defined `Intent.EXTRA_TEXT` as the identifier, but we didn't have to. We can use any key we want (you've seen this concept before if you're familiar with name/value pairs).

The key point about using name/value pairs is that you have to use the same name to get the data back out. That's why we used the same key identifier when we read the extra data with `getStringExtra()`.

The second activity was launched with the intent that we created, so it's simply a matter of getting the intent and checking for the data sent along with it. We do this in `onCreate()`:

```
textView.setText(getIntent().getStringExtra(Intent.EXTRA_TEXT));
```

There's more...

We aren't limited to just sending `String` data. The intent object is very flexible and already supports basic data types. Go back to Android Studio and click on the `putExtra` method. Then, hit *Ctrl* and the spacebar. Android Studio will bring up the auto-complete list so that you can see the different data types that you can store.

Returning a result from an activity

Being able to start one activity from another is very useful and commonly used, but there are times when we need to know the result from the called activity. The `startActivityForResult()` method provides the solution.

Getting ready

Returning a result from an activity is not very different from the way we just called the activity in the previous recipes. You can either use the project from the previous recipe or start a new project and call it `GettingResults`. Either way, once you have a project with two activities and the code needed to call the second activity, you're ready to begin.

How to do it...

There are only a few changes needed to get the results:

1. First of all, open `MainActivity.java` and add the following constant to the class:

   ```
   public static final String REQUEST_RESULT="REQUEST_RESULT";
   ```

2. Next, change the way the intent is called by modifying the `onClickSwitchActivity()` method to expect a result:

   ```
   public void onClickSwitchActivity(View view) {
       EditText editText = (EditText)findViewById(R.id.editTextData);
       String text = editText.getText().toString();
       Intent intent = new Intent(this, SecondActivity.class);
       intent.putExtra(Intent.EXTRA_TEXT,text);
       startActivityForResult(intent,1);
   }
   ```

3. Then, add this new method to receive the result:

```
@Override
protected void onActivityResult(int requestCode, int resultCode,
Intent data) {
    super.onActivityResult(requestCode, resultCode, data);
    if (resultCode==RESULT_OK) {
        Toast.makeText(this,
Integer.toString(data.getIntExtra(REQUEST_RESULT,
                0)), Toast.LENGTH_LONG).show();
    }
}
```

4. Finally, modify `onClickClose` in `SecondActivity.java` to set the return value as follows:

```
public void onClickClose(View view) {
    Intent returnIntent = new Intent();
    returnIntent.putExtra(MainActivity.REQUEST_RESULT, 42);
    setResult(RESULT_OK, returnIntent);
    finish();
}
```

How it works...

As you can see, getting the results back is relatively straightforward. We just call the intent with `startActivityForResult`, indicating we want a result back. We set up the `onActivityResult()` callback handler to receive the results. Finally, we make sure that the second activity returns a result with `setResult()` before closing the activity. In this example, we are just setting a result with a static value. We use a simple Toast to display the result back to the user.

It's good practice to check the result code to make sure that the user didn't cancel the action. It's technically an integer, but the system uses it as a Boolean value. Check for either `RESULT_OK` or `RESULT_CANCEL` and proceed accordingly. In our example, the second activity doesn't have a cancel button, so why bother to check? What if the user hits the back button? Android will set the result code to `RESULT_CANCEL` and the intent to null, which would cause our code to throw an exception if we attempt to access the null result.

We made use of the **Toast** object, which displays a convenient pop-up **message** to unobtrusively notify the user. It also functions as a handy method for debugging as it doesn't need a special layout or screen space.

There's more...

Besides the result code, `onActivityResults()` also includes a **Request Code**. Are you wondering where that came from? It is simply the integer value that was passed with the `startActivityForResult()` call, which takes this form:

```
startActivityForResult(Intent intent, int requestCode);
```

We didn't check the request code because we knew we had only one result to handle, but in non-trivial applications with several activities, this value can be used to identify which Activity is returning a result.

> If `startActivityForResult()` is called with a negative request code, it will behave the same as if we used `startActivity()`, that is, it will not return a result.

See also

- To learn more about creating new activity classes, refer to the *Switching between activities* recipe
- For more information about Toasts, check out the *Making a Toast* recipe in Chapter 8, *Alerts and Notifications*

Saving an activity's state

The mobile environment is very dynamic, with users changing tasks much more often than on desktops. With generally fewer resources on a mobile device, it should be expected that your application will be interrupted at some point. It's also very possible that the system will shut down your app completely to give additional resources to the task at hand. It's the nature of mobiles.

A user might start typing something in your app, be interrupted by a phone call, or switch over to send a text message, and by the time they get back to your app, the OS may have closed your app completely to free up the memory. To provide the best user experience, you need to expect such behavior and make it easier for your user to resume from where they left off. The good thing is that the Android OS makes this easier by providing callbacks to notify your app of state changes.

Simply rotating your device will cause the OS to destroy and recreate your activity. This might seem a bit heavy-handed, but it's done for a good reason: it's very common to have different layouts for portrait and landscape, so this ensures that your app is using the correct resources.

In this recipe, you'll see how to handle the onSaveInstanceState() and onRestoreInstanceState() callbacks to save your application's state. We will demonstrate this by creating a counter variable and increment it each time the **Count** button is pressed. We will also have an EditText and a TextView widget to see their default behavior.

Getting ready

Create a new project in Android Studio and name it StateSaver. We need only a single activity, so the auto-generated main activity is sufficient. However, we will need a few widgets, including EditText, Button, and TextView. Their layout (in activity_main.xml) will be as follows:

```
<EditText
    android:id="@+id/editText"
    android:layout_width="match_parent"
    android:layout_height="wrap_content"
    android:layout_alignParentTop="true"
    android:layout_alignParentStart="true"
    app:layout_constraintLeft_toLeftOf="parent"
    app:layout_constraintRight_toRightOf="parent"
    app:layout_constraintTop_toTopOf="parent"
    app:layout_constraintBottom_toTopOf="@+id/button"/>

<Button
    android:id="@+id/button"
    android:layout_width="wrap_content"
    android:layout_height="wrap_content"
    android:layout_centerInParent="true"
    android:text="Count"
    android:onClick="onClickCounter"
    app:layout_constraintLeft_toLeftOf="parent"
    app:layout_constraintRight_toRightOf="parent"
    app:layout_constraintTop_toTopOf="parent"
    app:layout_constraintBottom_toBottomOf="parent"/>

<TextView
    android:id="@+id/textViewCounter"
    android:layout_width="wrap_content"
```

```
android:layout_height="wrap_content"
android:layout_below="@id/button"
app:layout_constraintLeft_toLeftOf="parent"
app:layout_constraintRight_toRightOf="parent"
app:layout_constraintTop_toBottomOf="@id/button"
app:layout_constraintBottom_toBottomOf="parent"/>
```

How to do it...

Perform the following set of steps:

1. To keep track of the counter, we need to add a global variable to the project, along with a key for saving and restoring. Add the following code to the `MainActivity.java` class:

```
static final String KEY_COUNTER = "COUNTER";
private int mCounter=0;
```

2. Then, add the code needed to handle the button press; it increments the counter and displays the result in the `TextView` widget:

```
public void onClickCounter(View view) {
    mCounter++;
    ((TextView)findViewById(R.id.textViewCounter))
            .setText("Counter: " + Integer.toString(mCounter));
}
```

3. To receive notifications of application state change, we need to add the `onSaveInstanceState()` and `onRestoreInstanceState()` methods to our application. Open `MainActivity.java` and add the following:

```
@Override
protected void onSaveInstanceState(Bundle outState) {
    super.onSaveInstanceState(outState);
    outState.putInt(KEY_COUNTER,mCounter);
}

@Override
protected void onRestoreInstanceState(Bundle savedInstanceState) {
    super.onRestoreInstanceState(savedInstanceState);
    mCounter=savedInstanceState.getInt(KEY_COUNTER);
}
```

4. Run the program and try changing the orientation to see how it behaves (if you're using the emulator, *Ctrl* + *F11* will rotate the device).

How it works...

All activities go through multiple states during their lifetime. By setting up callbacks to handle the events, we can have our code save important information before the activity is destroyed.

Step 3 is where the actual saving and restoring occurs. The OS sends a **Bundle** (a data object that also uses name/value pairs) to the methods. We use the `onSaveInstanceState()` callback to save the data and pull it out in the `onRestoreInstanceState()` callback.

But wait! Did you try typing text in the `EditText` view before rotating the device? If so, you'd have noticed that the text was also restored, but we don't have any code to handle that view. By default, the system will automatically save the state, provided it has a unique ID.

 Note that if you want Android to automatically save and restore the state of a view, it must have a unique ID (specified with the `android:id=` attribute in the layout). Bur beware: not all view types automatically save and restore the state of a view.

There's more...

The `onRestoreInstanceState()` callback is not the only place where the state can be restored. Look at the signature of `onCreate()`:

```
onCreate(Bundle savedInstanceState)
```

Both methods receive the same `Bundle` instance named `savedInstanceState`. You could move the restore code to the `onCreate()` method and it would work the same. But one catch is that the `savedInstanceState` bundle will be null if there is no data, such as during the initial creation of the activity. If you want to move the code from the `onRestoreInstanceState()` callback, just check to make sure that the data is not null. Here's how that code would look:

```
if (savedInstanceState!=null) {
    mCounter = savedInstanceState.getInt(KEY_COUNTER);
}
```

See also

- The *Storing persistent activity data* recipe will introduce persistent storage
- Take a look at `Chapter 7`, Data Storage, for more examples on how to persist data
- The *Understanding the activity life cycle* recipe explains the Android Activity life cycle

Storing persistent activity data

Being able to store information about our activities on a temporary basis is very useful, but more often than not, we will want our application to remember information across multiple sessions.

Android supports SQLite, but that could be a lot of overhead for simple data, such as the user's name or a high score. Fortunately, Android also provides a lightweight option for these scenarios with `SharedPreferences`. (In a real-world application, you'll likely use both options for saving data.)

Getting ready

You can either use the project from the previous recipe or start a new project and call it `PersistentData`. In the previous recipe, we saved `mCounter` in the session state. In this recipe, we'll add a new method to handle `onPause()` and save `mCounter` to `SharedPreferences`. We'll restore the value in `onCreate()`.

How to do it...

We have only two changes to make, and both are in `MainActivity.java`:

1. Add the following `onPause()` method to save the data before the activity closes:

```
@Override
protected void onPause() {
    super.onPause();
    SharedPreferences settings = getPreferences(MODE_PRIVATE);
    SharedPreferences.Editor editor = settings.edit();
    editor.putInt(KEY_COUNTER, mCounter);
    editor.commit();
}
```

2. Then, add the following code at the end of `onCreate()` to restore the counter:

```
SharedPreferences settings = getPreferences(MODE_PRIVATE);
int defaultCounter = 0;
mCounter = settings.getInt(KEY_COUNTER, defaultCounter);
((TextView)findViewById(R.id.textViewCounter))
        .setText("Counter: " + Integer.toString(mCounter));
```

3. Run the program and try it out.

How it works...

As you can see, this is very similar to saving state data, because it also uses name/value pairs. Here, we just stored an `int`, but we can just as easily store one of the other primitive data types. Each data type has equivalent getters and setters, for example, `SharedPreferences.getBoolean()` or `SharedPreferences.setString()`.

Saving our data requires the services of `SharedPreferences.Editor`. This is evoked with `edit()` and accepts `remove()` and `clear()` procedures, as well as setters such as `putInt()`. Note that we must conclude any changes with the `commit()` statement.

There's more...

There is a slightly more sophisticated variant of the `getPreferences()` accessor: `getSharedPreferences()`. It can be used to store multiple preference sets.

Using more than one preference file

Using `getSharedPreferences()` is no different from using its counterpart, but it allows for more than one preference file. It takes the following form:

```
getSharedPreferences(String name, int mode)
```

Here, `name` is the file. The `mode` can be either `MODE_PRIVATE`, `MODE_WORLD_READABLE`, or `MODE_WORLD_WRITABLE` and describes the file's access levels.

See also

- Chapter 7, *Data Storage*, for more examples on data storage

Understanding the activity life cycle

As mobile hardware continues to improve, so too does the demand placed on that hardware. With increasingly more powerful applications and user multi-tasking, the already limited resources can be quite challenging. The Android OS has many features built in to help the user get the best performance from their device, such as limiting background processes, disabling application notifications, and allowing data limits. The OS will also manage application lifetime based on foreground tasks. If your application is in the foreground, the life cycle is straightforward. But as soon as your user switches tasks and your application is moved to the background, understanding the Android application life cycle becomes very important.

The following diagram shows the stages through which an activity passes during its lifetime:

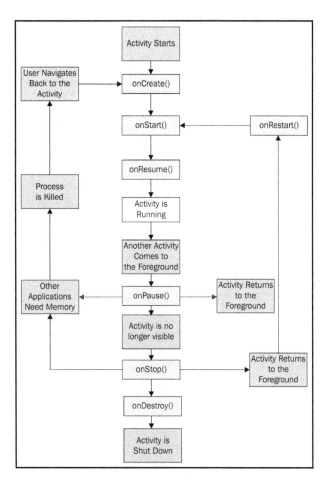

Along with the stages, the diagram also shows the methods that can be overridden. As you can see, we've already utilized most of these methods in the preceding recipes. Hopefully, getting the big picture will help your understanding.

Getting ready

Create a new project in Android Studio with a **Blank Activity**, and call it `ActivityLifecycle`. We will use the (auto-generated) `TextView` method to display the state information.

How to do it...

To see the application move through the various stages, we will create methods for all the stages:

1. Open `activity_main.xml` and add an ID to the auto-generated `TextView`:

   ```
   android:id="@+id/textViewState"
   ```

2. The remaining steps will be in `MainActivity.java`. Modify the `onCreate()` method to set the initial text:

   ```
   ((TextView)findViewById(R.id.textViewState)).setText("onCreate()n")
   ;
   ```

3. Add the following methods to handle the remaining events:

   ```
   @Override
   protected void onStart() {
       super.onStart();
   ((TextView)findViewById(R.id.textViewState)).append("onStart()\n");
   }

   @Override
   protected void onResume() {
       super.onResume();
   ((TextView)findViewById(R.id.textViewState)).append("onResume()\n")
   ;
   }

   @Override
   protected void onPause() {
       super.onPause();
   ((TextView)findViewById(R.id.textViewState)).append("onPause()\n");
   ```

```
    }

    @Override
    protected void onStop() {
        super.onStop();
        ((TextView)findViewById(R.id.textViewState)).append("onStop()\n");
    }

    @Override
    protected void onRestart() {
        super.onRestart();
        ((TextView)findViewById(R.id.textViewState)).append("onRestart()\n"
        );
    }

    @Override
    protected void onDestroy() {
        super.onDestroy();
        ((TextView)findViewById(R.id.textViewState)).append("onDestroy()\n"
        );
    }
```

4. Run the application and observe what happens when the activity is interrupted by pressing the Back and Home keys. Try other actions, such as task switching, to see how they impact your application.

How it works...

Our activity can exist in one of these three states: **active**, **paused**, or **stopped**. There is also a fourth state, **destroyed** (but there's no guarantee the OS will ever call it):

- An activity is in the active state when its interface is available for the user. It persists from onResume() until onPause(), which is brought about when another activity comes to the foreground. If this new activity does not entirely obscure our activity, then ours will remain in the paused state until the new activity is finished or dismissed. It will then immediately call onResume() and continue.

- When a newly started activity fills the screen or makes our activity invisible, then our activity will enter the stopped state, and resumption will always invoke a call to onRestart().

- When an activity is in either the paused or stopped state, the operating system can (and will) remove it from the memory when the memory is low or when other applications demand it.

- It is worth noting that we never actually see the results of the `onDestroy()` method, as the activity is removed by this point. If you want to explore these methods further, then it is well worth employing `Activity.isFinishing()` to see whether the activity is really finishing before `onDestroy()` is executed, as seen in the following snippet:

```
@Override
public void onPause() {
    super.onPause();
((TextView)findViewById(R.id.textViewState)).append("onPause()\n");
    if (isFinishing()){
        ((TextView)findViewById(R.id.textViewState)).append(" ...
finishing");
    }
}
```

When implementing these methods, always call the superclass before doing any work.

There's more...

To shut down an activity, directly call its `finish()` method, which in turn calls `onDestroy()`. To perform the same action from a child activity, use `finishFromChild(Activity child)`, where `child` is the calling subactivity.

It is often useful to know whether an activity is being shut down or merely paused, and the `isFinishing(boolean)` method returns a value that indicates which of these two states the activity is in.

2
Layouts

In this chapter, we will cover the following topics:

- Defining and inflating a layout
- Using `RelativeLayout`
- Using `LinearLayout`
- Creating tables—`TableLayout` and `GridLayout`
- `RecyclerView` replaces `ListView`
- Changing layout properties during runtime

Introduction

In Android, the user interface is defined in a **layout**. A layout can be declared in XML or created dynamically in code. (It's recommended to declare the layout in XML rather than in code to keep the presentation layer separate from the implementation layer.) A layout can define an individual `ListItem`, a fragment, or even the entire activity. Layout files are stored in the `/res/layout` folder and referenced in code with the following identifier: `R.layout.<filename_without_extension>`.

Android provides a useful variety of `Layout` classes that contain and organize individual elements of an activity (such as buttons, checkboxes, and other Views). The `ViewGroup` object is a container object that serves as the base class for Android's family of `Layout` classes. The Views placed in a layout form a hierarchy, with the topmost layout being the parent.

Android provides several built-in layout types designed for specific purposes, such as `RelativeLayout`, which allows Views to be positioned with respect to other elements. The `LinearLayout` can stack Views or align them horizontally, depending on the orientation specified. The `TableLayout` can be used for laying out a grid of Views. Within various layouts, we can also justify Views with `Gravity` and provide proportional size with `Weight` control. Layouts and `ViewGroups` can be nested within each other to create complex configurations. Over a dozen different Layout objects are provided for managing widgets, lists, tables, galleries, and other display formats, plus you can always derive from base classes to create your own custom layouts.

Google has released a new layout called `ConstraintLayout`. This layout is similar to `ReleativeLayout` in that Views are positioned relative to each other and to the parent, as well as a new element called guidelines. The focus of the layout is to keep the layout itself as flat as possible (deeply nested layouts can cause performance issues) and for a visual layout editor. Giving the best visual editing experience while keeping the editor in sync with the underlying class is such a priority for Google, that the same team develops both. `ConstraintLayout` is now the default layout created when using the Android Studio and is the basis for most of the examples in this book. (The other layouts are still available and are used when their layout provides the cleanest XML.) Here's the link to the `ConstraintLayout` class, but for the best experience, it's recommended to use the visual editor in Android Studio: `https://developer.android.com/reference/android/support/constraint/ConstraintLayout`.

Defining and inflating a layout

When using the Android Studio wizard to create a new project, it automatically creates the `res/layout/activity_main.xml` file (as shown in the following screenshot). It then inflates the XML file in the `onCreate()` callback with `setContentView(R.layout.activity_main)`:

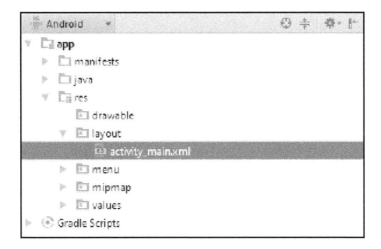

For this recipe, we will create two slightly different layouts and switch between them with a button.

Getting ready

Create a new project in Android Studio and call it `InflateLayout`. Once the project is created, expand the `res/layout` folder so we can edit the `activity_main.xml` file. Use the default **Phone & Tablet** settings on the **Target Android devices** and select **Empty Activity** on the **Add an Activity to Mobile** dialog.

How to do it...

1. Edit the `res/layout/activity_main.xml` file so it includes a button as defined here:

```
<Button
    android:id="@+id/buttonLeft"
    android:layout_width="wrap_content"
    android:layout_height="wrap_content"
    android:layout_alignParentLeft="true"
    android:layout_centerVertical="true"
    android:onClick="onClickLeft"
    android:text="Left Button"
    app:layout_constraintBottom_toBottomOf="parent"
    app:layout_constraintHorizontal_bias="0.0"
    app:layout_constraintLeft_toLeftOf="parent"
```

```
app:layout_constraintRight_toRightOf="parent"
app:layout_constraintTop_toTopOf="parent"/>
```

2. Now make a copy of `activity_main.xml` and call it `activity_main2.xml`. Change the button so it matches the following:

```
<Button
    android:id="@+id/buttonLeft"
    android:layout_width="wrap_content"
    android:layout_height="wrap_content"
    android:layout_alignParentLeft="true"
    android:layout_centerVertical="true"
    android:onClick="onClickRight"
    android:text="Right Button"
    app:layout_constraintBottom_toBottomOf="parent"
    app:layout_constraintHorizontal_bias="1.0"
    app:layout_constraintLeft_toLeftOf="parent"
    app:layout_constraintRight_toRightOf="parent"
    app:layout_constraintTop_toTopOf="parent"/>
```

3. Open `MainActivity.java` and add the following two methods to handle the button clicks:

```java
public void onClickLeft(View view) {
    setContentView(R.layout.activity_main2);
}

public void onClickRight(View view) {
    setContentView(R.layout.activity_main);
}
```

4. Run this application on a device or emulator to see it in action.

How it works...

The key here is the call to `setContentView()`, which we have come across before in the autogenerated `onCreate()` code. Just pass a layout ID to `setContentView()` and it automatically inflates the layout.

This code is meant to make the concept easy to understand but would be overkill for simply changing the property of a button (in this example, we could just change the alignment on the button click). Inflating the layout is usually needed once, in the `onCreate()` method, but there are times when you may want to manually inflate a layout, as we did here. (If you were manually handling orientation changes, it would be a good example.)

There's more...

As well as identifying a layout using a resource ID, as we did here, `setContentView()` can also take a View as an argument, for example:

```
findViewById(R.id.myView)
setContentView(myView);
```

See also

As mentioned previously, read about *Fragments* in `Chapter 5`, *Fragments*, for creating reusable screen components for your activities.

Using RelativeLayout

As mentioned in the *Introduction* section, `RelativeLayout` allows Views to be position-relative to each other and the parent. `RelativeLayout` is particularly useful for reducing the number of nested layouts, which is very important for reducing memory and processing requirements.

Getting ready

Create a new project and call it `RelativeLayout`. Android Studio defaults to using a `ConstraintLayout`, which we will replace with a `RelativeLayout` for this example. Use the default **Phone & Tablet** settings on the **Target Android devices** and select **Empty Activity** on the **Add an Activity to Mobile** dialog.

How to do it...

1. Open the `res/layout/activity_main.xml` file and change it as follows:

```
<?xml version="1.0" encoding="utf-8"?>
<RelativeLayout
    xmlns:android="http://schemas.android.com/apk/res/android"
    android:layout_width="match_parent"
    android:layout_height="match_parent" >
    <TextView
        android:id="@+id/textView1"
```

```
            android:layout_width="wrap_content"
            android:layout_height="wrap_content"
            android:text="Centered"
            android:layout_centerVertical="true"
            android:layout_centerHorizontal="true" />
    <TextView
            android:id="@+id/textView2"
            android:layout_width="wrap_content"
            android:layout_height="wrap_content"
            android:text="Below Left"
            android:layout_below="@+id/textView1"
            android:layout_toLeftOf="@id/textView1" />
    <TextView
            android:id="@+id/textView3"
            android:layout_width="wrap_content"
            android:layout_height="wrap_content"
            android:text="Bottom Right"
            android:layout_alignParentBottom="true"
            android:layout_alignParentRight="true" />
</RelativeLayout>
```

2. Run the code, or view the layout in the **Design** tab

How it works...

This is a very straightforward exercise but it demonstrates several of the `RelativeLayout` options: `layout_centerVertical`, `layout_centerHorizontal`, `layout_below`, `layout_alignParentBottom`, and so on.

The most commonly used `RelativeLayout` layout attributes include the following:

- `layout_below`: This View should be below the View specified.
- `layout_above`: This View should be above the View specified.
- `layout_alignParentTop`: Align this View to the top edge of the parent.
- `layout_alignParentBottom`: Align this View to the bottom edge of the parent.
- `layout_alignParentLeft`: Align this View to the left edge of the parent.
- `layout_alignParentRight`: Align this View to the right edge of the parent.
- `layout_centerVertical`: Center this View vertically within the parent.
- `layout_centerHorizontal`: Center this View horizontally within the parent.
- `layout_center`: Center this View both horizontally and vertically within the parent.

For the complete list of `RelativeLayout` parameters, visit `http://developer.android.com/reference/android/widget/Relat iveLayout.LayoutParams.html`.

There's more...

In contrast to what we saw earlier, here is an example using `LinearLayout` just to center `TextView` (creating the same effect as the `layout_center` parameter of `RelativeLayout`):

```xml
<?xml version="1.0" encoding="utf-8"?>
<LinearLayout xmlns:android="http://schemas.android.com/apk/res/android"
    android:orientation="horizontal"
    android:layout_width="match_parent"
    android:layout_height="match_parent"
    android:gravity="center">
    <LinearLayout
        android:layout_width="0dp"
        android:layout_height="wrap_content"
        android:layout_weight="1"
        android:gravity="center" >
        <TextView
            android:id="@+id/imageButton_speak"
            android:layout_width="wrap_content"
            android:layout_height="wrap_content"
            android:text="Centered" />
    </LinearLayout>
</LinearLayout>
```

Notice this layout is one level deeper than the equivalent `RelativeLayout` (which is `LinearLayout` nested within the parent `LinearLayout`.) Though a simple example, it's a good idea to avoid unnecessary nesting as it can impact performance, especially when a layout is being repeatedly inflated (such as `ListItem`).

See also

The next recipe, *Using LinearLayout*, will give you an alternative layout.

See the *Optimizing layouts with the Hierarchy Viewer* recipe for more information on efficient layout design.

Using LinearLayout

Another common layout option is `LinearLayout`, which arranges the child Views in a single column or single row, depending on the orientation specified. The default orientation (if not specified) is vertical, which aligns the Views in a single column.

`LinearLayout` has a key feature not offered in `RelativeLayout`—the `weight` attribute. We can specify a `layout_weight` parameter when defining a View to allow the View to dynamically size based on the available space. Options include having a View fill all the remaining space (if a View has a higher weight), having multiple Views fit within the given space (if all have the same weight), or spacing the Views proportionally by their weight.

We will create `LinearLayout` with three `EditText` Views to demonstrate how the `weight` attribute can be used. For this example, we will use three `EditText` Views-one to enter a `To Address` parameter, another to enter `Subject`, and the third to enter `Message`. The `To` and `Subject` Views will be a single line each, with the remaining space given to the `Message` View.

Getting ready

Create a new project and call it `LinearLayout`. We will replace the default `RelativeLayout` created in `activity_main.xml` with `LinearLayout`. Use the default **Phone & Tablet** settings on the **Target Android devices** and select **Empty Activity** on the **Add an Activity to Mobile** dialog.

How to do it...

1. Open the `res/layout/activity_main.xml` file and replace it as follows:

```
<LinearLayout
xmlns:android="http://schemas.android.com/apk/res/android"
    android:orientation="vertical"
    android:layout_width="match_parent"
    android:layout_height="match_parent">
    <EditText
        android:id="@+id/editTextTo"
        android:layout_width="match_parent"
        android:layout_height="wrap_content"
        android:hint="To" />
    <EditText
        android:id="@+id/editTextSubject"
```

```
            android:layout_width="match_parent"
            android:layout_height="wrap_content"
            android:hint="Subject" />
        <EditText
            android:id="@+id/editTextMessage"
            android:layout_width="match_parent"
            android:layout_height="0dp"
            android:layout_weight="1"
            android:gravity="top"
            android:hint="Message" />
    </LinearLayout>
```

2. Run the code, or view the layout in the **Design** tab.

How it works...

When using vertical orientation with LinearLayout, the child Views are created in a single column (stacked on top of each other). The first two Views use the android:layout_height="wrap_content" attribute, giving them a single line each. To specify the height, editTextMessage uses the following:

```
android:layout_height="0dp"
android:layout_weight="1"
```

When using LinearLayout, it tells Android to calculate the height based on the weight. A weight of 0 (the default if not specified) indicates the View should not expand. In this example, editTextMessage is the only View defined with a weight, so it alone will expand to fill any remaining space in the parent layout.

 When using the horizontal orientation, specify android:layout_height="0dp" (along with the weight) to have Android calculate the width.

It might be helpful to think of the weight attribute as a percentage. In this case, the total weight defined is 1, so this View gets 100 percent of the remaining space. If we assigned a weight of 1 to another View, the total would be 2, so this View would get 50 percent of the space. Try adding a weight to one of the other Views (make sure to change the height to 0dp as well) to see it in action.

If you added a weight to one (or both) of the other Views, did you notice the text position? Without specifying a value for `gravity`, the text just remains in the center of the View space. The `editTextMessage` View specifies `android:gravity="top"`, which forces the text to the top of the View.

There's more...

Multiple attribute options can be combined using bitwise OR. (Java uses the pipe character (|) for OR). For example, we could combine two gravity options to both align along the top of the parent and center within the available space:

```
android:layout_gravity="top|center"
```

It should be noted that the `layout_gravity` and `gravity` tags are not the same thing. Where `layout_gravity` dictates where in its parent a View should lie, `gravity` controls the positioning of the contents within a View, for example, the alignment of text on a button.

See also

The previous recipe, *Using RelativeLayout*.

Creating tables – TableLayout and GridLayout

When you need to create a table in your UI, Android provides two convenient layout options: `TableLayout` (along with `TableRow`) and `GridLayout` (added in API 14). Both layout options can create similar-looking tables, but each using a different approach. With `TableLayout`, rows and columns are added dynamically as you build the table. With `GridLayout`, row and column sizes are defined in the layout definition.

Neither layout is better, it's just a matter of using the best layout for your needs. We'll create a 3 x 3 grid using each layout to give a comparison, as you could easily find yourself using both layouts, even within the same application.

Getting ready

To stay focused on the layouts and offer an easier comparison, we will create two separate applications for this recipe. Create two new Android projects, the first called `TableLayout` and the other called `GridLayout`. Use the default **Phone & Tablet** settings on the **Target Android devices** and select **Empty Activity** on the **Add an Activity to Mobile** dialog.

How to do it...

1. Starting with the `TableLayout` project, open `activity_main.xml`. Change the root layout to `TableLayout`.

2. Add three `TableRow` objects with three sets of `TextView` objects to each `TableRow` to create a 3 x 3 matrix. For demonstration purposes, the columns are labeled A-C and the rows 1-3, so the first row of `TextView` objects will be A1, B1, and C1. The final result will look like this:

```
<TableLayout
    xmlns:android="http://schemas.android.com/apk/res/android"
    xmlns:tools="http://schemas.android.com/tools"
    android:layout_width="match_parent"
    android:layout_height="match_parent">
    <TableRow
        android:layout_width="match_parent"
        android:layout_height="match_parent">
        <TextView
            android:layout_width="wrap_content"
            android:layout_height="wrap_content"
            android:text="A1"
            android:id="@+id/textView1" />
        <TextView
            android:layout_width="wrap_content"
            android:layout_height="wrap_content"
            android:text="B1"
            android:id="@+id/textView2" />
        <TextView
            android:layout_width="wrap_content"
            android:layout_height="wrap_content"
            android:text="C1"
            android:id="@+id/textView3" />
    </TableRow>
    <TableRow
        android:layout_width="match_parent"
        android:layout_height="match_parent">
        <TextView
```

```
                    android:layout_width="wrap_content"
                    android:layout_height="wrap_content"
                    android:text="A2"
                    android:id="@+id/textView4" />
                <TextView
                    android:layout_width="wrap_content"
                    android:layout_height="wrap_content"
                    android:text="B2"
                    android:id="@+id/textView5" />
                <TextView
                    android:layout_width="wrap_content"
                    android:layout_height="wrap_content"
                    android:text="C2"
                    android:id="@+id/textView6" />
            </TableRow>
            <TableRow
                android:layout_width="match_parent"
                android:layout_height="match_parent">
                <TextView
                    android:layout_width="wrap_content"
                    android:layout_height="wrap_content"
                    android:text="A3"
                    android:id="@+id/textView7" />
                <TextView
                    android:layout_width="wrap_content"
                    android:layout_height="wrap_content"
                    android:text="B3"
                    android:id="@+id/textView8" />
                <TextView
                    android:layout_width="wrap_content"
                    android:layout_height="wrap_content"
                    android:text="C3"
                    android:id="@+id/textView9" />
            </TableRow>
        </TableLayout>
```

3. Now, open the `GridLayout` project to edit `activity_main.xml`. Change the root layout to `GridLayout`. Add the `columnCount=3` and `rowCount=3` attributes to the `GridLayout` element.

4. Now, add nine `TextView` objects to `GridLayout`. We will use the same text as the preceding `TableLayout` for a consistent comparison. Since `GridView` does not use `TableRow` objects, the first three `TextView` objects are in row 1, the next three are in row 2, and so on. The final result will look like this:

```
<GridLayout
    xmlns:android="http://schemas.android.com/apk/res/android"
```

```
android:layout_width="match_parent"
android:layout_height="match_parent"
android:columnCount="3"
android:rowCount="3">
<TextView
    android:layout_width="wrap_content"
    android:layout_height="wrap_content"
    android:text="A1"
    android:id="@+id/textView1" />
<TextView
    android:layout_width="wrap_content"
    android:layout_height="wrap_content"
    android:text="B1"
    android:id="@+id/textView2" />
<TextView
    android:layout_width="wrap_content"
    android:layout_height="wrap_content"
    android:text="C1"
    android:id="@+id/textView3" />
<TextView
    android:layout_width="wrap_content"
    android:layout_height="wrap_content"
    android:text="A2"
    android:id="@+id/textView4" />
<TextView
    android:layout_width="wrap_content"
    android:layout_height="wrap_content"
    android:text="B2"
    android:id="@+id/textView5" />
<TextView
    android:layout_width="wrap_content"
    android:layout_height="wrap_content"
    android:text="C2"
    android:id="@+id/textView6" />
<TextView
    android:layout_width="wrap_content"
    android:layout_height="wrap_content"
    android:text="A3"
    android:id="@+id/textView7" />
<TextView
    android:layout_width="wrap_content"
    android:layout_height="wrap_content"
    android:text="B3"
    android:id="@+id/textView8" />
<TextView
    android:layout_width="wrap_content"
    android:layout_height="wrap_content"
    android:text="C3"
```

```
                android:id="@+id/textView9" />
        </GridLayout>
```

5. You can either run the application or use the **Design** tab to see the results.

How it works...

As you can see when viewing the tables created, the tables basically look the same on screen. The main difference is the code to create them.

In the `TableLayout` XML, each row is added to the table using `TableRow`. Each View becomes a column. This is not a requirement as cells can be skipped or left empty. (See how to specify the cell location in `TableRow` in the following section.)

`GridLayout` uses the opposite approach. The number of rows and columns are specified when creating the table. We don't have to specify the row or column information (though we can, as discussed later). Android will automatically add each View to the cells in order.

There's more...

First, let's see more similarities between the layouts. Both layouts have the ability to stretch columns to use the remaining screen space. For `TableLayout`, add the following attribute to the XML declaration:

```
android:stretchColumns="1"
```

The `stretchColumns` attribute specifies the (zero-based) index of the columns to stretch (`android:shrinkColumns` is a zero-based index of columns that can shrink, so the table can fit the screen).

To achieve the same effect with `GridLayout`, add the following attribute to all the Views in the B column (`textView2`, `textView5`, and `textView8`):

```
android:layout_columnWeight="1"
```

All cells in a given column must define the weight or it will not stretch.

Now, let's look at some of the differences, as this is really the key to determining which layout to use for a given task. The first item to note is how the columns and rows are actually defined. In `TableLayout`, the rows are specifically defined, using `TableRow`. (Android will determine the number of columns in the table based on the row with the most cells.) Use the `android:layoutColumn` attribute when defining the View to specify the column.

In contrast, with `GridLayout`, the row and column counts are specified when defining the table (using `columnCount` and `rowCount` as shown previously).

In the preceding example, we just added `TextView` objects to `GridLayout` and let the system position them automatically. We can alter this behavior by specifying the row and column position when defining the View, such as the following:

```
android:layout_row="2"
android:layout_column="2"
```

 Android automatically increments the cell counter after adding each View, so the *next* View should also specify the row and column, otherwise, you may not get the intended result.

Like `LinearLayout`, shown in the *Using LinearLayout* recipe, `GridLayout` also offers the orientation attribute of supporting both horizontal (the default) and vertical. The orientation determines how the cells are placed. (Horizontal fills the columns first, then moves down to the next row. Vertical fills the first column on each row, then moves to the next column.)

RecyclerView replaces ListView

As the name implies, `ListView` is designed for displaying lists of information. If you have prior experience on Android, you've probably come across the `ListView` and possibly `GridView` controls before. If not while coding, most likely you've used it as an app, as it's one of the most commonly used controls available. For most applications and users, the old `ListView` was probably sufficient and didn't pose any problems. As an example, most users could probably see their list of emails in their inbox without any problems. But for some, they might have so many emails in their inbox that when scrolling through their list, their device would stutter (slight pauses when scrolling). Unfortunately, `ListView` has many such performance problems.

The most significant performance issue with ListView is caused by creating new item objects for each item when scrolling. Though much of the performance problem could be eliminated with a properly implemented data adapter, the implementation was optional. As the name implies, RecyclerView is based on recycling the list items (the part that was optional in the ListView adapter). There are other changes to the control as well. Whereas ListView has many features built-in, RecyclerView is very basic and relies on additional helper classes to achieve the same functionality. For some, this feels like a step backward with the new control but this design allows it to be expanded much easier.

Where RecylerView really shines is with the flexibility when extending it and animations. Our example here uses a static list so it doesn't show off the built-in animations, but with dynamic data, your list will take advantage of the Material Design look and feel. Though ListView is not officially deprecated, it is recommended to use RecyclerView for new projects. It's a bit more work to get started, but this recipe will give you all the code to get set up.

Getting ready

Create a new project in Android Studio called RecyclerView. Use the default **Phone & Tablet** settings on the **Target Android devices** and select **Empty Activity** on the **Add an Activity to Mobile** dialog.

How to do it...

Creating RecyclerView is as simple as placing the control on the screen. Most of the work is with the adapter, which we'll create from a static list. RecyclerView is distributed in a separate library so it needs to be added to the project as a dependency. The steps are as follows:

1. Either add the dependency through the Android Studio UI or add the following code to the dependencies section of the build.gradle (Module: app) file:
   implementation 'com.android.support:recyclerview-v7:27.1

   NOTE: v7:27.1 is current at the time of this writing, but should be updated to the latest version. (The IDE will likely give you a warning if you're not using the latest version.)

2. Open `activity_main.xml` and replace the existing `<TextView />` block with the following `RecyclerView` widget:

```
<android.support.v7.widget.RecyclerView
    android:id="@+id/recyclerView"
    android:layout_width="match_parent"
    android:layout_height="match_parent"
    app:layout_constraintBottom_toBottomOf="parent"
    app:layout_constraintLeft_toLeftOf="parent"
    app:layout_constraintRight_toRightOf="parent"
    app:layout_constraintTop_toTopOf="parent" />
```

3. We need another layout for the adapter to create the individual items in the list. To do this, create a new file in the `res\layout` folder called `item.xml` as follows:

```
<?xml version="1.0" encoding="utf-8"?>
<LinearLayout
xmlns:android="http://schemas.android.com/apk/res/android"
    android:layout_width="match_parent"
    android:layout_height="wrap_content"
    android:orientation="vertical">
    <TextView
        android:id="@+id/textView"
        android:layout_width="match_parent"
        android:layout_height="wrap_content"
        android:text="TextView" />
</LinearLayout>
```

4. Now comes the heart of `RecyclerView` – the adapter. Create a new Java file called `MyAdapter.java`. Our new class will extend from the `RecyclerView.Adapter` class so there are several key methods we need to override. We'll discuss the details of this class later, but the full code is as follows:

```
public class MyAdapter extends
RecyclerView.Adapter<MyAdapter.MyViewHolder> {

    private List<String> nameList;

    public MyAdapter(List<String> list) {
        nameList = list;
    }

    @Override
    public MyViewHolder onCreateViewHolder(ViewGroup parent, int
viewType) {
        LayoutInflater inflater =
```

```
LayoutInflater.from(parent.getContext());
        View view = inflater.inflate(R.layout.item, parent, false);
        MyViewHolder myViewHolder = new MyViewHolder(view);
        return myViewHolder;
    }

    @Override
    public void onBindViewHolder(@NonNull MyViewHolder holder,
final int position) {
        final String name = nameList.get(position);
        holder.textView.setText(name);
    }

    @Override
    public int getItemCount() {
        if (nameList==null) {
            return 0;
        } else {
            return nameList.size();
        }
    }

    public class MyViewHolder extends RecyclerView.ViewHolder {
        public TextView textView;

        public MyViewHolder(View itemvieww) {
            super(itemvieww);
            textView = itemView.findViewById(R.id.textView);
        }
    }
}
```

5. With all the pieces set up, the final step is to put it all together. Open the `MainActivity.java` file and add the following code to the existing `onCreate()` method:

```
List<String> list = new ArrayList<>();
list.add("China");
list.add("France");
list.add("Germany");
list.add("India");
list.add("Russia");
list.add("United Kingdom");
list.add("United States");

RecyclerView recyclerView = findViewById(R.id.recyclerView);

recyclerView.setHasFixedSize(true);
```

```
LinearLayoutManager linearLayoutManager = new
LinearLayoutManager(this);
linearLayoutManager.setOrientation(LinearLayoutManager.VERTICAL);
recyclerView.setLayoutManager(linearLayoutManager);

MyAdapter myAdapter = new MyAdapter(list);
recyclerView.setAdapter(myAdapter);
```

How it works...

We've purposely kept this recipe basic, but as you can see, there are still many steps even for this basic implementation. The good news is, with this foundation set, you can easily expand and modify `RecyclerView` as needed. Want your list to scroll sideways instead? You can easily accomplish this by using `LinearLayoutManager.HORIZONTAL` in the `setOrientation()` call.

If you have ever worked with Android `ListView` before, then the preceding steps will look very familiar. The concept is the same: we create an adapter to hold a list of items. Steps 1 and 2 set up `RecyclerView` on the activity. In step 3, we specify the visual layout and pass it to the adapter. In step 4, we created the adapter by extending the `RecycerView.Adapter` class. As you can see from the code, there are three methods we need to override: `onCreateViewHolder()`, `onBindViewHolder()`, and `getItemCount()`. The key concept behind `RecylerView` is to recycle or reuse the item Views. This means, when you have a very large list of items, instead of creating a new view object for each item (which is very costly in terms of performance and memory usage), the item Views are reused. So as a user scrolls through a long list, as a view goes off the screen, it's reused for the next item being shown. Even if we added all the countries in the world to our list, there wouldn't be enough items to see the performance difference, but when you're working with a list of thousands of items, especially if those items include images, the performance when scrolling will be noticeable.

Now that you understand the concept behind `RecyclerView`, hopefully the methods we need to override are self-explanatory. The adapter only calls `onCreateViewHolder()` to create enough items to show on the screen (plus a few extra for scrolling), whereas `onBindViewHolder()` is called for each item as it's displayed.

There's more...

If you ran the code, then you saw it's a very simple app. In fact, it doesn't do anything more than just display the list in a scrollable container. Most apps will require some interaction with the list so how do we respond to click events? Unlike the older ListView, RecyclerView does not have any click events built-in. It's up to you, the programmer, to create the events you need. (For basic items like in our example, this may seem like more work for the programmer, but when you get to complex list items with buttons and other interactive controls, ListView would often get in your way and you'd need to implement custom events anyway.)

To respond to item clicks, add the following code to the MyAdapter class:

```
private void remove(int position) {
    nameList.remove(position);
    notifyItemRemoved(position);
}
```

Then add the following code to the onBindViewHolder() method created in step 4:

```
holder.itemView.setOnClickListener(new View.OnClickListener() {
    @Override
    public void onClick(View v) {
        remove(position);
    }
});
```

Now, when you run the code, the app will respond to the click event by removing the clicked item. You may also notice the smooth animation when removing the item. By calling the notifyItemRemoved() and notifyItemInserted() methods of RecyclerView, we can take advantage of the widget's built-in Material Design animations.

Changing layout properties during runtime

In Android development, it's generally the preferred practice to define the UI with XML and the application code in Java, keeping the user interface code separate from the application code. There are times where it is much easier or more efficient, to alter (or even build) the UI from the Java code. Fortunately, this is easily supported in Android.

In this recipe, we will obtain a reference to the `LayoutParams` object to change the margin during runtime.

Getting ready

Here, we will set up a simple layout with XML and use a `LinearLayout.LayoutParams` object to change the margins of a View during runtime. Create a new project using with an **Empty Activity** called `RuntimeProperties`. Use the default **Phone & Tablet** settings on the **Target Android devices** and select **Empty Activity** on the **Add an Activity to Mobile** dialog.

How to do it...

We can create or manipulate any of the standard layouts or controls through code. For this example, we will work with `LinearLayout`:

1. Open the `activity_main.xml` file and change the layout as follows:

```
<?xml version="1.0" encoding="utf-8"?>
<LinearLayout
xmlns:android="http://schemas.android.com/apk/res/android"
    android:layout_width="match_parent"
    android:layout_height="match_parent" >

</LinearLayout>
```

2. Add `TextView` with an ID value of `textView`, as follows:

```
<TextView
    android:id="@+id/textView"
    android:layout_width="wrap_content"
    android:layout_height="wrap_content"
    android:text="TextView" />
```

3. Add `Button` with an ID value of `button`, as follows:

```
<Button
    android:id="@+id/button"
    android:layout_width="wrap_content"
    android:layout_height="wrap_content"
    android:text="Button" />
```

4. Open `MainActivity.java` and add the following code to the `onCreate()` method to respond to the button click:

```
Button button = (Button)findViewById(R.id.button);
button.setOnClickListener(new View.OnClickListener() {
    @Override
    public void onClick(View view) {
        ((TextView)findViewById(
                R.id.textView)).setText("Changed at runtime!");
        LinearLayout.LayoutParams params = (LinearLayout.
                LayoutParams)view.getLayoutParams();
        params.leftMargin += 5;
    }
});
```

5. Run the program on a device or emulator.

How it works...

Every View (and therefore `ViewGroup`) has a set of layout parameters associated with it. In particular, all Views have parameters to inform their parent of their desired height and width. These are defined with the `layout_height` and `layout_width` parameters. We can access this layout information from the code with the `getLayoutParams()` method. The layout information includes the layout height, width, margins, and any class-specific parameters.

In this example, we moved the button on each click by obtaining the current button `LayoutParams` and increasing the margin.

Views, Widgets, and Styles

3

In this chapter, we will cover the following topics:

- Inserting a widget into a layout
- Using graphics to show the button state
- Creating a widget at runtime
- Creating a custom component
- Applying a style to a View
- Turning a style into a theme
- Selecting a theme based on the Android OS version

Introduction

The term **widgets** can refer to several different concepts in Android. When most people talk about widgets, they are referring to **app widgets**, which are typically seen on the home screen. App widgets are like mini applications by themselves as they usually provide a subset of functionality, based on their main application. (Usually, most app widgets are installed along with an application, but that is not a requirement. They can be standalone apps in a widget format.) A common app widget example is a weather application that offers several different app widgets for the home screen. Chapter 6, *Beyond Your App - Home Screen Widgets, Search, and the System UI*, will discuss home screen app widgets and provide recipes to create your own.

When developing for Android, the term widgets generally refers to specialized Views placed in the layout files, such as a **Button**, **TextView**, **CheckBox**, and so on. This chapter will focus on widgets for screen layouts.

To see the list of widgets provided in the **Android SDK**, open a layout file in Android Studio, and click on the **Design** tab. Along the left-hand side of the **Design** view, you will see the list of items that can be placed on the layout: **Common**, **Text**, **Buttons**, **Widgets**, **Layouts**, **Containers**, **Google**, and **Legacy**. Even though many of the items are not in the **Widget** category, by definition, they are still widgets. As you can see in the following screenshot, the **Widgets** category groups the more complicated controls:

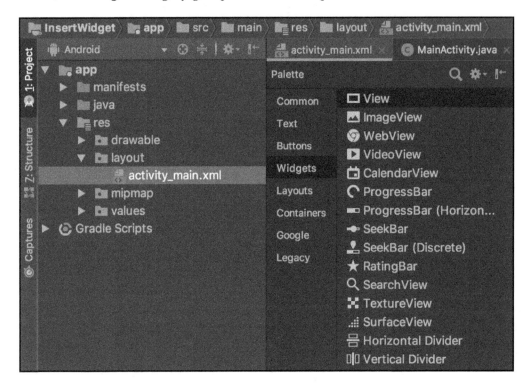

As you can see from the list, the Android SDK provides many useful widgets—from a simple **TextView**, **Button**, or **Checkbox**, to the much more complex widgets such as the **WebView**, **ProgressBar**, and **SearchView**. As useful as the built-in widgets are, it's also very easy to expand on what's provided in the SDK. We can extend an existing widget to customize its functionality, or we can create our own widget from scratch by extending the base View class. (We will provide an example of this in the *Creating a custom component* recipe later.)

The visual look of widgets can also be customized. These settings can be used to create **styles**, which in turn can be used to create **themes**. Just like with other development environments, creating a theme offers the benefit of easily changing the appearance throughout our entire application with minimal effort. Lastly, the Android SDK also provides many built-in themes and variations, such as the Material theme introduced in Android 5 and later the Material Design 2.0.

Inserting a widget into a layout

As you may have seen from previous recipes, **widgets** are declared in a layout file, or created in code. For this recipe, we will go step by step to add a button with the Android Studio Designer. (For later recipes, we will just show the layout XML.) After creating the button, we will create a method to receive the button click events using `onClickListener()`.

Getting ready

Start a new project in Android Studio and call it `InsertWidget`. Use the default options for creating a **Phone and Tablet** project and select **Empty Activity** when prompted for the **Activity Type**. You can delete the default `TextView` (or leave it) as it will not be needed for this recipe.

How to do it...

To insert a widget into a layout, follow these steps:

1. Open the `activity_main.xml` file in Android Studio and click on the **Design** tab. As you can see, by default, Android Studio adds a `TextView` to the layout. Select the `TextView` and delete it:

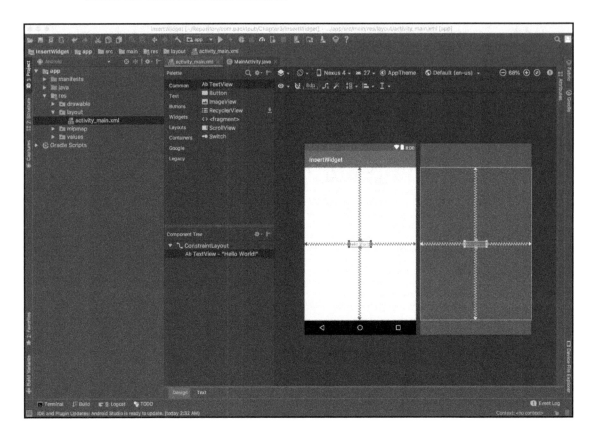

2. Find **Button** in the widget list and drag it to the center of the activity screen on the right:

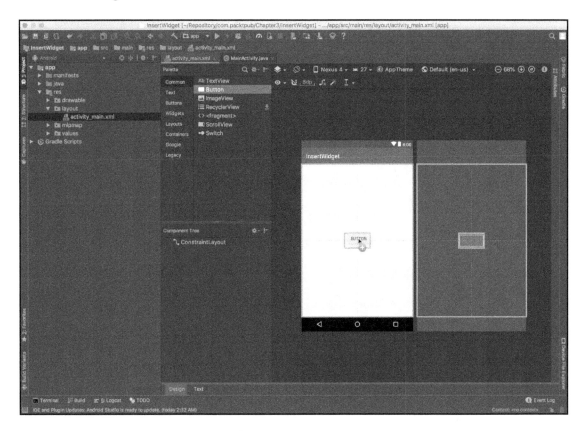

3. Though we placed the button in the center of the screen, the button will not actually be centered when you run the app. If we want it centered, we need to set the layout properties accordingly. (Currently, the button is just centered in the design tool to make it easier to work with but this has no affect when the app is running.) To center the button, start by selecting the button in the design view. When it is selected, you will see the edge nodes. Drag each edge node to the corresponding edge of the screen as shown in the following screenshot:

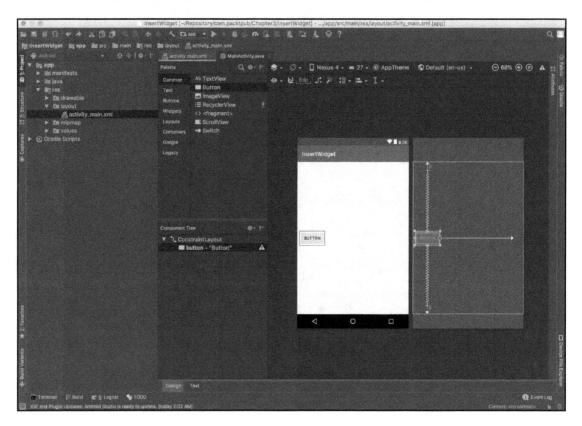

4. To view the xml created, click on the **Text** tab as shown in the following screenshot. See how the button is centered using the ConstraintLayout parameters. Also, take note of the default ID as we will need it for the next step:

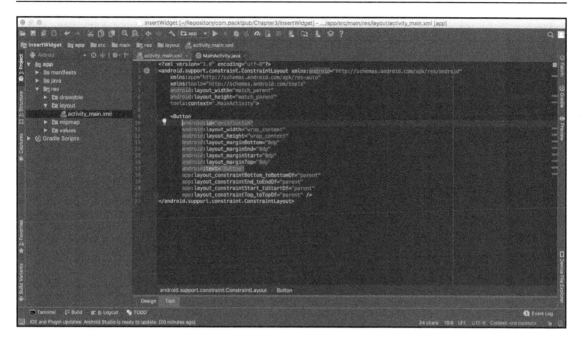

5. Now, open the `MainActivity.java` file to edit the code. Add the following code to the `onCreate()` method to set up `onClickListener()`:

```java
Button button = (Button)findViewById(R.id.button);
button.setOnClickListener(new View.OnClickListener() {
    @Override
    public void onClick(View view) {
        Toast.makeText(MainActivity.this,"Clicked",
            Toast.LENGTH_SHORT).show();
    }
});
```

6. Run the application on a device or emulator.

How it works...

Creating the UI with the Android Studio is as simple as dragging and dropping Views. You can also edit the properties of the Views directly in the **Design** tab. Switching to the XML code is as simple as hitting the **Text** tab.

What we did here is very common in Android development – creating the UI in XML, then hooking up the UI components (Views) in the Java code. To reference a View from code, it must have a resource identifier associated with it. This is done using the `id` parameter:

```
android:id="@+id/button"
```

Our `onClickListener` function displays a pop-up message on the screen called **Toast**, when the button is pressed.

There's more...

Take a look again at the format of the identifier we created previously, `@+id/button`. The `@` sign specifies this is going to be a resource and the + sign indicates a new resource. (If we failed to include the plus sign, we would get a compile-time error stating **No resource matched the indicated name**).

See also

- *Butter Knife – Field and method binding for Android views* (open source project): `http://jakewharton.github.io/butterknife/`

Using graphics to show button state

We've talked about the versatility of Android Views and how behavior and visual appearance can be customized. In this recipe, we will create a drawable **state selector**, which is a resource defined in XML that specifies the drawable to use based on the View's state.

The most commonly used states, along with the possible values, include the following:

- `state_pressed=["true" | "false"]`
- `state_focused=["true" | "false"]`
- `state_selected=["true" | "false"]`
- `state_checked=["true" | "false"]`
- `state_enabled=["true" | "false"]`

To define a state selector, create an XML file with the `<selector>` element, as shown:

```xml
<?xml version="1.0" encoding="utf-8"?>
<selector xmlns:android="http://schemas.android.com/apk/res/android" >
</selector>
```

Within the `<selector>` element, we define an `<item>` element to identify the drawable to be used based on the specified state(s). Here's an example `<item>` element using multiple states:

```xml
<item
    android:drawable="@android:color/darker_gray"
    android:state_checked="true"
    android:state_selected="false"/>
```

It's important to remember the file is read from top to bottom so the first item that meets the state requirements will be used. A default drawable, one with no states included, would need to go last.

For this recipe, we will use a state selector to change the background color based on the `ToggleButton` state.

Getting ready

Create a new project in Android Studio and call it `StateSelector` using the default **Phone & Tablet** options. When prompted for the **Activity Type**, select **Empty Activity**. To make it easier to type the code for this recipe, we will use a color as the graphic to represent the button state.

How to do it...

We will start by creating the state selector, which is a resource file defined with XML code. We will then set up the button to use our new state selector. Here are the steps:

1. Create a new **Drawable resource file** in the `res/drawable` folder and call it: `state_selector.xml`. The file should contain the following code:

```xml
<?xml version="1.0" encoding="utf-8"?>
<selector
xmlns:android="http://schemas.android.com/apk/res/android">
    <item
        android:drawable="@android:color/darker_gray"
```

```
            android:state_checked="true"/>
        <item
            android:drawable="@android:color/white"
            android:state_checked="false"/>
    </selector>
```

2. Now open the `activity_main.xml` file and drop in `ToggleButton` as follows:

```
<ToggleButton
    android:layout_width="wrap_content"
    android:layout_height="wrap_content"
    android:text="New ToggleButton"
    android:id="@+id/toggleButton"
    android:layout_centerVertical="true"
    android:layout_centerHorizontal="true"
    android:background="@drawable/state_selector" />
```

3. Run the application on a device or emulator.

How it works...

The main concept to understand here is the Android State Selector. As shown in step 1, we created a resource file to specify a **drawable** (a color in this case) based on `state_checked`.

Android supports many other state conditions besides checked. While typing in `android:state`, look at the autocomplete drop-down menu to see the list of other options.

Once we have the drawable resource created (the XML from step 1), we just have to tell the view to use it. Since we want the background color to change based on the state, we use the `android:background` property. The `state_selector.xml` is a drawable resource that can be passed to any property that accepts a drawable. We could, for example, replace the check image of a checkbox with the following XML:

```
<CheckBox
    android:id="@+id/checkBox"
    android:layout_width="wrap_content"
    android:layout_height="wrap_content"
    android:button="@drawable/state_selector"
    android:text="CheckBox" />
```

There's more...

What if we wanted actual images for the graphics instead of just a color change? This is as easy as changing the drawable referenced in the item state. The source code available for download uses two graphics, downloaded from: `https://pixabay.com/` (this site was chosen because the images are free to use and don't require a login).

Once you have your desired images, place them in the `res/drawable` folder. Then, change the state item line in the XML to reference your images. Here's an example:

```
<item
    android:drawable="@drawable/checked_on"
    android:state_checked="true"/>
```

(Change `check_on` to match your image resource name)

Using designated folders for screen-specific resources

When Android encounters a `@drawable` reference, it expects to find the target in one of the `res/drawable` folders. These are designed for different screen densities - `ldpi` (low dots per inch), `mdpi` (medium), `hdpi` (high), and `xhdpi` (extra-high) - and they allow us to create resources for specific target devices. When an application is running on a specific device, Android will load resources from the designated folder that most closely matches the actual screen density.

If it finds this folder empty, it will try the next nearest match and so on until it finds the named resource. For tutorial purposes, a separate set of files for each possible density is not required, and so placing our images in the `drawable` folder is a simple way to run the exercise on any device.

For a complete list of resource identifiers available, visit `http://developer.android.com/guide/topics/resources/providing-re sources.html`.

See also

For another example of Android resource selection, see the *Selecting a theme based on the Android version* recipe

Creating a widget at runtime

As mentioned before, generally, the UI is declared in XML files and then modified during runtime through the Java code. It is possible to create the UI completely in Java code, though for a complex layout, it would generally not be considered best practice.

In this recipe, we are going to add a view to the existing layout defined in `activity_main.xml`.

Getting ready

Create a new project in Android Studio and call it `RuntimeWidget`. Select the **Empty Activity** option when prompted for the **Activity Type**.

How to do it...

We will start by adding an ID attribute to the existing layout so we can access the layout in code. Once we have a reference to the layout in code, we can add new views to the existing layout. Here are the steps:

1. Open `res/layout/activity_main.xml` and add an ID attribute to the root `ConstraintLayout`, as follows:

   ```
   android:id="@+id/layout"
   ```

2. Completely remove the default `<TextView>` element.
3. Open the `MainActivity.java` file so we can add code to the `onCreate()` method. Add the following code (after `setContentView()`) to get a reference to `ConstraintLayout`:

   ```
   ConstraintLayout layout = findViewById(R.id.layout);
   ```

4. Create `DatePicker` and add it to the layout with the following code:

   ```
   DatePicker datePicker = new DatePicker(this);
   layout.addView(datePicker);
   ```

5. Run the program on a device or emulator.

How it works...

This is hopefully very straightforward code. First, we get a reference to the parent layout using `findViewById`. We added the ID to the existing `ConstraintLayout` (in step 1) to get a reference. We create a `DatePicker` in code and add it to the layout with the `addView()` method.

There's more...

What if we wanted to create the entire layout from code? Though it may not be considered best practice, there are times when it is certainly easier (and less complex) to create the entire layout from code. Let's see how this example would look if we didn't use the layout from `activity_main.xml`. Here's how `onCreate()` would look:

```
@Override
protected void onCreate(Bundle savedInstanceState) {
    super.onCreate(savedInstanceState);
    ConstraintLayout layout = new ConstraintLayout(this);
    DatePicker datePicker = new DatePicker(this);
    layout.addView(datePicker);
    setContentView(layout);
}
```

In this example, it's really not that different. If you create a view in code and want to reference it later, you either need to keep a reference to the object, or assign the view an ID to use `findViewByID()`. To give a view an ID, use the `setID()` method by passing in `View.generateViewId()` (to generate a unique ID) or define the ID using `<resources>` in XML.

Creating a custom component

As we have seen in previous recipes, the Android SDK provides a wide range of components. But what happens when you can't find a prebuilt component that fits your unique needs? You can always create your own!

In this recipe, we will walk through creating a custom component that derives from the View class, just like the built-in widgets. Here's a high-level overview:

1. Create a new class that extends View.
2. Create custom constructor(s).
3. Override onMeasure(), as the default implementation returns a size of 100 x 100.
4. Override onDraw(), as the default implementation draws nothing.
5. Define custom methods and listeners (such as the onClick() event).
6. Implement custom functionality.

Overriding onMeasure() and onDraw() is not strictly required, but the default behavior is likely not what you would want.

Getting ready

Start a new project in Android Studio and call it CustomView. Use the default wizard options, including the **Phone & Tablet SDK** and select **Empty Activity** when prompted for the **Activity Type**. Once the project files are created and open in Android Studio, you are ready to begin.

How to do it...

We will create a new class for our custom component to derive from the Android View class. Our custom component could be a subclass of an existing class, such as the activity, but we will create it in a separate file to make it easier to maintain. Here are the steps:

1. Start by creating a new Java class and calling it CustomView. This is where we will implement our custom component, as described in the *Introduction*.
2. Change the class constructor so it extends View. It should look as follows:

```
public class CustomView extends View {
```

3. Define a `Paint` object for the class, which will be used in `onDraw()`:

```
final Paint mPaint = new Paint();
```

4. Create a default constructor, which requires the activity `Context`, so we can inflate the view. We will set the paint properties here as well. The constructor should look as follows:

```
public CustomView(Context context) {
    super(context);
    mPaint.setColor(Color.BLACK);
    mPaint.setTextSize(30);
}
```

5. Override the `onDraw()` method as follows:

```
@Override
protected void onDraw(Canvas canvas) {
    super.onDraw(canvas);
    setBackgroundColor(Color.CYAN);
    canvas.drawText("Custom Text", 100, 100, mPaint);
    invalidate();
}
```

6. Finally, inflate our custom view in `MainActivity.java` by replacing `setContentView()` in the `onCreate()` method with our view, as shown:

```
setContentView(new CustomView(this));
```

7. Run the application on a device or emulator to see it in action.

How it works...

We start by extending the `View` class, just as the built-in components do. Next, we create the default constructor. This is important as we need the context to pass down to the `super` class, which we do with the following call:

```
super(context);
```

We need to override `onDraw()`, otherwise, as mentioned in the *Introduction*, our custom view won't display anything. When `onDraw()` is called, the system passes in a **Canvas** object. The canvas is the screen area of our view. (Since we didn't override `onMeasure()`, our view would be 100 x 100, but since our entire activity consists of just this view, we get the whole screen as our canvas.)

We created the `Paint` object at the class level, and as `final`, to be more efficient with memory allocation. (`onDraw()` should be as efficient as possible since it can be called multiple times per second.) As you see from running the program, our `onDraw()` implementation just sets the background color to cyan and prints text to the screen (using `drawText()`).

There's more...

Actually, there's a lot more. We've just touched the surface of what you can do with a custom component. Fortunately, as you see from this example, it doesn't take a lot of code to get basic functionality. We could easily spend an entire chapter on topics such as passing layout parameters to the view, adding listener callbacks, overriding `onMeasure()`, using our view in the IDE, and so on. These are all features you can add as your needs dictate.

While a custom component is always an option, there are other options that might require less coding. Extending an existing widget is often enough without the overhead of creating a custom component from scratch. If what you need is a solution with multiple widgets, there's also the **compound control**. A compound control, such as a combo box, is just two or more controls grouped together as a single widget.

A compound control would generally extend from a layout, not a View, since you will be adding multiple widgets. You probably wouldn't need to override `onDraw()` and `onMeasure()`, as each widget would handle the drawing in their respective methods.

See also

- For more information on drawing, look at Chapter 10, *Graphics and Animation*.
- For full details on the View object, refer to the Android Developer resource at http://developer.android.com/reference/android/view/View.html.

Applying a style to a View

A **style** is a collection of property settings to define the look of a View. As you have already seen while defining layouts, a view offers many settings to determine how it looks, as well as functions. We have already set a view height, width, background color, and padding, plus there are many more settings such as text color, font, text size, margin, and so on. Creating a style is as simple as pulling these settings from the layout and putting them in a style resource.

In this recipe, we will go through the steps of creating a style and hooking it up to a view.

Similar to Cascading Style Sheets, Android Styles allow you to specify your design settings separate from the UI code.

Getting ready

Create a new Android Studio project and call it Styles. Use the default wizard options to create a **Phone & Tablet** project and select **Empty Activity** when prompted for the Activity type. We haven't looked at it before, but by default, the wizard also creates a styles.xml file, which we will use for this recipe.

How to do it...

We will create our own style resource to change the appearance of `TextView`. We can add our new style to the `styles.xml` resource created by Android Studio using the following steps:

1. Open the default `styles.xml` file located in `res/values`, as shown here:

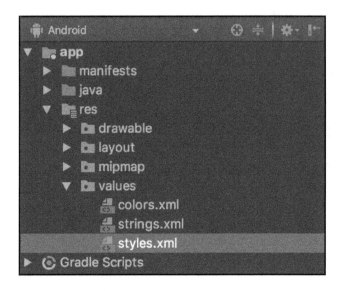

2. We will create a new style called `MyStyle` by adding the following XML below the existing `AppTheme` style:

```xml
<style name="MyStyle">
    <item name="android:layout_width">match_parent</item>
    <item name="android:layout_height">wrap_content</item>
    <item name="android:background">#000000</item>
    <item name="android:textColor">#AF0000</item>
    <item name="android:textSize">20sp</item>
    <item name="android:padding">8dp</item>
    <item name="android:gravity">center</item>
</style>
```

3. Now tell the view to use this style. Open the `activity_main.xml` file and add the following attribute to the existing `<TextView>` element:

```xml
style="@style/MyStyle"
```

4. Either run the application or view the results in the **Design** tab.

How it works...

A style is a resource, defined by using the `<style>` element in a `<resources>` element of an XML file. We used the existing `styles.xml` file, but that is not a requirement, as we can use whatever filename we want. As seen in this recipe, multiple `<style>` elements can be included in one XML file.

Once the style is created, you can easily apply it to any number of other views as well. What if you wanted to have a button with the same style? Just drop a button in the layout and assign the same style.

What if we created a new button, but wanted the button to expand the full width of the view? How do we override the style for just that view? Simply specify the attribute in the layout as you've always done. The local attribute will take priority over the attribute in the style.

There's more...

There is another feature of styles: **inheritance**. By specifying a parent when defining the style, we can have styles build on each other, creating a hierarchy of styles. If you look at the default style in `styles.xml`: `AppTheme`, you will see the following line:

```
<style name="AppTheme" parent="Theme.AppCompat.Light.DarkActionBar">
```

`AppTheme` inherits from a theme defined in the Android SDK.

 If you want to inherit from a style you have created yourself, there is a shortcut method. Instead of using the parent attribute, you can specify the parent name first, followed by a period, then the new name, such as the following:
`<style name="MyParent.MyStyle" >`

You saw how to specify a style for a view, but what if we wanted all the `TextView` objects in our application to use a specific style? We'd have to go back to each `TextView` and specify the style. But there's another way. We can include a `textViewStyle` item in a style to automatically assign a style to all `TextView` objects. (There's a style for each of the widget types so you can do this for `Button`, `ToggleButton`, `TextView`, and so on.)

To set the style for all `TextView` objects, add the following line to the `AppTheme` style:

```
<item name="android:textViewStyle">@style/MyStyle</item>
```

Since the theme for our application already uses AppTheme, we only have to add that single line to AppTheme to have all our TextView objects styled with our custom MyStyle.

See also

The Android Design Support Library at https://www.google.com/design/spec/material-design/introduction.html.

Turning a style into a theme

A **theme** is a style applied to an activity or the whole application. To set a theme, use the android:theme attribute in the AndroidManifest.xml file. The theme attribute applies to the <Application> element as well as the <Activity> elements. All views within that element will be styled with the theme specified.

It's common to set the application theme, but then override a specific activity with a different theme.

In the previous recipe, we set textViewStyle using the AppTheme style (which the wizard created automatically). In this recipe, you will learn how to set both the application and activity themes.

Along with the style settings we have already explored, there are additional style options we didn't discuss because they don't apply to a View, they apply to the window as a whole. Settings such as hiding the application title or action bar and setting the window background, just to name a few, apply to the window and therefore must be set as a theme.

For this recipe, we are going to create a new theme based on the autogenerated AppTheme. Our new theme will modify the window appearance to make it a **dialog**. We will also look at the theme settings in the AndroidManifest.xml.

Getting ready

Start a new project in Android Studio and call it Themes. Use the default wizard options and select **Empty Activity** when prompted for the **Activity type**.

How to do it...

We start by adding a new theme to the existing `styles.xml` file to make our activity look like a dialog. Here are the steps to create the new theme and set the activity to use the new theme:

1. Since themes are defined in the same resource as styles, open the `styles.xml` file located in `res/values` and create a new style. We will create a new style based on the `AppTheme` already provided, and set `windowIsFloating`. The XML will be as follows:

```
<style name="AppTheme.MyDialog">
    <item name="android:windowIsFloating">true</item>
</style>
```

2. Next, set the activity to use this new dialog theme. Open the `AndroidManifest.xml` file and add a `theme` attribute to the activity element, as shown:

```
<activity android:name=".MainActivity"
    android:theme="@style/AppTheme.MyDialog">
```

 Note that both application and activity will now have a theme specified.

3. Now run the application on a device or emulator to see the dialog theme in action.

How it works...

Our new theme, `MyDialog`, inherits the base `AppTheme` using the alternative parent declaration, since `AppTheme` is defined in our code (and not a system theme). As mentioned in the *Introduction*, some settings apply to the window as a whole, which is what we see with the `windowIsFloating` setting. Once our new theme is declared, we assign our theme to the activity in the `AndroidManifest` file.

There's more...

You might have noticed we could have just added `windowIsFloating` to the existing `AppTheme` and been done. Since this application only has one activity, the end result would be the same, but then any new activities would also appear as a dialog.

Selecting a theme based on the Android version

Most users prefer to see apps using the latest themes provided by Android. To be competitive with the many other apps in the market, you'll probably want to upgrade your app as well, but what about your users who are still running older versions of Android? By setting up our resources properly, we can use **resource selection** in Android to automatically define the parent theme based on the Android OS version the user is running.

First, let's explore the three main themes available in Android:

- Theme - Gingerbread and earlier
- Theme.Holo - Honeycomb (API 11)
- Theme.Material - Lollipop (API 21)

This recipe will show how to properly set up the resource directories for Android to use the most appropriate theme based on the API version the app is running on.

Getting ready

Start a new project in Android Studio and call it `AutomaticThemeSelector`. Use the default wizard option to make a **Phone & Tablet** project. Select the **Empty Activity** when prompted for the **Activity Type**. On the **Configure Activity** dialog, deselect the **Backwards Compatibility (AppCompat)** checkbox.

How to do it...

Normally, we use the **AppCompat** option when creating a project but in the preceding *Getting ready* section, we deselected this option as we need to explicitly set our resources manually. We will verify we are extending from the generic `Activity` class, then we can add our new style resources to select the theme based on the API. Here are the steps:

1. We need to make sure `MainActivity` extends from `Activity` and not `AppCompatActivity`. Open `ActivityMain.java` and if necessary, change it to read as follows:

   ```
   public class MainActivity extends Activity {
   ```

2. Open `activity_main.xml` and drop in two views: `Button` and `Checkbox`.

3. Open `styles.xml` and remove `AppTheme` as it will not be used. Add our new theme so the file reads as follows:

   ```
   <resources>
       <style name="AutomaticTheme" parent="android:Theme.Light">
       </style>
   </resources>
   ```

4. We need to create two new values folders for API 11 and 21. To do this, we need to change Android Studio to use the project view rather than the Android view. (Otherwise, we won't see the new folders in the next step.) At the top of the **Project** window, it shows **Android**; change this to **Project** for the project view. See the following screenshot:

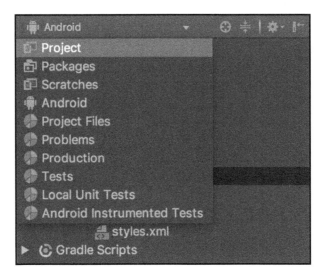

5. Create a new directory by right-clicking on the `res` folder and navigating to **New** | **Directory**, as shown in the following screenshot:

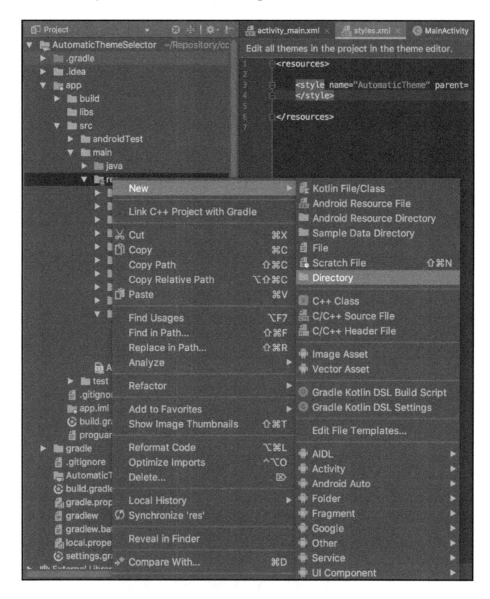

Use the following name for the first directory: `values-v11`.

Repeat this for the second directory using `values-v21`.

6. Now create a `styles.xml` file in each of the new directories. (Right-click on the `values-v11` directory and go to the **New** | **File** option.) For `values-v11`, use the following style to define the Holo theme:

```
<resources> <style name="AutomaticTheme"
 parent="android:Theme.Holo.Light"> </style>
</resources>
```

For `values-v21`, use the following code to define the Material theme:

```
<resources> <style name="AutomaticTheme"
    parent="android:Theme.Material.Light"> </style>
</resources>
```

7. The last step is to tell the application to use our new theme. To do this, open `AndroidManifest.xml` and change the application `android:theme` attribute to `AutomaticTheme`. It should read as follows:

```
android:theme="@style/AutomaticTheme"
```

8. Now run the application on a physical device or emulator. If you want to see the three different themes, you will need to have a device or emulator running the different versions of Android.

How it works...

In this recipe, we are using the Android resource selection process to assign the appropriate theme (which is a resource) based on the API version. Since we need to choose the theme based on the OS version in which it was released, we created two new values folders specifying the API version. This gives us a total of three `styles.xml` files: the default style, one in the `values-v11` directory, and the last in the `values-v21` directory.

Notice the same theme name is defined in all three `styles.xml` files. This is how the resource selection works. Android will use the resource from the directory that best fits our values. Here we are using the API level, but other criteria are available as well. It is very common to define separate resources based on other criteria, such as screen size, screen density, and even orientation.

The last step was to specify our new theme as the application theme, which we did in the Android Manifest.

There's more...

For more information on resource selection, see the *Using designated folders for screen-specific resources* section as well as the *Using graphics to show button state* recipe.

4
Menus and Action Mode

In this chapter, we will cover the following topics:

- Creating an options menu
- Modifying menus and menu items during runtime
- Enabling Contextual Action Mode for a view
- Using Contextual Batch Mode with `RecyclerView`
- Creating a pop-up menu

Introduction

The Android OS is an ever-changing environment. The earliest Android devices (prior to Android 3.0), were required to have a hardware menu button. Though a hardware button is no longer required, menus are no less important. In fact, the Menu API has expanded to now support three different types of menus:

- **Options menu and action bar**: This is the standard menu, which is used for global options of your application. Use this for additional features such as search, settings, and so on.
- **ContextualMode** (**Contextual Action Mode**): This is generally activated by a long press. (Think of this as similar to a right-click on the desktop.) This is used to take an action on the pressed item, such as replying to an email or deleting a file.
- **Pop-up menu**: This provides a pop-up selection (like a spinner) for an additional action. The menu options are not meant to affect the item pressed; instead, use Contextual Mode as described previously. An example would be hitting the share button and getting an additional list of share options.

Menu resources are similar to other Android UI components; they are generally created in XML, but can be created in code as well. Our first recipe, as shown in the following section, will show the XML menu format and how to inflate it.

Creating an options menu

Before we actually create and display a menu, let's look at a menu to see the end result. The following is a screenshot showing the menu section of the Chrome app:

The most obvious feature to note is that the menu will look different based on the screen size. By default, menu items will be added to the overflow menu—that's the menu you see when you press the three dots at the far right edge.

Menus are typically created in resource files using XML (like many other Android resources) stored in the `res/menu` directory, though they can also be created in code. To create a menu resource, use the `<menu>` element as shown:

```
<menu xmlns:android="http://schemas.android.com/apk/res/android">
</menu>
```

The `<item>` element defines each individual menu item and is enclosed in the `<menu>` element. A basic menu item looks as follows:

```
<item
    android:id="@+id/settings"
    android:title="@string/settings" />
```

The most common `<item>` attributes are the following:

- `id`: This is the standard resource identifier
- `title`: This indicates the text to display
- `icon`: This is a drawable resource
- `showAsAction`: This is explained in the following paragraph
- `enabled`: This is enabled by default

Let's look at `showAsAction` in more detail.

The `showAsAction` attribute controls how the menu item is shown. The options include the following:

- `ifRoom`: This menu item should be included in the action bar if there's enough space
- `withText`: This indicates that both the title and the icon should be shown
- `never`: This indicates that the menu item should never be included in the action bar; it is always shown in the overflow menu
- `always`: This indicates that the menu item should be always included in the action bar (use sparingly as space is limited)

 Multiple options can be combined using the pipe (`|`) separator, such as `showAsAction="ifRoom|withText"`.

With the fundamentals of the menu resource covered, we are now ready to create a standard options menu and inflate it.

Getting ready

Use Android Studio to create a new project called `OptionsMenu`. Use the default **Phone & Tablet** option and select the **Empty Activity** option when prompted for the **Activity Type**. The Android Studio wizard does not create the `res/menu` folder by default. You can create it manually using **File** | **New** | **Directory,** or create it using the **Android Resource Directory** wizard.

Here are the steps to use the wizard:

1. First, right-click on the `res` folder and select **New** | **Android Resource Directory** as shown here:

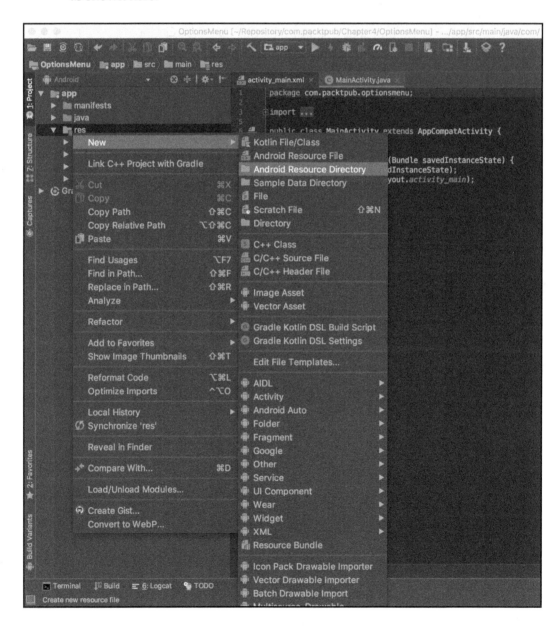

2. On the **New Resource Directory** dialog, select the **Resource type** drop-down menu and choose the **menu** option:

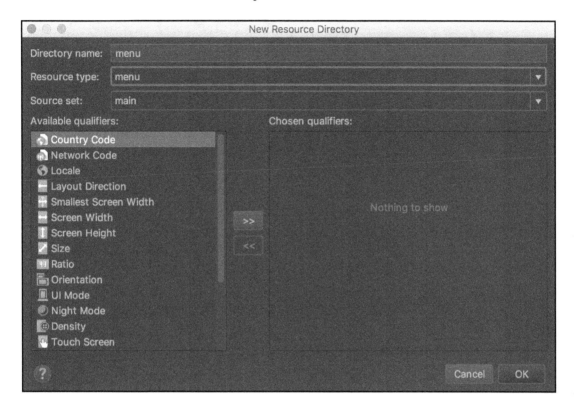

How to do it...

With the new project created as described in the preceding section, you are ready to create a menu. First, we will add a string resource to `strings.xml`. We will use the new string for the menu title when we create the XML for the menu. Here are the steps:

1. Start by opening the `strings.xml` file and adding the following `<string>` element to the `<resources>` element:

```
<string name="menu_settings">Settings</string>
```

2. Create a new file in the `res/menu` directory and call it `menu_main.xml`.

3. Open the `menu_main.xml` file and add the following XML to define the menu:

```xml
<?xml version="1.0" encoding="utf-8"?>
<menu xmlns:android="http://schemas.android.com/apk/res/android"
    xmlns:app="http://schemas.android.com/apk/res-auto">
    <item android:id="@+id/menu_settings"
        android:title="@string/menu_settings"
        app:showAsAction="never">
    </item>
</menu>
```

4. With the menu now defined in the XML, we just have to override the `onCreateOptionsMenu()` method in `ActivityMain.java` to inflate the menu:

```java
@Override
public boolean onCreateOptionsMenu(Menu menu) {
    getMenuInflater().inflate(R.menu.menu_main, menu);
    return true;
}
```

5. Run the program on a device or emulator to see the menu in the action bar.

How it works...

There are two basic steps here:

1. Define the menu in XML
2. Inflate the menu when the activity is created

As a good programming habit, we define the string in the `strings.xml` file rather than hard coding it in the XML. We then use the standard Android string identifier to set the title for the menu in step 3. Since this is a **Settings** menu item, we used the `showAsAction="never"` option so it wouldn't be shown as an individual menu option in the action bar.

With the menu defined, we will use the menu inflater in step 4 to load the menu during the activity creation. Notice the `R.menu.menu_main` menu resource syntax? This is why we create the XML in the `res/menu` directory—so the system will know this is a menu resource.

In step 4, we used `app:showAsAction` rather than Android: `android:showAsAction`. This is because we are using the `AppCompat` library (also referred to as the Android Support Library). By default, the Android Studio new project wizard includes the support library in the project.

There's more...

If you ran the program in step 5, then you must have seen the **Settings** menu item when you pressed the menu overflow button. But that was it. Nothing else happened. Obviously, menu items aren't very useful if the application doesn't respond to them. Responding to the **Options** menu is done through the `onOptionsItemSelected()` callback.

Add the following method to the application to see a Toast when the **Settings** menu is selected:

```
@Override
public boolean onOptionsItemSelected(MenuItem item) {
    if (item.getItemId() == R.id.menu_settings) {
        Toast.makeText(this, "Settings", Toast.LENGTH_LONG).show();
    } else {
        return super.onContextItemSelected(item);
    }
    return true;
}
```

That's it. You now have a working menu!

 As shown in the preceding example, return `true` when you've handled the callback; otherwise, call the super class as shown in the `else` statement.

Using a menu item to launch an activity

In the above example, we show a Toast in response to the menu click; however, we could just as easily launch a new activity if needed. To start an activity, create an Intent and call it with `startActivity()` as shown in the *Starting a new activity with an Intent object* recipe in `Chapter 1`, *Activities*.

Creating submenus

Submenus are created and accessed in almost exactly the same manner as other menu elements. They can be placed in any of the provided menus but not within other submenus. To define a submenu, include a <menu> element within an <item> element. Here is the XML for this recipe with two submenu items added:

```xml
<?xml version="1.0" encoding="utf-8"?>
<menu
    xmlns:android="http://schemas.android.com/apk/res/android"
    xmlns:app="http://schemas.android.com/apk/res-auto">
    <item android:id="@+id/menu_settings"
        android:title="@string/menu_settings"
        app:showAsAction="never">
        <menu>
            <item android:id="@+id/menu_sub1"
                android:title="Storage Settings" />
            <item android:id="@+id/menu_sub2"
                android:title="Screen Settings" />
        </menu>
    </item>
</menu>
```

Grouping menu items

Another menu feature that Android supports is grouping menu items. Android provides several methods for groups, including the following:

- `setGroupVisible()`: Show or hide all items
- `setGroupEnabled()`: Enable or disable all items
- `setGroupCheckable()`: Set the checkable behavior

Android will keep all grouped items with `showAsAction="ifRoom"` together. This means all items in the group with `showAsAction="ifRoom"` will be in the action bar or all items will be in the overflow.

To create a group, add the <item> menu elements to a <group> element. Here is an example using the menu XML from this recipe with two additional items in a group:

```xml
<?xml version="1.0" encoding="utf-8"?>
<menu xmlns:android="http://schemas.android.com/apk/res/android"
    xmlns:app="http://schemas.android.com/apk/res-auto">
    <group android:id="@+id/group_one" >
```

```
        <item android:id="@+id/menu_item1"
            android:title="Item 1"
            app:showAsAction="ifRoom"/>
        <item android:id="@+id/menu_item2"
            android:title="Item 2"
            app:showAsAction="ifRoom"/>
    </group>
    <item android:id="@+id/menu_settings"
        android:title="@string/menu_settings"
        app:showAsAction="never"/>
</menu>
```

See also

- For complete details on the menu, visit the Android Developer Menu Resources site at
  `http://developer.android.com/guide/topics/resources/menu-resource.html`

Modifying menus and menu items during runtime

Though it's been stated many times it's considered the *best* programming practice to create UIs in XML rather than in Java, there are still times when using code is the better option. This is especially true if you wanted a menu item to be visible (or enabled) based on some external criteria. Menus can also be included in resource folders, but there are times when you need code to perform the logic of which resource to use. One example might be if you wanted to offer an upload menu item only if the user is logged in to your app.

In this recipe, we will create and modify the menu only through code.

Getting ready

Create a new project in Android Studio and call it `RuntimeMenu` using the default **Phone & Tablet** option. Select the **Empty Activity** option when prompted to add an activity. Since we will create and modify the menu completely in code, we will not need to create a `res/menu` directory.

How to do it...

To start, we will add string resources for our menu items and a button to toggle the menu visibility. Open the res/strings.xml file and follow these steps:

1. Add the following two strings to the existing `<resources>` element:

```
<string name="menu_download">Download</string>
<string name="menu_settings">Settings</string>
```

2. Delete the existing TextView and add a button to activity_main.xml with onClick() set to toggleMenu as shown here:

```
<Button
    android:id="@+id/buttonToggleMenu"
    android:layout_width="wrap_content"
    android:layout_height="wrap_content"
    android:text="Toggle Menu"
    app:layout_constraintBottom_toBottomOf="parent"
    app:layout_constraintEnd_toEndOf="parent"
    app:layout_constraintStart_toStartOf="parent"
    app:layout_constraintTop_toTopOf="parent" />
```

3. Open ActivityMain.java and add the following three lines of code just below the class declaration:

```
private final int MENU_DOWNLOAD = 1;
private final int MENU_SETTINGS = 2;
private boolean showDownloadMenu = false;
```

4. Add the following method for the button click callback:

```
public void toggleMenu(View view) {
    showDownloadMenu=!showDownloadMenu;
}
```

5. When the activity is first created, Android calls onCreateOptionsMenu() to create the menu. Here is the code to dynamically build the menu:

```
@Override
public boolean onCreateOptionsMenu(Menu menu) {
    menu.add(0, MENU_DOWNLOAD, 0, R.string.menu_download);
    menu.add(0, MENU_SETTINGS, 0, R.string.menu_settings);
    return true;
}
```

6. For best programming practice, don't use `onCreateOptionsMenu()` to update or change your menu; instead, use `onPrepareOptionsMenu()`. Here is the code to change the visibility of the **Download** menu item based on our flag:

```
@Override
public boolean onPrepareOptionsMenu(Menu menu) {
    MenuItem menuItem = menu.findItem(MENU_DOWNLOAD);
    menuItem.setVisible(showDownloadMenu);
    return true;
}
```

7. Though not technically required for this recipe, this `onOptionsItemSelected()` code shows how to respond to each menu item:

```
@Override
public boolean onOptionsItemSelected(MenuItem item) {
    switch (item.getItemId()) {
        case MENU_DOWNLOAD:
            Toast.makeText(this, R.string.menu_download,
            Toast.LENGTH_LONG).show();
            break;
        case MENU_SETTINGS:
            Toast.makeText(this, R.string.menu_settings,
            Toast.LENGTH_LONG).show();
            break;
        default:
            return super.onContextItemSelected(item);
    }
    return true;
}
```

8. Run the program on a device or emulator to see the menu changes.

How it works...

We created an override for `onCreateOptionsMenu()`, just like we did in the previous recipe, *Creating an options menu*. But instead of inflating an existing menu resource, we created the menu using the `Menu.add()` method. Since we want to modify the menu items later as well as respond to the menu item events, we defined our own menu IDs and passed them to the `add()` method. The `onOptionsItemSelected()` object is called for all the menu items, so we get the menu ID and use a `switch` statement based on the ID. We return `true` if we are handling the menu event, otherwise we pass the event to the super class.

Changing the menu occurs in the `onPrepareOptionsMenu()` method. To simulate an external event, we created a button to toggle a Boolean flag. The visibility of the **Download** menu is determined by the flag. This is where you would want to create your custom code based on whatever criteria you set. Your flag could be set using the current player level or maybe when a new level is ready for release, you send a push message to enable the menu item.

There's more...

What if we wanted the **Download** option to stand out when it's available? We could tell Android we want the menu in the action bar by adding the following code to `onPrepareOptionsMenu()` (before the return statement):

```
menuItem.setShowAsAction(MenuItem.SHOW_AS_ACTION_ALWAYS);
```

Now if you run the code, you will see the **Download** menu item in the action bar, but the behavior isn't correct.

Earlier, when we didn't have a menu item in the action bar, Android called `onPrepareOptionsMenu()` each time we opened the overflow menu so the visibility was always updated. To correct this behavior, add the following line of code to the `toggleMenu()` method:

```
invalidateOptionsMenu();
```

The `invalidateOptionsMenu()` call tells Android that our option menu is no longer valid, which then forces a call to `onPrepareOptionsMenu()`, giving us the behavior we expect.

 Android considers the menu as always open if a menu item is displayed in the action bar.

Enabling Contextual Action Mode for a view

A context menu provides additional options related to a specific view—the same concept as a right-click on the desktop. Android currently supports two different approaches: the floating context menu and Contextual Mode. Contextual Action Mode was introduced in Android 3.0. The older floating context menu could lead to confusion since there was no indication of the currently selected item and it didn't support actions on multiple items—such as selecting multiple emails to delete in one action.

Creating a floating context menu

If you need to use the old-style context menu, for example to support pre-Android 3.0 devices, it's very similar to the Option Menu API, you just different method names. To create the menu, use `onCreateContextMenu()` instead of `onCreateOptionsMenu()`. To handle the menu item selection, use `onContextItemSelected()` instead of `onOptionsItemSelected()`. Finally, call `registerForContextMenu()` to let the system know you want context menu events for the view.

Since Contextual Mode is considered the preferred way to display context options, this recipe will focus on the newer API. Contextual Mode offers the same features as the floating context menu, but also adds additional functionality by allowing multiple item selection when using batch mode.

This recipe will demonstrate the setup of Contextual Mode for a single view. Once activated, with a long press in our example, a **contextual action bar** (**CAB**) will replace the action bar until Contextual Mode is finished.

 The CAB is not the same as the action bar and your activity does not need to include an action bar.

Getting ready

Use Android Studio to create a new project and call it `ContextualMode`. Use the default **Phone & Tablet** option and select **Empty Activity** when prompted to add an activity. Create a menu directory (`res/menu`) as we did in the first recipe, *Creating an options menu*, to store the XML for the contextual menu.

How to do it...

We will create `ImageView` to serve as the host view to initialize Contextual Mode. Since Contextual Mode is usually triggered with a long press, we will set up a long click listener in `onCreate()` for `ImageView`. When called, we will start Contextual Mode and pass an `ActionMode` callback to handle the Contextual Mode events. Here are the steps:

1. We will start by adding two new string resources. Open the `strings.xml` file and add the following:

```
<string name="menu_cast">Cast</string>
<string name="menu_print">Print</string>
```

2. With the strings created, we can now create the menu by creating a new file in `res/menu` called `context_menu.xml` using the following XML:

```
<?xml version="1.0" encoding="utf-8"?>
<menu xmlns:android="http://schemas.android.com/apk/res/android"
xmlns:app="http://schemas.android.com/apk/res-auto">
    <item android:id="@+id/menu_cast"
        android:title="@string/menu_cast" />
    <item android:id="@+id/menu_print"
        android:title="@string/menu_print" />
</menu>
```

3. Now add `ImageView` to `activity_main.xml` to serve as the source for initiating Contextual Mode. Here is the XML for `ImageView`:

```
<ImageView
    android:id="@+id/imageView"
    android:layout_width="wrap_content"
    android:layout_height="wrap_content"
    app:layout_constraintBottom_toBottomOf="parent"
    app:layout_constraintEnd_toEndOf="parent"
    app:layout_constraintStart_toStartOf="parent"
    app:layout_constraintTop_toTopOf="parent"
    app:srcCompat="@mipmap/ic_launcher" />
```

4. With the UI now set up, we can add the code for Contextual Mode. First, we need a global variable to store the `ActionMode` instance returned when we call `startActionMode()`. Add the following line of code to `MainActivity.java` below the class constructor:

```
ActionMode mActionMode;
```

5. Next, create an `ActionMode` callback to pass to `startActionMode()`. Add the following code to the `MainActivity` class below the code in the previous step:

```
private ActionMode.Callback mActionModeCallback = new
ActionMode.Callback() {
    @Override
    public boolean onCreateActionMode(ActionMode mode, Menu menu) {
        mode.getMenuInflater().inflate(R.menu.context_menu, menu);
        return true;
    }

    @Override
    public boolean onPrepareActionMode(ActionMode mode, Menu menu)
    {
        return false;
    }

    @Override
    public boolean onActionItemClicked(ActionMode mode, MenuItem
    item) {
        switch (item.getItemId()) {
            case R.id. menu_cast:
                Toast.makeText(MainActivity.this, "Cast",
                Toast.LENGTH_SHORT).show();
                mode.finish();
                return true;
            case R.id. menu_print:
                Toast.makeText(MainActivity.this, "Print",
                Toast.LENGTH_SHORT).show();
                mode.finish();
                return true;
            default:
                return false;
        }
    }

    @Override
    public void onDestroyActionMode(ActionMode mode) {
        mActionMode = null;
    }
};
```

6. With the `ActionMode` callback created, we just need to call `startActionMode()` to begin Contextual Mode. Add the following code to the `onCreate()` method to set up the long click listener:

```
ImageView imageView = findViewById(R.id.imageView);
imageView.setOnLongClickListener(new View.OnLongClickListener() {
    public boolean onLongClick(View view) {
        if (mActionMode != null) return false;
        mActionMode = startSupportActionMode(mActionModeCallback);
        return true;
    }
});
```

7. Run the program on a device or emulator to see the CAB in action.

How it works...

As you saw in step 2, we used the same menu XML to define the contextual menu as the other menus.

The main piece of code to understand is the `ActionMode` callback. This is where we handle the Contextual Mode events: initializing the menu, handling menu item selections, and cleaning up. We start Contextual Mode in the long press event with a call to `startActionMode()` by passing in the `ActionMode` callback created in step 5.

When action mode is triggered, the system calls the `onCreateActionMode()` callback, which inflates the menu and displays it in the CAB. The user can dismiss the CAB by pressing the back arrow or the back key. The CAB is also dismissed when the user makes a menu selection. We show a Toast to give a visual feedback for this recipe but this is where you would implement your functionality.

There's more...

In this example, we store `ActionMode` returned from the `startActionMode()` call. We use it to prevent a new instance from being created when the Action Mode is already active. We could also use this instance to make changes to the CAB itself, such as changing the title with the following:

```
mActionMode.setTitle("New Title");
```

This is particularly useful when working with multiple item selections as we'll see in the next recipe.

See also

- See the next recipe, *Using Contextual Batch Mode with RecyclerView*, to work with multiple item selection

Using Contextual Batch Mode with RecyclerView

As discussed in the previous recipe, Contextual Mode supports two forms of use: single View mode (as demonstrated) and multiple selection (or batch) mode. Batch mode is where Contextual Mode outperforms the old-style context menu as multiple selections were not supported.

If you've ever used an email app such as Gmail or a file browser, you've probably seen Contextual Mode when selecting multiple items. Here is a screenshot from Solid Explorer, which shows an excellent implementation of Material Theme and Contextual Mode:

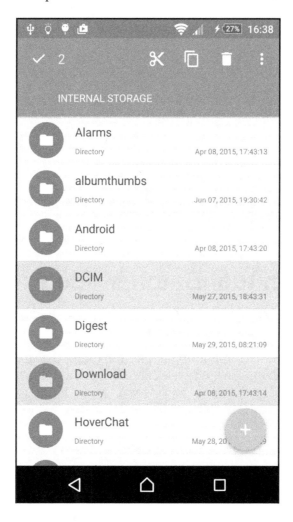

When we introduced `RecyclerView` in `Chapter 2`, *Layouts*, we discussed how many features from the old `ListView` were not already included in the new `RecyclerView`. Multiple item selection is one of the most missed features. In this recipe, we will demonstrate multiple item selection with the `RecyclerView` using Action Mode.

Getting ready

We will use the `RecyclerView` example created in `Chapter 2`, *Layouts* as the base for this recipe. If you have not already done so, go back to the *RecyclerView replaces ListView* recipe in that chapter, then add the menu directory (`res/menu`) for the contextual menu as demonstrated previously. From this point, you can perform the following steps to add multiple item selection to `RecyclerView`. The project will be called `RecyclerViewActionMode`.

How to do it...

We'll be combining several concepts already learned in previous recipes to enable multiple item selection with `RecyclerView`. We'll start by adding the menu and related code, then modify the `RecyclerView` item to show the state selection. Finally, we'll modify the `RecyclerView` adapter to support click notification, which will start Action Mode. Here are the steps:

1. Open the `strings.xml` file and add two new string resources for the menu items as follows:

```
<string name="delete_all">Delete All</string>
```

2. Create a new file called `contextual_menu.xml` in the `res/menu` folder with the following XML:

```xml
<?xml version="1.0" encoding="utf-8"?>
<menu xmlns:android="http://schemas.android.com/apk/res/android" >
    <item android:id="@+id/delete_all"
        android:title="@string/delete_all" />
</menu>
```

3. Next, add a new file to the `res/drawable` folder called `item_selector.xml` with the following XML:

```xml
<?xml version="1.0" encoding="utf-8"?>
<menu xmlns:android="http://schemas.android.com/apk/res/android" >
    <item android:id="@+id/delete_all"
    android:title="@string/delete_all" />
</menu>
```

4. Open the `item.xml` file in `res/layout` and add the following line to the `LinearLayout`:

```
android:background="@drawable/item_selector"
```

5. Next, create a new Java file called `SelectMode` to server as the click event interface. The code is as follows:

```
public interface SelectMode {
    void onSelect();
}
```

6. Now open the `MyAdapter` file and add `implements SelectMode` to the class. The final result will be as follows:

```
public class MyAdapter extends
RecyclerView.Adapter<MyAdapter.MyViewHolder>
    implements SelectMode {
```

7. Add the `onSelect` method to the class using the following code:

```
@Override
public void onSelect() {
    if (mListener!=null) {
        mListener.onSelect();
    }
}
```

8. Add the following declaration to the class to hold the list of selected items:

```
private SparseArray<Boolean> selectedList = new SparseArray<>();
```

9. We'll add another method to the adapter to handle the actual `delete` method called from the Action Mode:

```
public void deleteAllSelected() {
    if (selectedList.size()==0) { return; }
    for (int index = nameList.size()-1; index >=0; index--) {
        if (selectedList.get(index,false)) {
            remove(index);
        }
    }
    selectedList.clear();
}
```

10. The final change to make to the `MyAdapter` class is to replace the existing `onClick()`. The final code will be as follows:

```
@Override
public void onClick(View v) {
    holder.itemView.setSelected(!holder.itemView.isSelected());
    if (holder.itemView.isSelected()) {
        selectedList.put(position, true);
    } else {
        selectedList.remove(position);
    }
    onSelect();
}
```

11. Now that we have the menu created and the adapter updated, we need to hook it all up in the `MainActivity` class. To start, modify the `MainActivity` declaration to implement the `SelectMode` interface. The final code will be as follows:

```
public class MainActivity extends AppCompatActivity
implements SelectMode {
```

12. Below the class declaration, add the following two variable declarations:

```
MyAdapter myAdapter;
ActionMode mActionMode;
```

13. Then add the `ActionMode` callback declaration:

```
private ActionMode.Callback mActionModeCallback = new
ActionMode.Callback() {
    @Override
    public boolean onCreateActionMode(ActionMode mode, Menu menu) {
        mode.getMenuInflater().inflate(R.menu.context_menu, menu);
        return true;
    }

    @Override
    public boolean onPrepareActionMode(ActionMode mode, Menu menu)
    {
        return false;
    }

    @Override
    public boolean onActionItemClicked(ActionMode mode, MenuItem
    item) {
        switch (item.getItemId()) {
```

```
                case R.id. delete_all:
                    myAdapter.deleteAllSelected();
                    mode.finish();
                    return true;
                default:
                    return false;
            }
        }

        @Override
        public void onDestroyActionMode(ActionMode mode) {
            mActionMode = null;
        }
    };
```

14. We need to store the `MyAdapter` reference so it can be called from `ActionMode`. To do this, modify the `myAdapter` instantiation call in the `onCreate()` method as follows:

```
myAdapter = new MyAdapter(list, this);
```

15. The final code is to implement the `onSelect` method to connect the adapter callback to the Action Mode. Add the following method to the `MainActivity` class:

```
@Override
public void onSelect() {
    if (mActionMode != null) return;
    mActionMode = startSupportActionMode(mActionModeCallback);
}
```

16. Run the program on a device or emulator to see the CAB in action.

How it works...

As mentioned in the *Introduction* to this recipe, multiple item selection is one of the most missed features of `RecyclerView` and the one that receives the most questions. As you can see from this example, even a basic implementation requires many steps but the end result can be the exact implementation required for your task. You won't be limited to an existing feature set since you'll be creating it yourself.

This recipe combines several concepts learned from previous recipes, including the following:

- RecyclerView
- The RecyclerView adapter
- The contextual menu
- The action mode callback

To tie everything together, we created a custom interface so the adapter could notify when an item was selected. MainActivity receives the onSelect() event to trigger ActionMode. The ActionMode menu item calls the adapter when the user clicks the **Delete All** menu item and then closes the CAB.

This is just one-way ActionMode could be implemented. We could start ActionMode with a long press, a checkbox on the item, or maybe a menu item. The choice is yours.

There's more...

If you ran the application using the code shown previously, everything works as you'd expect. But there's a problem. Our example only has a few items in the list—probably not enough to even allow scrolling. The point of RecyclerView though is to efficiently handle many items when scrolling. If you add many more items to the list, enough to allow scrolling a screen or two, you'll see the problem. RecyclerView does exactly what it says: it recycles the views. If you select the first item, then scroll down, you'll see the problem - items you didn't select are selected.

What's happening is a common issue and confuses many developers new to RecyclerView. Because the view is being reused, it's showing the state from the previous item. The solution is simple: just set the state appropriately when binding a new item. We can fix the preceding problem just by setting the initial state in the onBindViewHolder() call. Add the following line of code to the onBindViewHolder() method in the MyAdapter class:

```
holder.itemView.setSelected(selectedList.get(position,false));
```

As you can see, we set the initial state by checking our list to see if the item was selected.

See also

- For more information on `RecyclerView`, refer to `Chapter 2`, *Layouts*
- For more information on the SparseArray, refer to `https://developer.android.com/reference/android/util/SparseArray`

Creating a pop-up menu

A pop-up menu is attached to a view similar to the drop-down menu on a spinner. The idea of a pop-up menu is to provide additional options to complete an action. A common example might be a **Reply** button in an email app. When pressed, several reply options are shown, such as: **Reply**, **Reply All**, and **Forward**.

Here is an example of the pop-up menu from the following recipe:

Android will show the menu options below the anchor view if there is room; otherwise, the menu will be shown above the view.

A pop-up menu is *not* meant to affect the view itself. That is the purpose of a Context Menu. Instead refer to the Floating Menu/Context Mode described in the *Enabling Contextual Action Mode for a view* recipe.

In this recipe, we will create the pop-up menu shown previously, using `ImageButton` as the anchor view.

Getting ready

Create a new project in Android Studio and call it `PopupMenu`. Use the default **Phone & Tablet** option and select **Empty Activity** on the **Add an Activity to Mobile** dialog. As detailed in the first exercise of this chapter, create a menu directory (`res/menu`) to store the menu XML.

How to do it...

We start by creating the XML menu to inflate on the button press. After inflating the pop-up menu, we call `setOnMenuItemClickListener()` by passing in the callback to handle the menu item selection. Start by opening the `strings.xml` file located in the `res/values` folder, then follow these steps:

1. Add the following strings:

```xml
<string name="menu_reply">Reply</string>
<string name="menu_reply_all">Reply All</string>
<string name="menu_forward">Forward</string>
```

2. Create a new file in the `res/menu` directory called `menu_popup.xml` using the following XML:

```xml
<?xml version="1.0" encoding="utf-8"?>
<menu xmlns:android="http://schemas.android.com/apk/res/android">
    <item android:id="@+id/menu_reply"
        android:title="@string/menu_reply" />
    <item android:id="@+id/menu_reply_all"
        android:title="@string/menu_reply_all" />
    <item android:id="@+id/menu_forward"
        android:title="@string/menu_forward" />
</menu>
```

3. Create `ImageButton` in `activity_main.xml` to provide the anchor view for the pop-up menu. Create it as shown in the following XML code:

```xml
<ImageButton
    android:id="@+id/imageButtonReply"
    android:layout_width="wrap_content"
    android:layout_height="wrap_content"
    android:layout_marginStart="8dp"
    android:layout_marginTop="8dp"
    app:layout_constraintStart_toStartOf="parent"
    app:layout_constraintTop_toTopOf="parent"
```

```
app:srcCompat="@android:drawable/ic_menu_revert"
android:onClick="showPopupMenu"/>
```

4. Open `MainActivity.java` and add the following `OnMenuItemClickListener` below the class constructor:

```
private PopupMenu.OnMenuItemClickListener mOnMenuItemClickListener
= new
        PopupMenu.OnMenuItemClickListener() {
            @Override
            public boolean onMenuItemClick(MenuItem item) {
                switch (item.getItemId()) {
                    case R.id.menu_reply:
                        Toast.makeText(MainActivity.this,  "Reply",
                        Toast.LENGTH_SHORT).show();
                        return true;
                    case R.id.menu_reply_all:
                        Toast.makeText(MainActivity.this,"Reply
                        All",Toast.LENGTH_SHORT).show();
                        return true;
                    case R.id.menu_forward:
                        Toast.makeText(MainActivity.this,"Forward",
                        Toast.LENGTH_SHORT).show();
                        return true;
                    default:
                        return false;
                }
            }
        };
```

5. The final code is to handle the button `onClick()` event, as follows:

```
public void showPopupMenu(View view) {
    PopupMenu popupMenu = new PopupMenu(MainActivity.this,view);
    popupMenu.inflate(R.menu.menu_popup);
    popupMenu.setOnMenuItemClickListener(mOnMenuItemClickListener);
    popupMenu.show();
}
```

6. Run the program on a device or emulator to see the pop-up menu.

How it works...

If you read the previous menu recipes, this will probably look very familiar. Basically, we just inflate a pop-up menu when `ImageButton` is pressed. We set up a menu item listener to respond to the menu selection.

The key is to understand each of the menu options available in Android so you can use the correct menu type for a given scenario. This will help your application by providing a consistent user experience and reducing the learning curve for the user as they will already be familiar with the *standard* way of doing things.

5
Fragments

In this chapter, we will cover the following topics:

- Creating and using a Fragment
- Adding and removing Fragments during runtime
- Passing data between Fragments
- Handling the Fragment back stack

Introduction

With a firm understanding of layouts from `Chapter 2`, *Layouts*, we'll dig deeper into UI development with Fragments. Fragments are a way to separate your UI into smaller sections that can easily be reused. Think of Fragments as mini-activities, complete with their own classes, layouts, and life cycle. Instead of designing your screen in one Activity Layout, possibly duplicating functionality across multiple layouts, you can break the screen into smaller, logical sections and turn them into Fragments. Your Activity Layout can then reference one or multiple Fragments, as needed.

Creating and using a Fragment

Android didn't always support Fragments. The early versions of Android were designed for phones when screens had relatively small displays. It wasn't until Android started being used on tablets that there was a need to split the screen into smaller sections. Android 3.0 introduced the `Fragments` class and the Fragment Manager.

Along with a new class, also came the Fragment Lifecycle. The Fragment Lifecycle is similar to the Activity Lifecycle introduced in `Chapter 1`, *Activities*, as most events parallel the Activity Lifecycle.

Here's a brief overview of the main callbacks:

- `onAttach()`: It's called when the Fragment is associated with an Activity.
- `onCreate()`: It's called when the Fragment is first created.
- `onCreateView()`: It's called when the Fragment is about to be displayed for the first time.
- `onActivityCreated()`: It's called when the associated Activity is created.
- `onStart()`: It's called when the Fragment will become visible to the user.
- `onResume()`: It's called just before a Fragment is displayed.
- `onPause()`: It's called when the Fragment is first suspended. The user may return to the Fragment, but this is where you should persist any user data.
- `onStop()`: It's called when the Fragment is no longer visible to the user.
- `onDestroyView()`: It's called to allow final cleanup.
- `onDetach()`: It's called when the Fragment is no longer associated with the Activity.

For our first exercise, we will create a new Fragment derived from the standard `Fragment` class. But there are several other Fragment classes we could derive from, including the following:

- `DialogFragment`: It's used for creating a floating dialog
- `ListFragment`: It creates a `ListView` in a Fragment, similar to `ListActivity`
- `PreferenceFragment`: It creates a list of `Preference` objects, commonly used for a **Settings** page

In this recipe, we will walk through creating a basic Fragment derived from the `Fragment` class and include it in an Activity Layout.

Getting ready

Create a new project in Android Studio and call it `CreateFragment`. Use the default **Phone & Tablet** option and select **Empty Activity** on the **Add an Activity to Mobile** dialog.

How to do it...

In this recipe, we will create a new `Fragment` class with an accompanying layout file. We will then add the Fragment to the Activity Layout so it will be visible when the activity starts.

Here are the steps to create and display a new Fragment:

1. Create a new layout called `fragment_one.xml` using the following XML:

```xml
<?xml version="1.0" encoding="utf-8"?>
<RelativeLayout
xmlns:android="http://schemas.android.com/apk/res/android"
    android:layout_height="match_parent"
    android:layout_width="match_parent">
    <TextView
        android:layout_width="wrap_content"
        android:layout_height="wrap_content"
        android:text="Fragment One"
        android:id="@+id/textView"
        android:layout_centerVertical="true"
        android:layout_centerHorizontal="true" />
</RelativeLayout>
```

2. Create a new Java class called `FragmentOne.java` with the following code:

```java
public class FragmentOne extends Fragment {
    @Override
    public View onCreateView(LayoutInflater inflater, ViewGroup container,
                             Bundle savedInstanceState) {
        return inflater.inflate(R.layout.fragment_one, container, false);
    }
}
```

3. Open the `activity_main.xml` file and replace the existing `<TextView>` element with the following `<fragment>` element:

```xml
<fragment
    android:name="com.packtpub.createfragment.FragmentOne"
    android:id="@+id/fragment"
    android:layout_width="wrap_content"
    android:layout_height="wrap_content"
    android:layout_centerVertical="true"
    android:layout_centerHorizontal="true"
    app:layout_constraintBottom_toBottomOf="parent"
    app:layout_constraintLeft_toLeftOf="parent"
    app:layout_constraintRight_toRightOf="parent"
    app:layout_constraintTop_toTopOf="parent" />
```

4. Run the program on a device or emulator.

How it works...

We start by creating a new class, the same as we do for an Activity. In this recipe, we only create an overwrite for the `onCreateView()` method to load our Fragment layout. But, just like with the Activity events, we can override the other events as we need them. Once the new Fragment is created, we then add it to the Activity Layout. Since the original `Activity` class was created before Fragments existed, they do not support Fragments. That's why, unless otherwise indicated, all the examples for this book extend from `AppCompatActivity`. (If you used the Android Studio New Project Wizard, then by default `MainActivity` extends `AppCompatActivity`.)

There's more...

We're only creating a single, simple Fragment in this recipe to teach the fundamentals of Fragments. But this is a good time to point out the power of Fragments. If we are creating multiple Fragments (and usually we are, as that's the point of using Fragments), when creating the Activity Layouts as we did in step 4, we could create different layout configurations using the Android Resource Folders. The portrait layout may have only a single Fragment while the landscape may have two or more. The Master/Detail layout typically uses Fragments, thus only requiring each screen section to be designed and coded once, then included in the layout as appropriate.

See also

- For more information on the Master/Detail pattern, see the *Passing data between Fragments* recipe later in this chapter.

Adding and removing Fragments during runtime

Defining a Fragment in the layout, as we did in the previous recipe, is known as a static Fragment, which doesn't allow the fragment to be changed during runtime. Rather than using the `<fragment>` element, we will create a container to hold the Fragment, then create the Fragment dynamically in the Activity's `onCreate()` method.

The FragmentManager provides the APIs for adding, removing, and changing Fragments during runtime using a FragmentTransaction. A Fragment transaction consists of the following:

1. Starting a transaction
2. Performing one or multiple actions
3. Committing the transaction

This recipe will demonstrate the Fragment Manager by adding and removing Fragments during runtime.

Getting ready

Create a new project in Android Studio and call it: `RuntimeFragments`. Use the default **Phone & Tablet** option and select **Empty Activity** on the **Add an Activity to Mobile** dialog.

How to do it...

To demonstrate adding and removing Fragments, we first need to create the Fragments, which we will do by extending the `Fragment` class. After creating the new Fragments, we need to alter the layout for the Main Activity to include the Fragment container. From there, we just add the code to handle the Fragment transactions. Here are the steps:

1. Create a new layout file called `fragment_one.xml` and include the following XML:

```xml
<?xml version="1.0" encoding="utf-8"?>
<RelativeLayout
xmlns:android="http://schemas.android.com/apk/res/android"
    android:layout_height="match_parent"
    android:layout_width="match_parent">
    <TextView
        android:layout_width="wrap_content"
        android:layout_height="wrap_content"
        android:text="Fragment One"
        android:id="@+id/textView"
        android:layout_centerVertical="true"
        android:layout_centerHorizontal="true" />
</RelativeLayout>
```

2. The second layout file called `fragment_two.xml` is almost identical, with the only difference being the text:

```
android:text="Fragment Two"
```

3. Create a new Java class called `FragmentOne.java` with the following code:

```
public class FragmentOne extends Fragment {
    @Override
    public View onCreateView(LayoutInflater inflater,
                             ViewGroup container, Bundle
savedInstanceState) {
        return inflater.inflate(R.layout.fragment_one,
                container, false);
    }
}
```

- Import from the support library as follows:

```
import android.support.v4.app.Fragment;
```

4. Create the second Java class called `FragmentTwo` with the following code:

```
public class FragmentTwo extends Fragment {
    @Override
    public View onCreateView(LayoutInflater inflater,
                             ViewGroup container, Bundle
savedInstanceState) {
        return inflater.inflate(R.layout.fragment_two,
                container, false);
    }
}
```

- As before, import from the support library:

```
import android.support.v4.app.Fragment;
```

5. Now we need to add a container and a button to the Main Activity layout. Change `activity_main.xml` as follows:

```
<?xml version="1.0" encoding="utf-8"?>
<RelativeLayout
xmlns:android="http://schemas.android.com/apk/res/android"
    android:layout_width="match_parent"
    android:layout_height="match_parent">
    <FrameLayout
        android:id="@+id/frameLayout"
        android:layout_width="match_parent"
```

```
        android:layout_height="wrap_content"
        android:layout_above="@+id/buttonSwitch"
        android:layout_alignParentTop="true">
    </FrameLayout>
    <Button
        android:id="@+id/buttonSwitch"
        android:layout_width="wrap_content"
        android:layout_height="wrap_content"
        android:text="Switch"
        android:layout_alignParentBottom="true"
        android:layout_centerInParent="true"
        android:onClick="switchFragment"/>
</RelativeLayout>
```

6. With the Fragments created and the container added to the layout, we are now ready to write the code to manipulate the Fragments. Open `MainActivity.java` and add the following code below the class constructor:

```
FragmentOne mFragmentOne;
FragmentTwo mFragmentTwo;
int showingFragment=0;
```

7. Add the following code to the existing `onCreate()` method, below `setContentView()`:

```
mFragmentOne = new FragmentOne();
mFragmentTwo = new FragmentTwo();
FragmentManager fragmentManager = getSupportFragmentManager();
FragmentTransaction fragmentTransaction =
        fragmentManager.beginTransaction();
fragmentTransaction.add(R.id.frameLayout, mFragmentOne);
fragmentTransaction.commit();
showingFragment=1;
```

- Import from the support libraries:

```
            import android.support.v4.app.FragmentManager;
            import android.support.v4.app.FragmentTransaction;
```

8. The last code we need to add handles the Fragment switching, called by the button:

```
public void switchFragment(View view) {
    FragmentManager fragmentManager = getSupportFragmentManager();
    FragmentTransaction fragmentTransaction =
fragmentManager.beginTransaction();
    if (showingFragment==1) {
        fragmentTransaction.replace(R.id.frameLayout,
```

```
        mFragmentTwo);
            showingFragment = 2;
        } else {
            fragmentTransaction.replace(R.id.frameLayout,
    mFragmentOne);
            showingFragment=1;
        }
        fragmentTransaction.commit();
    }
```

9. Run the program on a device or emulator.

How it works...

Most of the steps for this recipe involve setting up the Fragments. Once the Fragments are declared, we create them in the `onCreate()` method. Though the code can be condensed to a single line, it's shown in the long form as it makes it easier to read and understand.

First, we get `FragmentManager` so we can begin `FragmentTransaction`. Once we have `FragmentTransaction`, we start the transaction with `beginTransaction()`. Multiple actions can occur within the transaction, but all we need here is to `add()` our initial Fragment. We call the `commit()` method to finalize the transaction.

Now that you understand the Fragment transaction, here is the succinct version for `onCreate()`:

```
getSupportFragmentManager().beginTransaction().add(R.id.frameLayout,
mFragmentOne).commit();
```

Our `switchFragment()` method does basically the same type of Fragment transaction. Instead of calling the `add()` method, we call the `replace()` method with the existing Fragment. We keep track of the current Fragment with the `showingFragment` variable so we know which Fragment to show next. We are not limited to switching between two Fragments either. If we needed additional Fragments, we just need to create them.

There's more...

In the *Switching between activities* recipe from Chapter 1, *Activities*, we discussed the back stack. Most users would expect the back key to move backward through the "screens" and they don't know or care if those screens are activities or Fragments. Fortunately, Android makes it very easy to add Fragments to the back stack just by adding a call to `addToBackStack()` before calling `commit()`.

When a Fragment is removed or replaced without adding it to the back stack, it is immediately destroyed. If it is added to the back stack, it is stopped and, if the user returns to the Fragment, it is restarted, instead of recreated.

See also

- For more information on managing the Fragment back stack, see the *Handling the Fragment back stack* recipe later in this chapter.

Passing data between Fragments

Often, the need arises to pass information between Fragments. An email application serves as a classic example. It's common to have the list of emails in one Fragment and show the email details in another Fragment (this is commonly referred to as a Master/Detail pattern). Fragments make creating this pattern easier because we only have to code each Fragment once, then include them in different layouts. We can easily have a single Fragment in a portrait layout with the ability to swap out the master Fragment with the detail Fragment when an email is selected. We can also create a two-panel layout where both the list and detail Fragments are side by side. Either way, when the user clicks the email in the list, the email opens up in the detail panel. This is when we need to communicate between two Fragments.

Since one of the primary goals of Fragments is that they be completely self-contained, direct communication between Fragments is discouraged, and for good reason. If Fragments had to rely on other Fragments, your code would likely break when the layouts changed and only one Fragment was available. Fortunately, direct communication is not required for this scenario either. All Fragment communication should pass through the host activity. The host activity is responsible for managing the Fragments and can properly route the messages.

Now the question becomes: How do Fragments communicate with the activity? The answer is with an interface. You're probably already familiar with an interface, as that's how a view communicates an event back to an activity. One of the most common examples is the button `onClick()` interface.

In this recipe, we will create two Fragments to demonstrate passing data from one Fragment to another via the host activity. We'll also build on what we learned from the previous recipe by including two different Activity Layouts-one for portrait and one for landscape. When in portrait mode, the activity will swap the Fragments as needed. Here is a screenshot of when the application first runs in portrait mode:

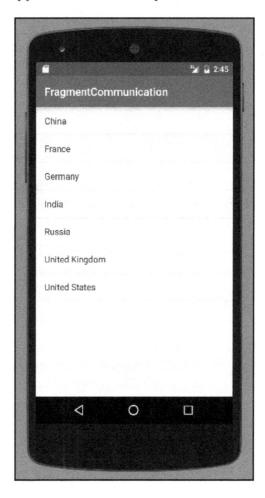

This is the screen showing the detail Fragment when you click on a country name:

When in landscape, both Fragments will be side by side, as shown in the landscape screenshot:

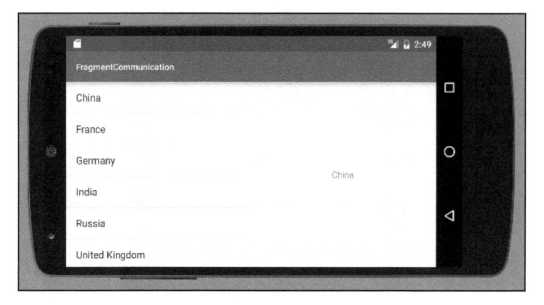

Since the Master/Detail pattern generally involves a list for the master, we'll take advantage of `ListFragment` (mentioned in the *Creating and using a Fragment* section). When an item in the list is selected, the item text (country name in our example) will be sent to the detail Fragment via the host activity.

Getting ready

Create a new project in Android Studio and call it `FragmentCommunication`. Use the default **Phone & Tablet** option and select **Empty Activity** on the **Add an Activity to Mobile** dialog.

How to do it...

To fully demonstrate working Fragments, we'll need to create two Fragments. The first Fragment will extend from `ListFragment` so it will not need a layout. We're going to go one step further by creating both portrait and landscape layouts for our Activity. For portrait mode, we'll swap Fragments and for landscape mode, we'll show both Fragments side by side.

When typing this code, Android Studio will offer two different library import options. Since the New Project Wizard automatically references the AppCompat library, we need to use the support library APIs instead of the framework APIs. Though very similar, the following code uses the support Fragment APIs.

Here are the steps, starting with the first Fragment:

1. Create a new Java class called `MasterFragment` and change it so it extends `ListFragment` as shown:

   ```
   public class MasterFragment extends ListFragment
   ```

   - Import from the following library:

     ```
     android.support.v4.app.ListFragment
     ```

2. Create the following interface inside the `MasterFragment` class:

   ```
   public interface OnMasterSelectedListener {
       public void onItemSelected(String countryName);
   }
   ```

3. Set up the interface callback listener with the following code:

   ```
   private OnMasterSelectedListener mOnMasterSelectedListener=null;

   public void setOnMasterSelectedListener(OnMasterSelectedListener
   listener) {
       mOnMasterSelectedListener=listener;
   }
   ```

4. The last step for the `MasterFragment` is to create `ListAdapter` to populate `ListView`, which we do in the `onViewCreated()` method. When a country name is selected, we'll use `setOnItemClickListener()` to call our `OnMasterSelectedListener` interface with the following code:

   ```
   public void onViewCreated(View view, Bundle savedInstanceState) {
       super.onViewCreated(view, savedInstanceState);

       String[] countries = new String[]{"China", "France",
               "Germany", "India", "Russia", "United Kingdom",
               "United States"};

       ListAdapter countryAdapter = new ArrayAdapter<String>(
               getActivity(), android.R.layout.simple_list_item_1,
               countries);
   ```

```
        setListAdapter(countryAdapter);

        getListView().setChoiceMode(ListView.CHOICE_MODE_SINGLE);

        getListView().setOnItemClickListener(new
    AdapterView.OnItemClickListener() {
            @Override
            public void onItemClick(AdapterView<?> parent, View
                    view, int position, long id) {
                if (mOnMasterSelectedListener != null) {
                    mOnMasterSelectedListener.onItemSelected(((
                            TextView) view).getText().toString());
                }
            }
        });
    }
```

5. Next, we need to create `DetailFragment`, starting with the layout. Create a new layout file called `fragment_detail.xml` with the following XML:

```
<?xml version="1.0" encoding="utf-8"?>
<RelativeLayout
    xmlns:android="http://schemas.android.com/apk/res/android"
    android:layout_width="match_parent"
    android:layout_height="match_parent">
    <TextView
        android:id="@+id/textViewCountryName"
        android:layout_width="wrap_content"
        android:layout_height="wrap_content"
        android:layout_centerVertical="true"
        android:layout_centerHorizontal="true" />
</RelativeLayout>
```

6. Create a new Java class called `DetailFragment` extending from `Fragment` as follows:

```
public class DetailFragment extends Fragment
```

- Import from the following library:

```
android.support.v4.app.Fragment
```

7. Add the following constant to the class:

```
public static String KEY_COUNTRY_NAME="KEY_COUNTRY_NAME";
```

8. Override `onCreateView()` as follows:

```
@Override
public View onCreateView(LayoutInflater inflater,
                         ViewGroup container,
                         Bundle savedInstanceState) {
    return inflater.inflate(R.layout.fragment_detail, container,
false);
}
```

9. Code `onViewCreated()` as follows:

```
@Override
public void onViewCreated(@NonNull View view, @Nullable Bundle
savedInstanceState) {
    super.onViewCreated(view, savedInstanceState);

    Bundle bundle = getArguments();

    if (bundle != null && bundle.containsKey(KEY_COUNTRY_NAME)) {
        showSelectedCountry(bundle.getString(KEY_COUNTRY_NAME));
    }
}
```

10. The last step for this Fragment is to update `TextView` when we receive the selected country name. Add the following method to the class:

```
public void showSelectedCountry(String countryName) {
((TextView)getView().findViewById(R.id.textViewCountryName)).setTex
t(countryName);
}
```

11. The existing `activity_main.xml` layout will handle the portrait mode layout. Remove the existing `<TextView>` and replace with the following `<FrameLayout>`:

```
<FrameLayout
    android:id="@+id/frameLayout"
    android:layout_width="match_parent"
    android:layout_height="match_parent"
    android:layout_marginTop="8dp"
    app:layout_constraintBottom_toBottomOf="parent"
    app:layout_constraintLeft_toLeftOf="parent"
    app:layout_constraintRight_toRightOf="parent"
    app:layout_constraintTop_toTopOf="parent" />
```

12. For the landscape layout, create a new directory called `layout-land` in the `res` folder. The final result will be `res/layout-land`.

 If you do not see the new `res/layout-land` directory, change from Android view to project view.

13. Create a new `activity_main.xml` layout in `res/layout-land` as follows:

```xml
<?xml version="1.0" encoding="utf-8"?>
<LinearLayout
xmlns:android="http://schemas.android.com/apk/res/android"
    xmlns:tools="http://schemas.android.com/tools"
    android:layout_width="match_parent"
    android:layout_height="match_parent"
    android:orientation="horizontal">
    <FrameLayout
        android:id="@+id/frameLayoutMaster"
        android:layout_width="0dp"
        android:layout_weight="1"
        android:layout_height="match_parent"/>
    <FrameLayout
        android:id="@+id/frameLayoutDetail"
        android:layout_width="0dp"
        android:layout_weight="1"
        android:layout_height="match_parent"/>
</LinearLayout>
```

14. The final steps are to set up `MainActivity` to handle the Fragments. Open the `MainActivity.java` file and add the following class variable to track single/dual pane:

```java
boolean mDualPane;
```

15. Next, change `onCreate()` as follows:

```java
@Override
protected void onCreate(Bundle savedInstanceState) {
    super.onCreate(savedInstanceState);

    setContentView(R.layout.activity_main);

    MasterFragment masterFragment = null;
    FrameLayout frameLayout = findViewById(R.id.frameLayout);
    if (frameLayout != null) {
        mDualPane = false;
```

```java
        FragmentTransaction fragmentTransaction =
getSupportFragmentManager().beginTransaction();
        masterFragment = (MasterFragment)
getSupportFragmentManager()
                .findFragmentByTag("MASTER");
        if (masterFragment == null) {
            masterFragment = new MasterFragment();
            fragmentTransaction.add(R.id.frameLayout,
masterFragment, "MASTER");
        }
        DetailFragment detailFragment = (DetailFragment)
getSupportFragmentManager().findFragmentById(R.id.frameLayoutDetail
);
        if (detailFragment != null) {
            fragmentTransaction.remove(detailFragment);
        }
        fragmentTransaction.commit();
    } else {
        mDualPane = true;
        FragmentTransaction fragmentTransaction =
getSupportFragmentManager().beginTransaction();
        masterFragment = (MasterFragment)
getSupportFragmentManager()
                .findFragmentById(R.id.frameLayoutMaster);
        if (masterFragment == null) {
            masterFragment = new MasterFragment();
            fragmentTransaction.add(R.id.frameLayoutMaster,
masterFragment);
        }
        DetailFragment detailFragment = (DetailFragment)
getSupportFragmentManager()
                .findFragmentById(R.id.frameLayoutDetail);
        if (detailFragment == null) {
            detailFragment = new DetailFragment();
            fragmentTransaction.add(R.id.frameLayoutDetail,
detailFragment);
        }
        fragmentTransaction.commit();
    }
    masterFragment.setOnMasterSelectedListener(new
MasterFragment.OnMasterSelectedListener() {
        @Override
        public void onItemSelected(String countryName) {
            sendCountryName(countryName);
        }
    });
}
```

16. The last code to add is the `sendCountryName()` method, which handles sending the country name to `DetailFragment`:

```
private void sendCountryName(String countryName) {
    DetailFragment detailFragment;
    if (mDualPane) {
        //Two pane layout
        detailFragment = (DetailFragment)
getSupportFragmentManager().findFragmentById(R.id.frameLayoutDetail
);
        detailFragment.showSelectedCountry(countryName);
    } else {
        // Single pane layout
        detailFragment = new DetailFragment();
        Bundle bundle = new Bundle();
        bundle.putString(DetailFragment.KEY_COUNTRY_NAME,
countryName);
        detailFragment.setArguments(bundle);
        FragmentTransaction fragmentTransaction =
getSupportFragmentManager().beginTransaction();
        fragmentTransaction.replace(R.id.frameLayout,
detailFragment);
        fragmentTransaction.addToBackStack(null);
        fragmentTransaction.commit();
    }
}
```

17. Run the program on a device or emulator.

How it works...

We start by creating `MasterFragment`. In the Master/Detail pattern we are using, this usually represents a list, so we create a list by extending `ListFragment`. `ListFragment` is the Fragment equivalent of `ListActivity`. Other than extending from a Fragment, it's basically the same.

As stated in the recipe introduction, we shouldn't attempt to communicate directly with other Fragments.

To provide a means to communicate the list item selection, we expose the interface: OnMasterSelectedListener. We call onItemSelected() every time an item is selected in the list.

Most of the work for passing data between Fragments is done in the host activity but, ultimately, the receiving Fragment needs a way to receive the data. DetailFragment supports this in two ways:

- Passing the country name in the argument bundle, available at creation time
- A public method for the activity to call directly.

When the activity creates the Fragment, it also creates a bundle to hold the data we want to send. Here we add the country name using KEY_COUNTRY_NAME defined in step 7. We retrieve this bundle with getArguments() in onViewCreated(). If the key is found in the bundle, it is extracted and displayed using the showSelectedCountry() method. This is the same method the activity will call directly if the Fragment is already visible (in the two-panel layout).

Most of the work for this recipe is in the activity. We created two layouts: one for portrait and one for landscape. When in landscape orientation, Android will choose the landscape layout from the res/layout-land directory created in step 12. Both layouts use a <FrameLayout> placeholder, similar to the previous exercise. We manage the Fragments in both onCreate() and sendCountryName().

In onCreate(), we set the mDualPane flag by checking whether the current layout includes the frameLayout view. If frameLayout is found (meaning it's not null), then we have only a single panel because frameLayout is only defined in the portrait layout. If frameLayout is not found, then we have two <FrameLayout> elements instead: one for MasterFragment and another for DetailFragment.

The last thing we do in onCreate() is to set up the MasterFragment listener by creating an anonymous callback, which passes the country name to the sendCountryName() method. The sendCountryName() method is where the data is actually passed to DetailFragment. If we are in portrait (or single-pane) mode, we need to create DetailFragment and replace the existing MasterFragment. This is where we create the bundle with the country name and call setArguments(). Notice how we call addToBackStack() before committing the transaction? This allows the back key to bring the user back to the list (MasterFragment). If we are in landscape mode, DetailFragment is already visible so we call the howSelectedCountry() public method directly.

There's more...

In `MasterFragment`, before sending the `onItemSelected()` event, we check to make sure the listener is not null with the following code:

```
if (mOnMasterSelectedListener != null)
```

Though it's the job of the activity to set up the callback to receive the events, we don't want this code to crash if there's no listener. An alternative approach would be to verify the activity extends our interface in the Fragment's `onAttach()` callback.

The objective for this recipe was to demonstrate the proper pattern for communicating between fragments (by using an interface) and how to pass data. We used the `ListView` fragment because it made typing this example easier, but for real-world applications, it's probably better to use `RecyclerView`. `RecyclerView` does not have a pre-made `Fragment` class (or `Activity` class) so you need to roll your own but it's no different than the examples shown in earlier chapters.

See also

- For `RecyclerView` examples, refer to the *RecyclerView replaces ListView* section in `Chapter 2`, *Layouts* and the *Using Contextual Batch Mode with RecyclerView* section in `Chapter 4`, *Menus and Action Mode*.
- For more information on resource directories, see the *Selecting themes based on the Android version* section in `Chapter 3`, *Views, Widgets, and Styles*.

Handling the Fragment back stack

In several of the previous recipes, it was mentioned that you should call the `addToBackStack()` method in the Fragment transaction to enable Android to maintain a Fragment back stack. This is the first step, but may not be enough to provide a rich user experience. In this recipe, we'll explore two other callbacks: `onBackPressed()` and `onBackStackChanged()`. As you'll see, by implementing these callbacks, your application can provide specific behavior for the Fragment back stack. The `onBackPressed()` callback allows the app to check the back stack state and provide custom behavior, such as closing the app when appropriate.

The `onBackStackChanged()` callback is called whenever the actual back stack changes - such as when a Fragment is popped from the back stack. By overriding this callback, your app can check the current Fragment and update the UI (such as the *Home* key back arrow) as appropriate.

Getting ready

Create a new project in Android Studio and call it `FragmentBackStack`. Use the default **Phone & Tablet** option and select **Empty Activity** on the **Add an Activity to Mobile** dialog.

How to do it...

To demonstrate handling the Fragment back stack, we'll create two fragments with a **Next** button to create a back stack. With that setup, we'll implement the `onBackPressed()` callback to exit the app when the user reaches the top Fragment. We'll be using the Fragment Manager from the support library, so be sure to choose the support library version when prompted for the import library. We'll need two layout files - one for each fragment - along with two fragment classes. Here are the steps in detail:

1. Create a new layout file called `fragment_one.xml` with the following XML:

```xml
<?xml version="1.0" encoding="utf-8"?>
<RelativeLayout
xmlns:android="http://schemas.android.com/apk/res/android"
    android:layout_height="match_parent"
    android:layout_width="match_parent">
    <TextView
        android:id="@+id/textView"
        android:layout_width="wrap_content"
        android:layout_height="wrap_content"
        android:text="Fragment One"
        android:layout_centerVertical="true"
        android:layout_centerHorizontal="true" />
</RelativeLayout>
```

2. Create the second fragment layout file called `fragment_two.xml` with the same XML as above, changing the following text property:

```
android:text="Fragment Two"
```

3. With the layout files created, it's time to create the classes for the fragments. Create a new Java class called `FragmentOne.java` with the following code:

```
public class FragmentOne extends Fragment {
    @Override
    public View onCreateView(LayoutInflater inflater,
                            ViewGroup container, Bundle
savedInstanceState) {
        return inflater.inflate(R.layout.fragment_one,
            container, false);
    }
}
```

4. Create the second Java class called `FragmentTwo` with the following code:

```
public class FragmentTwo extends Fragment {
    @Override
    public View onCreateView(LayoutInflater inflater,
                            ViewGroup container, Bundle
savedInstanceState) {
        return inflater.inflate(R.layout.fragment_two,
            container, false);
    }
}
```

5. Now we need to add a container and a button to the Main Activity layout. Change `activity_main.xml` as follows:

```
<?xml version="1.0" encoding="utf-8"?>
<RelativeLayout
xmlns:android="http://schemas.android.com/apk/res/android"
    android:layout_width="match_parent"
    android:layout_height="match_parent">
    <FrameLayout
        android:id="@+id/frameLayout"
        android:layout_width="match_parent"
        android:layout_height="wrap_content"
        android:layout_above="@+id/buttonNext"
        android:layout_alignParentTop="true">
    </FrameLayout>
    <Button
        android:id="@+id/buttonNext"
        android:layout_width="wrap_content"
        android:layout_height="wrap_content"
        android:text="Next"
        android:layout_alignParentBottom="true"
        android:layout_centerInParent="true"/>
</RelativeLayout>
```

6. With the Fragments created and the container added to the layout, we are now ready to write the code to manipulate the Fragments.
   Open `MainActivity.java` and add the following code below the class constructor:

```
Button mButtonNext;
```

7. Add the following code to the existing `onCreate()` method, below `setContentView()`:

```
mButtonNext = findViewById(R.id.buttonNext);
mButtonNext.setOnClickListener(new View.OnClickListener() {
    @Override
    public void onClick(View view) {
        FragmentManager fragmentManager =
getSupportFragmentManager();
        FragmentTransaction fragmentTransaction =
                fragmentManager.beginTransaction();
        fragmentTransaction.replace(R.id.frameLayout,  new
FragmentTwo());
        fragmentTransaction.addToBackStack(null);
        fragmentTransaction.commit();
        mButtonNext.setVisibility(View.INVISIBLE);
    }
});

FragmentManager fragmentManager = getSupportFragmentManager();
FragmentTransaction fragmentTransaction =
        fragmentManager.beginTransaction();
fragmentTransaction.add(R.id.frameLayout,  new FragmentOne());
fragmentTransaction.addToBackStack(null);
fragmentTransaction.commit();
```

8. The last method to implement is the `onBackPressed()` callback:

```
@Override
public void onBackPressed() {
    if(getSupportFragmentManager().getBackStackEntryCount() == 2 )
{
        super.onBackPressed();
        mButtonNext.setVisibility(View.VISIBLE);
    } else {
        finish();
    }
}
```

9. Run the program on a device or emulator.

How it works...

Most of the steps are similar to the *Adding and removing Fragments during runtime* recipe discussed previously, until step 8. The first seven steps just set up the app to create the fragments for our demonstration. In step 8, we implement the `onBackPressed()` callback. This is where we code for our specific situation. For this sample, all we need to do is make the **Next** button visible again.

There's more...

With the basics covered for handling the back stack, it's time to discuss the other callback: `onBackStackChanged()`. This is where you can implement custom behavior when the stack changes. One common example is changing the Home icon to a back arrow. We get this behavior automatically with an Activity when we set the parent property (in AndroidManifest), but Android doesn't do this for fragments. What if we wanted to have a back arrow on `FragmentTwo`? Add this line of code to the NextButton `onClick()`:

```
getSupportActionBar().setDisplayHomeAsUpEnabled(true);
```

If you run the app now, you'll see the back arrow when you go to `FragmentTwo`. The problem is, the back arrow doesn't actually do anything. The next problem you may notice is that if you use the back key, you still see the back arrow when you return to `FragmentOne`.

To make the back arrow work, add the following code to `MainActivity`:

```
@Override
public boolean onOptionsItemSelected(MenuItem menuItem) {
    if (menuItem.getItemId() == android.R.id.home) {
            onBackPressed();
            return true;
    } else {
        return super.onOptionsItemSelected(menuItem);
    }
}
```

Now the app will respond to the back arrow and treat it the same as the back key. What about the second issue? The Home icon still shows the back arrow. This is where we can use the `onBackStackChanged()` callback. Instead of modifying the NextButton `onClick()` as we did earlier, we can put all our code in `onBackStackChanged()`.

To do this, we need to implement the `OnBackStackChangedListener` interface in the class definition. Change the `MainActivity` declaration as follows:

```
public class MainActivity extends AppCompatActivity
        implements FragmentManager.OnBackStackChangedListener {
```

Then add this line to the `onCreate()` method (below `setContentView()`) to add the listener:

```
getSupportFragmentManager().addOnBackStackChangedListener(this);
```

Now we can implement the `onBackStackChanged()` callback:

```
@Override
public void onBackStackChanged() {
    Fragment fragment =
getSupportFragmentManager().findFragmentById(R.id.frameLayout);
    if (fragment instanceof FragmentOne) {
        getSupportActionBar().setDisplayHomeAsUpEnabled(false);
    } else if (fragment instanceof FragmentTwo) {
        getSupportActionBar().setDisplayHomeAsUpEnabled(true);
    }
}
```

Now when you run the app, you'll see the back arrow when you go to `FragmentTwo`. You can press the back arrow icon or use the back key to return to the first screen. Thanks to the `onBackStackChanged()` callback, you won't see the back arrow when you're on `FragmentOne`.

Home Screen Widgets, Search, and the System UI

6

In this chapter, we will cover the following topics:

- Creating a shortcut on the Home screen
- Creating a Home screen widget
- Adding Search to the Action Bar
- Showing your app full-screen
- Lock screen shortcuts

Introduction

With an understanding of Fragments from the previous chapter, we're ready to expand on our discussion of widgets. In Chapter 3, *Views, Widgets, and Styles*, we discussed how to add widgets to your own app. Now, we'll look at how to create an App Widget so users can add your app on their Home screen.

The remaining recipes in this chapter will explore System UI options. There's a recipe for adding a Search option to the Action Bar using the Android SearchManager API. Another recipe will explore Full Screen mode and several additional variations on altering the System UI. The final recipe will showcase the new Lock Screen shortcuts introduced in Android O (API 26).

Creating a shortcut on the Home screen

This recipe explains how to create a link or create a shortcut for your app on the user's Home screen. So as not to be too obtrusive, it's generally best to make this an option for the user to initiate, such as in the settings.

The following is a screenshot showing our shortcut on the Home screen:

As you can see, this is just a shortcut to your app. The next recipe will go deeper by creating a Home screen (AppWidget).

Getting ready

Create a new project in Android Studio and call it `HomeScreenShortcut`. Use the default Phone & Tablet options and select the **Empty Activity** option when prompted for the Activity Type.

How to do it...

For an app to create a shortcut, it must have the `INSTALL_SHORTCUT` permission. With the appropriate permission, it's a simple matter of calling an intent with your app properties. The following are the steps:

1. Open the `AndroidManifest` file and add the following permission:

```
<uses-permission
    android:name="com.android.launcher.permission.INSTALL_SHORTCUT" />
```

2. Next, open `activity_main.xml` and replace the existing TextView with the following button:

```
<Button
    android:id="@+id/button"
    android:layout_width="wrap_content"
    android:layout_height="wrap_content"
    android:text="Create Shortcut"
    android:onClick="createShortcut"
    app:layout_constraintBottom_toBottomOf="parent"
    app:layout_constraintLeft_toLeftOf="parent"
    app:layout_constraintRight_toRightOf="parent"
    app:layout_constraintTop_toTopOf="parent" />
```

3. Add the following method to `ActivityMain.java`:

```
public void createShortcut(View view) {
    Intent shortcutIntent = new Intent(this, MainActivity.class);
    shortcutIntent.setAction(Intent.ACTION_MAIN);
    Intent intent = new Intent();
    intent.putExtra(Intent.EXTRA_SHORTCUT_INTENT, shortcutIntent);
    intent.putExtra(Intent.EXTRA_SHORTCUT_NAME,
        getString(R.string.app_name));
```

```
intent.putExtra(Intent.EXTRA_SHORTCUT_ICON_RESOURCE,
        Intent.ShortcutIconResource.fromContext(this,
R.mipmap.ic_launcher));
intent.setAction("com.android.launcher.action.INSTALL_SHORTCUT");
    sendBroadcast(intent);
}
```

4. Run the program on a device or emulator. Notice that, each time you press the button, the app will make a shortcut on the Home screen.

How it works...

Once you set up the proper permission, this is a rather straightforward task. When the button is clicked, the code creates two intents. The first intent broadcasts to the OS that you want a shortcut created. The second intent is the intent that launches your app when the icon is pressed. One important consideration to keep in mind is that Home screens vary and may not support the INSTALL_SHORTCUT intent.

There's more...

If you also wanted to remove the shortcut, you would need the following permission:

```
<uses-permission
android:name="com.android.launcher.permission.UNINSTALL_SHORTCUT" />
```

Instead of using the INSTALL_SHORTCUT action, you would set the following action instead:

```
com.android.launcher.action.UNINSTALL_SHORTCUT
```

Creating a Home screen widget

Before we dig into the code for creating an App Widget, let's cover the basics. There are three required and one optional component:

- The AppWidgetProviderInfo file: It's an XML resource (described later)
- The AppWidgetProvider class: This is a Java class
- The View layout file: It's a standard layout XML file, with some restrictions (explained later)

- The App Widget configuration Activity (optional): This is an Activity the OS will launch when placing the widget to provide configuration options

The `AppWidgetProvider` must also be declared in the `AndroidManifest` file. Since `AppWidgetProvider` is a helper class based on the Broadcast Receiver, it is declared in the manifest with the `<receiver>` element. Here is an example manifest entry:

```
<receiver android:name=".HomescreenWidgetProvider" >
    <intent-filter>
        <action android:name="android.appwidget.action.APPWIDGET_UPDATE" />
    </intent-filter>
    <meta-data android:name="android.appwidget.provider"
        android:resource="@xml/appwidget_info" />
</receiver>
```

The metadata points to the `AppWidgetProviderInfo` file, which is placed in the `res/xml` directory. Here is a sample `AppWidgetProviderInfo.xml` file:

```
<appwidget-provider
xmlns:android="http://schemas.android.com/apk/res/android"
    android:minWidth="40dp"
    android:minHeight="40dp"
    android:updatePeriodMillis="0"
    android:initialLayout="@layout/widget"
    android:resizeMode="none"
    android:widgetCategory="home_screen">
</appwidget-provider>
```

The following is a brief overview of the available attributes:

- `minWidth`: The default width when placed on the Home screen
- `minHeight`: The default height when placed on the Home screen
- `updatePeriodMillis`: It's part of the `onUpdate()` polling interval (in milliseconds)
- `initialLayout`: The AppWidget layout
- `previewImage` (optional): The image shown when browsing App Widgets
- `configure` (optional): The activity to launch for configuration settings
- `resizeMode` (optional): The flags indicate resizing options: horizontal, vertical, none
- `minResizeWidth` (optional): The minimum width allowed when resizing
- `minResizeHeight` (optional): The minimum height allowed when resizing
- `widgetCategory` (optional): Android 5+ only supports Home screen widgets

The `AppWidgetProvider` extends the `BroadcastReceiver` class, which is why the `<receiver>` element is used when declaring the AppWidget in the Manifest. As it's `BroadcastReceiver`, the class still receives OS broadcast events, but the helper class filters those events down to those applicable for an App Widget.
The `AppWidgetProvider` class exposes the following methods:

- `onUpdate()`: It's called when initially created and at the interval specified.
- `onAppWidgetOptionsChanged()`: It's called when initially created and any time the size changes.
- `onDeleted()`: It's called any time a widget is removed.
- `onEnabled()`: It's called the first time a widget is placed (it isn't called when adding second and subsequent widgets).
- `onDisabled()`: It's called when the last widget is removed.
- `onReceive()`: It's called on every event received, including the preceding event. Usually not overridden as the default implementation only sends applicable events.

The last required component is the layout. An App Widget uses a Remote View, which only supports a subset of the available layouts:

- AdapterViewFlipper
- FrameLayout
- GridLayout
- GridView
- LinearLayout
- ListView
- RelativeLayout
- StackView
- ViewFlipper

And it supports the following widgets:

- AnalogClock
- Button
- Chronometer
- ImageButton
- ImageView
- ProgressBar
- TextClock

- TextView

With App Widget basics covered, it's now time to start coding. Our example will cover the basics so you can expand the functionality as needed. This recipe uses a View with a clock, which, when pressed, opens our activity.

The following screenshot shows the widget in the widget list when adding it to the Home screen:

The purpose of the image is to show how to add a widget to the home screen

The widget list's appearance varies by the launcher used.

Here's a screenshot showing the widget after it is added to the Home screen:

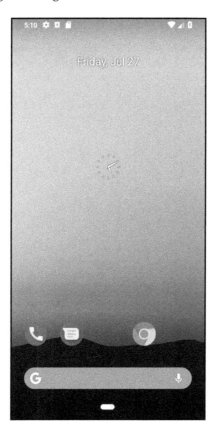

Getting ready

Create a new project in Android Studio and call it AppWidget. Use the default Phone & Tablet options and select the **Empty Activity** option when prompted for the Activity Type.

How to do it...

We'll start by creating the widget layout, which resides in the standard layout resource directory. Then, we'll create the XML resource directory to store the `AppWidgetProviderInfo` file. We'll add a new Java class and extend `AppWidgetProvider`, which handles the `onUpdate()` call for the widget. With the receiver created, we can then add it to the Android Manifest.

Here are the detailed steps:

1. Create a new file in `res/layout` called `widget.xml` using the following XML:

```xml
<?xml version="1.0" encoding="utf-8"?>
<RelativeLayout
xmlns:android="http://schemas.android.com/apk/res/android"
    android:layout_width="match_parent"
    android:layout_height="match_parent">
    <AnalogClock
        android:id="@+id/analogClock"
        android:layout_width="wrap_content"
        android:layout_height="wrap_content"
        android:layout_centerVertical="true"
        android:layout_centerHorizontal="true" />
</RelativeLayout>
```

2. Create a new directory called XML in the resource directory. The final result will be `res/xml`.

3. Create a new file in `res/xml` called `appwidget_info.xml` using the following XML:

```xml
<?xml version="1.0" encoding="utf-8"?>
<appwidget-provider
xmlns:android="http://schemas.android.com/apk/res/android"
    android:minWidth="40dp"
    android:minHeight="40dp"
    android:updatePeriodMillis="0"
    android:initialLayout="@layout/widget"
    android:resizeMode="none"
    android:widgetCategory="home_screen">
</appwidget-provider>
```

If you cannot see the new XML directory, switch from Android view to Project view in the Project panel drop-down.

4. Create a new Java class
called `HomescreenWidgetProvider`, **extending from** `AppWidgetProvider`.

5. Add the following `onUpdate()` method to
the `HomescreenWidgetProvider` class:

```
@Override
public void onUpdate(Context context, AppWidgetManager
appWidgetManager, int[] appWidgetIds) {
    super.onUpdate(context, appWidgetManager, appWidgetIds);

    for (int count=0; count<appWidgetIds.length; count++) {
        RemoteViews appWidgetLayout = new
                RemoteViews(context.getPackageName(),
                R.layout.widget);
        Intent intent = new Intent(context, MainActivity.class);
        PendingIntent pendingIntent =
PendingIntent.getActivity(context, 0, intent, 0);
        appWidgetLayout.setOnClickPendingIntent(R.id.analogClock,
pendingIntent);
        appWidgetManager.updateAppWidget(appWidgetIds[count],
appWidgetLayout);
    }
}
```

6. Add the `HomescreenWidgetProvider` to the AndroidManifest using the
following XML declaration within the `<application>` element:

```
<receiver android:name=".HomescreenWidgetProvider" >
    <intent-filter>
        <action
android:name="android.appwidget.action.APPWIDGET_UPDATE" />
    </intent-filter>
    <meta-data android:name="android.appwidget.provider"
        android:resource="@xml/appwidget_info" />
</receiver>
```

7. Run the program on a device or emulator. After first running the application, the
widget will then be available to add to the Home screen.

How it works...

Our first step is to create the layout file for the widget. This is a standard layout resource with the restrictions based on the App Widget being a Remote View, as discussed in the recipe introduction. Although our example uses an Analog Clock widget, this is where you'd want to expand the functionality based on your application needs.

The XML resource directory serves to store the AppWidgetProviderInfo, which defines the default widget settings. The configuration settings determine how the widget is displayed when initially browsing the available widgets. We use very basic settings for this recipe, but they can easily be expanded to include additional features, such as a preview image to show
a functioning widget and sizing options. The `updatePeriodMillis` attribute sets the update frequency. Since the update will wake up the device, it's a trade-off between having up-to-date data and battery life. (This is where the optional Settings Activity is useful by letting the user decide.)

The `AppWidgetProvider` class is where we handle the `onUpdate()` event triggered by the `updatePeriodMillis` polling. Our example doesn't need any updating so we set the polling to zero. The update is still called when initially placing the widget. `onUpdate()` is where we set the pending intent to open our app when the clock is pressed.

Since the `onUpdate()` method is probably the most complicated aspect of AppWidgets, we'll explain this in some detail. First, it's worth noting that `onUpdate()` will occur only once each polling interval for all the widgets is created by this provider. (All additional widgets created will use the same cycle as the first widget created.) This explains the for loop, as we need it to iterate through all the existing widgets. This is where we create a pending intent, which calls our app when the clock widget is pressed. As discussed earlier, an AppWidget is a Remote View. Therefore, to get the layout, we call `RemoteViews()` with our fully qualified package name and the layout ID. Once we have the layout, we can attach the pending intent to the clock view using `setOnClickPendingIntent()`. We call the AppWidgetManager named `updateAppWidget()` to initiate the changes we made.

The last step to make all this work is to declare the widget in the Android Manifest. We identify the action we want to handle with the `<intent-filter>`. Most App Widgets will likely want to handle the Update event, as ours does. The other item to note in the declaration is the following line:

```
<meta-data android:name="android.appwidget.provider"

    android:resource="@xml/appwidget_info" />
```

This tells the system where to find our configuration file.

There's more...

Adding an App Widget configuration Activity allows greater flexibility with your widget. Not only can you offer polling options, but you could offer different layouts, click behaviors, and so on. Users tend to really appreciate flexible App Widgets.

Adding a configuration Activity requires a few additional steps. The Activity needs to be declared in the Manifest as usual, but needs to include the `APPWIDGET_CONFIGURE` action, as shown in the following example:

```
<activity android:name=".AppWidgetConfigureActivity">
    <intent-filter>
        <action
android:name="android.appwidget.action.APPWIDGET_CONFIGURE"/>
    </intent-filter>
</activity>
```

The Activity also needs to be specified in the `AppWidgetProviderInfo` file using the configure attribute, as shown in this example:

```
android:configure="com.packtpub.appwidget.AppWidgetConfigureActivity"
```

The configure attribute requires the fully qualified package name as this Activity will be called from outside of your application.

Remember, the `onUpdate()` method will not be called when using a configuration Activity. The configuration Activity is responsible for handling any initial setup if required.

See also

- For App Widget Design Guidelines, visit Google's page: http://developer.android.com/design/patterns/widgets.html
- For detailed information on RemoteViews, visit https://developer.android.com/reference/android/widget/RemoteViews

Adding Search to the Action Bar

Along with the Action Bar, Android 3.0 introduced the SearchView widget, which can be included as a menu item when creating a menu. This is now the recommended UI pattern to provide a consistent user experience.

The following screenshot shows the initial appearance of the Search icon in the Action Bar:

The following screenshot shows how the Search option expands when pressed:

If you want to add Search functionality to your application, this recipe will walk you through the steps to set up your User Interface and properly configure the Search Manager API.

Getting ready

Create a new project in Android Studio and call it `SearchView`. Use the default Phone & Tablet options and select **Empty Activity** when prompted for the Activity Type.

How to do it...

To set up the Search UI pattern, we need to create the Search menu item and a resource called searchable. We'll create a second activity to receive the search query. Then, we'll hook it all up in the `AndroidManifest` file. To get started, open the `strings.xml` file in `res/values` and follow these steps:

1. Add the following string resources:

```
<string name="search_title">Search</string>
<string name="search_hint">Enter text to search</string>
```

2. Create the menu directory: `res/menu`.

3. Create a new menu resource called `menu_search.xml` in `res/menu` using the following XML:

```xml
<?xml version="1.0" encoding="utf-8"?>
<menu xmlns:android="http://schemas.android.com/apk/res/android"
    xmlns:app="http://schemas.android.com/apk/res-auto">
    <item android:id="@+id/menu_search"
        android:title="@string/search_title"
        android:icon="@android:drawable/ic_menu_search"
        app:showAsAction="collapseActionView|ifRoom"
        app:actionViewClass="android.support.v7.widget.SearchView"
/>
</menu>
```

4. Open ActivityMain and add the following `onCreateOptionsMenu()` to inflate the menu and set up the Search Manager:

```java
@Override
public boolean onCreateOptionsMenu(Menu menu) {
    MenuInflater inflater = getMenuInflater();
    inflater.inflate(R.menu.menu_search, menu);
    SearchManager searchManager = (SearchManager)
getSystemService(Context.SEARCH_SERVICE);
    MenuItem searchItem = menu.findItem(R.id.menu_search);
    SearchView searchView = (SearchView)
searchItem.getActionView();
searchView.setSearchableInfo(searchManager.getSearchableInfo(getCom
ponentName()));
    return true;
}
```

5. Create a new XML resource directory: `res/xml`.

6. Create a new file in `res/xml` called `searchable.xml` using the following XML:

```xml
<?xml version="1.0" encoding="utf-8"?>
<searchable
xmlns:android="http://schemas.android.com/apk/res/android"
    android:label="@string/app_name"
    android:hint="@string/search_hint" />
```

7. Create a new layout called `activity_search_result.xml` using this XML:

```xml
<?xml version="1.0" encoding="utf-8"?>
<RelativeLayout
xmlns:android="http://schemas.android.com/apk/res/android"
    android:layout_width="match_parent"
```

```
android:layout_height="match_parent" >
<TextView
    android:id="@+id/textViewSearchResult"
    android:layout_width="wrap_content"
    android:layout_height="wrap_content"
    android:layout_centerInParent="true" />
</RelativeLayout>
```

8. Add a new **Empty Activity** to the project called `SearchResultActivity`.

9. Add the following variable to the class:

```
TextView mTextViewSearchResult;
```

10. Change `onCreate()` to load our layout, set the TextView, and check for the **QUERY** action:

```
@Override
protected void onCreate(Bundle savedInstanceState) {
    super.onCreate(savedInstanceState);
    setContentView(R.layout.activity_search_result);
    mTextViewSearchResult =
findViewById(R.id.textViewSearchResult);
    if (Intent.ACTION_SEARCH.equals(getIntent().getAction())) {
handleSearch(getIntent().getStringExtra(SearchManager.QUERY));
    }
}
```

11. Add the following method to handle the search:

```
private void handleSearch(String searchQuery) {
    mTextViewSearchResult.setText(searchQuery);
}
```

12. With the User Interface and code now complete, we just need to hook everything up correctly in the AndroidManifest. Here is the complete manifest, including both activities:

```
<?xml version="1.0" encoding="utf-8"?>
<manifest
xmlns:android="http://schemas.android.com/apk/res/android"
    package="com.packtpub.searchview">
    <application
        android:allowBackup="true"
        android:icon="@mipmap/ic_launcher"
        android:label="@string/app_name"
        android:roundIcon="@mipmap/ic_launcher_round"
        android:supportsRtl="true"
```

```
            android:theme="@style/AppTheme">
            <meta-data android:name="android.app.default_searchable"
                android:value=".SearchResultActivity" />
            <activity android:name=".MainActivity">
                <intent-filter>
                    <action android:name="android.intent.action.MAIN"
    />
                    <category
    android:name="android.intent.category.LAUNCHER" />
                </intent-filter>
            </activity>
            <activity android:name=".SearchResultActivity">
                <intent-filter>
                    <action android:name="android.intent.action.SEARCH"
    />
                </intent-filter>
                <meta-data android:name="android.app.searchable"
                    android:resource="@xml/searchable" />
            </activity>
        </application>
    </manifest>
```

13. Run the application on a device or emulator. Type in a search query and hit the Search button (or press *Enter*). The **SearchResultActivity** will be displayed, showing the search query entered.

How it works...

Since the New Project Wizard uses the AppCompat library, our example uses the support library API. Using the support library provides the greatest device compatibility as it allows the use of modern features (such as the Action Bar) on older versions of the Android OS. This can sometimes provide an extra challenge as often the official documentation focuses on the framework API. Although usually the support library closely follows the framework API, they are not always interchangeable. The Search UI pattern is one of those situations, so it's worth paying extra attention to the steps outlined previously.

We start by creating string resources for the Search View (which is declared later in step 6.)

In step 3, we create the menu resource, as we've done many times. One difference is that we use the app namespace for the `showAsAction` and `actionViewClass` attributes. The earlier versions of the Android OS don't include these attributes in the Android namespace, which is why we create an app namespace. This serves as a way to bring new functionality to older versions of the Android OS.

In step 4, we set up the SearchManager, using the support library APIs.

Step 6 is where we define the searchable XML resource, which is used by the SearchManager. The only required attribute is the label, but a hint is recommended so the user will have an idea of what they should type in the field.

> The android:label must match the application name or the activity name and must use a string resource (as it does not work with a hardcoded string).

Steps 7-11 are for the SearchResultActivity. Calling the second activity is not a requirement of the SearchManager, but is commonly done to provide a single activity for all searches initiated in your application.

If you ran the application at this point, you would see the search icon, but nothing would work. Step 12 is where we put it all together in the AndroidManifest file. The first item to note is the following:

```
<meta-data android:name="android.app.default_searchable"
    android:value=".SearchResultActivity" />
```

Notice this is in the <application> element and not in either of the <activity> elements. By defining it at the <application> level, it will automatically apply to all <activities>. If we moved it to the MainActivity element, it would behave exactly the same in our example.

> You can define styles for your application in the <application> node and still override individual activity styles in the <activity> node.

We specify the searchable resource in the SearchResultActivity <meta-data> element:

```
<meta-data android:name="android.app.searchable"
    android:resource="@xml/searchable" />
```

We also need to set the intent filter for SearchResultActivity as we do here:

```
<intent-filter>
    <action android:name="android.intent.action.SEARCH" />
</intent-filter>
```

The SearchManager broadcasts the SEARCH intent when the user initiates the search. This declaration directs the intent to the SearchResultActivity activity. Once the search is triggered, the query text is sent to the SearchResultActivity using the SEARCH intent. We check for the SEARCH intent in the `onCreate()` and extract the query string using the following code:

```
if (Intent.ACTION_SEARCH.equals(getIntent().getAction())) {
    handleSearch(getIntent().getStringExtra(SearchManager.QUERY));
}
```

You now have the Search UI pattern fully implemented. With the UI pattern complete, what you do with the search results is specific to your application needs. Depending on your application, you might search a local database or maybe a web service.

See also

To take your search to the internet, see internet queries in `Chapter 13`, *Telephony, Networks, and the Web*.

Showing your app full-screen

Android 4.4 (API 19) introduced a UI feature called Immersive Mode. Unlike the previous full-screen flag, your app receives all touch events while in Immersive Mode. This mode is ideal for certain activities, such as reading books and news, full-screen drawing, gaming, or watching a video. There are several different approaches to full-screen, and each has a best use case:

- Reading books/articles, and so on: Immersive Mode with easy access to the System UI
- Game/drawing app: Immersive Mode for full-screen use but minimal System UI
- Watching video: Full-screen and normal System UI

The key difference between the modes is how the System UI responds. In the first two scenarios, your app is expecting user interaction, so the System UI is hidden to make it easier for your user (such as not hitting the back button while playing a game). While using full-screen with a normal System UI, such as watching a video, you wouldn't expect your user to use the screen at all, so when they do the System UI should respond normally. In all modes, the user can bring back the System UI with a swipe inward across the hidden System Bar.

Since watching a video doesn't require the new Immersive Mode, full-screen mode can be achieved using two
flags, SYSTEM_UI_FLAG_FULLSCREEN and SYSTEM_UI_FLAG_HIDE_NAVIGATION, available since Android 4.0 (API 14).

Our recipe will demonstrate setting up Immersive Mode. We're also going to add the ability to toggle the System UI with a tap on the screen.

Getting ready

Create a new project in Android Studio and call it ImmersiveMode. Use the default Phone & Tablet options and select **Empty Activity** when prompted for the Activity Type. When selecting the Minimum API Level, choose API 19 or higher.

How to do it...

We'll create two functions for handling the System UI visibility, then we'll create a gesture listener to detect when the user taps on the screen. All the steps for this recipe are adding code to MainActivity.java, so open the file and let's begin:

1. Add the following method to hide the System UI:

```
private void hideSystemUi() {
getWindow().getDecorView().setSystemUiVisibility(View.SYSTEM_UI_FLA
G_IMMERSIVE |
        View.SYSTEM_UI_FLAG_FULLSCREEN |
        View.SYSTEM_UI_FLAG_LAYOUT_STABLE |
        View.SYSTEM_UI_FLAG_LAYOUT_HIDE_NAVIGATION |
        View.SYSTEM_UI_FLAG_LAYOUT_FULLSCREEN |
        View.SYSTEM_UI_FLAG_HIDE_NAVIGATION);
}
```

2. Add the following method to show the System UI:

```
private void showSystemUI() {
    getWindow().getDecorView().setSystemUiVisibility(
        View.SYSTEM_UI_FLAG_LAYOUT_STABLE |
        View.SYSTEM_UI_FLAG_LAYOUT_HIDE_NAVIGATION |
        View.SYSTEM_UI_FLAG_LAYOUT_FULLSCREEN);
}
```

3. Add the following class variable:

```
private GestureDetectorCompat mGestureDetector;
```

4. Add the following `GestureListener` class at the class level, below the previous class variable:

```
private class GestureListener extends
GestureDetector.SimpleOnGestureListener {
    @Override
    public boolean onDown(MotionEvent event) {
        return true;
    }
    @Override
    public boolean onFling(MotionEvent event1, MotionEvent event2,
                            float velocityX, float velocityY) {
        return true;
    }
    @Override
    public boolean onSingleTapUp(MotionEvent e) {
        if (getSupportActionBar() != null &&
getSupportActionBar().isShowing()) {
            hideSystemUi();
        } else {
            showSystemUI();
        }
        return true;
    }
}
```

5. Override the `onTouchEvent()` callback with the following:

```
@Override
public boolean onTouchEvent(MotionEvent event) {
    mGestureDetector.onTouchEvent(event);
    return super.onTouchEvent(event);
}
```

6. Add the following code to the `onCreate()` method to set the GestureListener and hide the System UI:

```
mGestureDetector = new GestureDetectorCompat(this, new
GestureListener());
hideSystemUi();
```

7. Run the application on a device or emulator. Tapping the screen will toggle the System UI. Depending on your version of the Android OS, you can either swipe up from the bottom or swipe down from the top to reveal the System UI.

How it works...

We call `setSystemUiVisibility()` with the appropriate flags in the `showSystemUI()` and `hideSystemUI()` methods to set the application window state. The flags we set (and don't set) control what is visible and what is hidden. When we set the visibility without the `SYSTEM_UI_FLAG_IMMERSIVE` flag, we in effect disable Immersive Mode.

If all we wanted to do was hide the System UI, we could just add `hideSystemUI()` to `onCreate()` and we'd be done. The problem is it wouldn't stay hidden. Once the user left Immersive Mode, it would stay in the regular display mode. That's why we created the `GestureListener`. (We'll discuss gestures again in `Chapter 9`, *Using the Touchscreen and Sensors*.) Since we only want to respond to the `onSingleTapUp()` gesture, we don't implement the full range of gestures. When `onSingleTapUp` is detected, we toggle the System UI.

There's more...

Let's look at some other important tasks that can be performed.

Sticky Immersion

There's another option we can use if we want the System UI to stay hidden automatically. Instead of using `SYSTEM_UI_FLAG_IMMERSIVE` to hide the UI, we can use `SYSTEM_UI_FLAG_IMMERSIVE_STICKY`.

Dimming the System UI

If all you need is to reduce the visibility of the Navigation bar, there's also `SYSTEM_UI_FLAG_LOW_PROFILE` to dim the UI.

Use this flag with the same `setSystemUiVisibility()` call as the Immersive Mode flag:

```
getWindow().getDecorView().setSystemUiVisibility(View.SYSTEM_UI_FLAG_LOW_PR
OFILE);
```

Call `setSystemUiVisibility()` with 0 to clear all flags:

```
getWindow().getDecorView().setSystemUiVisibility(0);
```

Setting the Action Bar as an overlay

If you just need to hide or show the Action Bar, use these methods:

```
getActionBar().hide();
```

```
getActionBar().show();
```

One problem with this approach is that the system resizes the layout each time either method is called. Instead, you might want to consider using a theme option to make the System UI behave as an overlay. To enable overlay mode, add the following to the theme:

```
<item name="android:windowActionBarOverlay">true</item>
```

Translucent system bars

The following two themes enable translucent settings:

```
Theme.Holo.NoActionBar.TranslucentDecor
```

```
Theme.Holo.Light.NoActionBar.TranslucentDecor
```

If you are creating your own theme, use the following theme settings:

```
<item name="android:windowTranslucentNavigation">true</item>
```

```
<item name="android:windowTranslucentStatus">true</item>
```

See also

For more on handling gestures, refer to `Chapter 9`, *Using the Touchscreen and Sensors*.

7
Data Storage

In this chapter, we will cover the following topics:

- Storing simple data
- Read and writing a text file to internal storage
- Read and writing a text file to external storage
- Including resource files in your project
- Creating and using an SQLite database
- Accessing data in the background using a Loader
- Accessing external storage with scoped directories

Introduction

Since most applications, big or small, require saving data – from default user selections to user accounts – Android offers many options. From saving a simple value to creating full databases using SQLite, storage options include the following:

- Shared preferences: Simple name/value pairs
- Internal storage: Data files in private storage
- External storage: Data files in private or public storage
- SQLite database: Private data (can be made public through a Content Provider)
- Cloud storage: Private server or service provider

There are benefits and trade-offs to using internal and external storage. We will list some of the differences here to help you decide which option best fits your needs:

Internal storage:

- Unlike external storage, internal storage is always available but generally has less free space
- Files are not accessible to the user (unless the device has root access)
- Files are automatically deleted when your app is uninstalled (or with the **Clear Cache/Cleanup File** option in the App Manager)

External storage:

- The device may not have external storage or it may be inaccessible (such as when it's connected to a computer)
- Files are accessible to the user (and other apps) without requiring root access
- Files are not deleted when your app is uninstalled (unless you use `getExternalFilesDir()` to get app-specific public storage)

In this chapter, we will demonstrate working with shared preferences, internal and external storage, and SQLite databases. For cloud storage, take a look at the internet recipes in `Chapter 12`, *Telephony, Networks*.

Storing simple data

It's a common requirement to store simple data, and Android makes it simple using the Preferences API. It's not limited to just user preferences either; you can store any of the primitive data types using a name/value pair.

We'll demonstrate saving a name from an `EditText` and displaying it when the application starts. The following screenshots shows how the application looks the first time with no saved name:

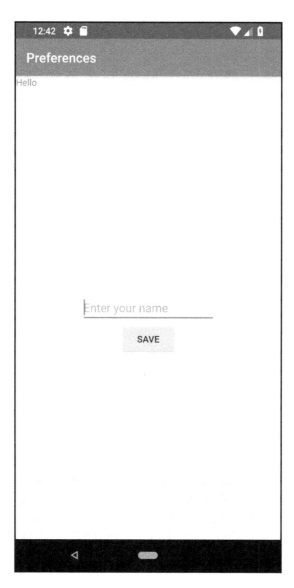

This is an example of how it looks after saving a name:

Getting ready

Create a new project in Android Studio and call it Preferences. Use the default **Phone & Tablet** options and select **Empty Activity** in the **Add an Activity to Mobile** dialog.

How to do it...

We'll use the existing **TextView** to display a **Welcome back** message and create a new `EditText` button to save the name. Start by opening `activity_main.xml`:

1. Replace the existing **TextView** with the following new views:

```
<TextView
    android:id="@+id/textView"
    android:layout_width="wrap_content"
    android:layout_height="wrap_content"
    app:layout_constraintLeft_toLeftOf="parent"
    app:layout_constraintTop_toTopOf="parent" />

<EditText
    android:id="@+id/editTextName"
    android:layout_width="wrap_content"
    android:layout_height="wrap_content"
    android:ems="10"
    android:hint="Enter your name"
    app:layout_constraintBottom_toBottomOf="parent"
    app:layout_constraintLeft_toLeftOf="parent"
    app:layout_constraintRight_toRightOf="parent"
    app:layout_constraintTop_toTopOf="parent"/>

<Button
    android:id="@+id/button"
    android:layout_width="wrap_content"
    android:layout_height="wrap_content"
    android:text="Save"
    app:layout_constraintTop_toBottomOf="@+id/editTextName"
    app:layout_constraintLeft_toLeftOf="parent"
    app:layout_constraintRight_toRightOf="parent"
    android:onClick="saveName"/>
```

2. Open `ActivityMain.java` and add the following global declarations:

```
private final String NAME="NAME";
private EditText mEditTextName;
```

3. Add the following code to `onCreate()` to save a reference to `EditText` and to load any saved name:

```
TextView textView = (TextView)findViewById(R.id.textView);
SharedPreferences sharedPreferences = getPreferences(MODE_PRIVATE);
String name = sharedPreferences.getString(NAME,null);
if (name==null) {
```

```
        textView.setText("Hello");
    } else {
        textView.setText("Welcome back " + name + "!");
    }
    mEditTextName = findViewById(R.id.editTextName);
```

4. Add the following `saveName()` method:

```
public void saveName(View view) {
    SharedPreferences.Editor editor =
getPreferences(MODE_PRIVATE).edit();
    editor.putString(NAME, mEditTextName.getText().toString());
    editor.commit();
}
```

5. Run the program on a device or emulator. Since we are demonstrating persisting data, it loads the name during `onCreate()`, so save a name and restart the program to see it load.

How it works...

To load the name, we first get a reference to `SharedPreference` and call the `getString()` method. We pass in the key for our name/value pair (we created a constant called NAME) and the default value to return if the key is not found.

To save the preference, we first need to get a reference to the Preference Editor. We use `putString()` with our NAME constant and follow it with `commit()`. Without `commit()`, the change will not be saved.

There's more...

Our example stores all the preferences in a single file. We can also store preferences in different files using `getSharedPreferences()` and passing in the name. One example where this option could be useful is you wanted to have separate profiles in a multi-user app.

Read and write a text file to internal storage

When simple name/value pairs are not sufficient, Android also supports regular file operations, including working with text and binary data.

The following recipe demonstrates how to read and write a file to internal or private storage.

Getting ready

Create a new project in Android Studio and call it `InternalStorageFile`. Use the default **Phone & Tablet** options and select **Empty Activity** in the **Add an Activity to Mobile** dialog.

How to do it...

To demonstrate both reading and writing text, we'll need a layout with an `EditText` and two buttons. Start by opening `main_activity.xml` and follow these steps:

1. Replace the existing `<TextView>` element with the following views:

```xml
<EditText
    android:id="@+id/editText"
    android:layout_width="wrap_content"
    android:layout_height="wrap_content"
    android:inputType="textMultiLine"
    android:ems="10"
    app:layout_constraintTop_toTopOf="parent"
    app:layout_constraintBottom_toTopOf="@+id/buttonRead"
    app:layout_constraintLeft_toLeftOf="parent"
    app:layout_constraintRight_toRightOf="parent" />
<Button
    android:id="@+id/buttonRead"
    android:layout_width="wrap_content"
    android:layout_height="wrap_content"
    android:text="Read"
    app:layout_constraintLeft_toLeftOf="parent"
    app:layout_constraintRight_toRightOf="parent"
    app:layout_constraintBottom_toTopOf="@+id/buttonWrite"
    android:onClick="readFile"/>
<Button
    android:id="@+id/buttonWrite"
    android:layout_width="wrap_content"
```

```
        android:layout_height="wrap_content"
        android:text="Write"
        app:layout_constraintLeft_toLeftOf="parent"
        app:layout_constraintRight_toRightOf="parent"
        app:layout_constraintBottom_toBottomOf="parent"
        android:onClick="writeFile"/>
```

2. Now, open `ActivityMain.java` and add the following global variables:

```
private final String FILENAME="testfile.txt";
EditText mEditText;
```

3. Add the following to the `onCreate()` method, after `setContentView ()`:

```
mEditText = (EditText)findViewById(R.id.editText);
```

4. Add the following `writeFile()` method:

```
public void writeFile(View view) {
    try {
        FileOutputStream fileOutputStream =
openFileOutput(FILENAME, Context.MODE_PRIVATE);
fileOutputStream.write(mEditText.getText().toString().getBytes());
        fileOutputStream.close();
    } catch (java.io.IOException e) {
        e.printStackTrace();
    }
}
```

5. Now, add the `readFile()` method:

```
public void readFile(View view) {
    StringBuilder stringBuilder = new StringBuilder();
    try {
        InputStream inputStream = openFileInput(FILENAME);
        if ( inputStream != null ) {
            InputStreamReader inputStreamReader = new
InputStreamReader(inputStream);
            BufferedReader bufferedReader = new
BufferedReader(inputStreamReader);
            String newLine = null;
            while ((newLine = bufferedReader.readLine()) != null )
{
                stringBuilder.append(newLine+"\n");
            }
            inputStream.close();
        }
    } catch (java.io.IOException e) {
```

```
                    e.printStackTrace();
            }
        mEditText.setText(stringBuilder);
    }
```

6. Run the program on a device or emulator.

How it works...

We use the `InputStream` and `FileOutputStream` classes to read and write, respectively. Writing to the file is as simple as getting the text from `EditText` and calling the `write()` method.

Reading back the contents is a little more involved. We could use the `FileInputStream` class for reading, but when working with text, the helper classes make it easier. In our example, we open the file with `openFileInput()`, which returns an `InputStream` object. We then use `InputStream` to get a `BufferedReader`, which offers the `ReadLine()` method. We loop through each line in the file and append it to our `StringBuilder`. When we're finished reading the file, we assign the text to `EditText`.

There's more...

The previous example used the private storage to save the file. Here's how you can use the cache folder.

Caching files

If all you need is to temporarily store data, you can also use the cache folder. The following method returns the cache folder as a `File` object (the next recipe demonstrates working with the `File` object):

```
getCacheDir()
```

The main benefit of the cache folder is that the system can clear the cache if running low on storage space. (The user can also clear the cache folder from **Apps Management** in **Settings**.)

For example, if your app downloads news articles, you could store those in the cache. When your app starts, you can display the news already downloaded. These are files that are not required to make your app work. If the system is low on resources, the cache can be cleared without adversely affecting your app. (Even though the system may clear the cache, it's still a good idea for your app to remove old files as well.)

See also

- The next recipe, *Read and write a text file to external storage*.

Read and write a text file to external storage

The process of reading and writing files to external storage is basically the same as using internal storage. The difference is in obtaining a reference to the storage location. Also, as mentioned in the *Introduction*, external storage may not be available, so it's best to check availability before attempting to access it.

This recipe will read and write a text file, as we did in the previous recipe. We'll also demonstrate how to check the external storage state before we access it.

Getting ready

Create a new project in Android Studio and call it `ExternalStorageFile`. Use the default **Phone & Tablet** options and select **Empty Activity** on the **Add an Activity to Mobile** dialog. We will use the same layout as the previous recipe, so you can just copy and paste if you typed it in already. Otherwise, use the layout from step 1 in the previous recipe, *Read and write a text file to internal storage*.

How to do it...

As mentioned previously in the *Getting ready* section, we'll use the layout from the previous recipe. With the layout file done, the first step will be to add permission to access the write to external storage. Here are the steps:

1. Open the **Android Manifest** and add the following permission:

```
<uses-permission
android:name="android.permission.READ_EXTERNAL_STORAGE" />
<uses-permission
android:name="android.permission.WRITE_EXTERNAL_STORAGE" />
```

2. Next, open `ActivityMain.java` and add the following global variables:

```
private final String FILENAME="testfile.txt";
private final String[] PERMISSIONS_STORAGE = {
        Manifest.permission.READ_EXTERNAL_STORAGE,
        Manifest.permission.WRITE_EXTERNAL_STORAGE
};
EditText mEditText;
```

3. Add the following to the `onCreate()` method, after `setContentView()`:

```
mEditText = (EditText)findViewById(R.id.editText);
```

4. Add the following two methods to check the storage state:

```
public boolean isExternalStorageWritable() {
    if
(Environment.MEDIA_MOUNTED.equals(Environment.getExternalStorageSta
te())) {
        return true;
    }
    return false;
}

public boolean isExternalStorageReadable() {
    if
(Environment.MEDIA_MOUNTED.equals(Environment.getExternalStorageSta
te()) ||
Environment.MEDIA_MOUNTED_READ_ONLY.equals(Environment.getExternalS
torageState())) {
        return true;
    }
    return false;
}
```

5. Add the following method to verify the app has permission to access the external storage:

```
public void checkStoragePermission() {
    int permission = ActivityCompat.checkSelfPermission(this,
            Manifest.permission.WRITE_EXTERNAL_STORAGE);

    if (permission != PackageManager.PERMISSION_GRANTED) {
        ActivityCompat.requestPermissions(this,
PERMISSIONS_STORAGE,101);
    }
}
```

6. Add the following `writeFile()` method:

```
public void writeFile(View view) {
    if (isExternalStorageWritable()) {
        checkStoragePermission();
        try {
            File textFile = new
File(Environment.getExternalStorageDirectory(), FILENAME);
            FileOutputStream fileOutputStream = new
FileOutputStream(textFile);
fileOutputStream.write(mEditText.getText().toString().getBytes());
            fileOutputStream.close();
        } catch (java.io.IOException e) {
            e.printStackTrace();
            Toast.makeText(this, "Error writing file",
Toast.LENGTH_LONG).show();
        }
    } else {
        Toast.makeText(this, "Cannot write to External Storage",
Toast.LENGTH_LONG).show();
    }
}
```

7. Add the following `readFile()` method:

```
public void readFile(View view) {
    if (isExternalStorageReadable()) {
        checkStoragePermission();
        StringBuilder stringBuilder = new StringBuilder();
        try {
            File textFile = new
File(Environment.getExternalStorageDirectory(), FILENAME);
            FileInputStream fileInputStream = new
FileInputStream(textFile);
            if (fileInputStream != null ) {
```

```
            InputStreamReader inputStreamReader = new
InputStreamReader(fileInputStream);
            BufferedReader bufferedReader = new
BufferedReader(inputStreamReader);
            String newLine = null;
            while ( (newLine = bufferedReader.readLine()) !=
null ) {

                stringBuilder.append(newLine+"\n");
            }
            fileInputStream.close();
        }
        mEditText.setText(stringBuilder);
    } catch (java.io.IOException e) {
        e.printStackTrace();
        Toast.makeText(this, "Error reading file",
Toast.LENGTH_LONG).show();
        }
    } else {
        Toast.makeText(this, "Cannot read External Storage",
            Toast.LENGTH_LONG).show();
    }
```

8. Run the program on a device or emulator with external storage.

How it works...

Reading and writing files are basically the same for both internal and external storage. The main difference is that we should check for the availability of the external storage before attempting to access it, which we do with the isExternalStorageWritable() and isExternalStorageReadable() methods. When checking the storage state, MEDIA_MOUNTED means we can read and write to it.

Unlike the internal storage example, we request the working path, which we do in this line of code:

```
File textFile = new File(Environment.getExternalStorageDirectory(),
FILENAME);
```

The actual reading and writing is done with the same classes, as it is just the location that is different.

 It is not safe to hard code an external folder path. The path can vary between versions of the OS and especially between hardware manufacturers. It is always best to call `getExternalStorageDirectory()` as shown.

There's more...

You probably noticed the `checkStoragePermission()` function from step 5 wasn't mentioned. This is because permissions aren't specific to storage but are required for the app to access various device features. Unlike the previous recipe, which used local app storage, "external" storage is considered risky for the user. (It wouldn't be good if just any app could go through a user's private files.) For that reason, the app must make additional effort to check if it has the required permission to access storage. If it does not, the user will be prompted. Note that this additional dialog is coming from the OS, not the app itself.

When you first run the app, if you are prompted for permission but still get an error writing, exit the app and restart. For a more in-depth explanation and handling of the new Android permission model, see the *See also...* section.

Getting public folders

The `getExternalStorageDirectory()` method returns the root folder of the external storage. If you want to obtain specific public folders, such as the `Music` or `Ringtone` folder, use `getExternalStoragePublicDirectory()` and pass in the desired folder type, for example:

```
getExternalStoragePublicDirectory(Environment.DIRECTORY_MUSIC)
```

Checking available space

One issue consistent between internal and external storage is limited space. If you know how much space you will need ahead of time, you can call the `getFreeSpace()` method on the `File` object. (`getTotalSpace()` will return the total space.) Here is a simple example, using the call to `getFreeSpace()`:

```
if (Environment.getExternalStorageDirectory().getFreeSpace() <
RQUIRED_FILE_SPACE) {
    //Not enough space
} else {
    //We have enough space
}
```

Deleting a file

There are many helper methods available through the `File` object, including deleting a file. If we wanted to delete the text file we created in the example, we could call `delete()` as follows:

```
textFile.delete()
```

Working with directories

Although it's called a `File` object, it supports directory commands as well, such as making and removing directories. If you want to make or remove a directory, build the `File` object, then call the respective methods: `mkdir()` and `delete()`. (There's also a method called `mkdirs()` (plural) that will create parent folders as well.)

Refer to the link in the *See also* section for a complete list.

Preventing files from being included in galleries

Android employs a **media scanner** that automatically includes sound, video, and image files in system collections, such as the **Image Gallery**. To exclude your directory, create an empty file called `.nomedia` (note the preceding period) in the same directory as the files you wish to exclude.

See also

- For more information on the Android 6.0 permission model, see the corresponding recipe in `Chapter 15`, *Getting Your App Ready for the Play Store*
- For a complete list of methods available in the `File` class, visit `http://developer.android.com/reference/java/io/File.html`

Including resource files in your project

Android provides two options for including files in your project: the `raw` folder and the `assets` folder. Which option you use depends on your requirements. To start, we'll give a brief overview of each option to help you decide the best use:

- **Raw files**
    - Included in the resource directory: `/res/raw`
    - As a resource, accessed through the raw identifier: `R.raw.<resource>`
    - A good place for storing media files such as MP3, MP4, and OGG files
- **Asset files**

    - Creates a file compiled in your APK (does not provide a resource ID)
    - Access files using their filenames, generally making them easier to use with dynamically created names
    - Some APIs do not support a Resource Identifier and therefore require including as an Asset

Generally, `raw` files are easier to work with since they are accessed through the resource identifier. As we'll demonstrate in this recipe, the main difference is how you access the file. In this example, we will load both a `raw` text file and an `asset` text file and display the contents.

Getting ready

Create a new project in **Android Studio** and call it `ReadingResourceFiles`. Use the default **Phone & Tablet** options and select **Empty Activity** in the **Add an Activity to Mobile** dialog.

How to do it...

To demonstrate reading content from both resource locations, we'll create a split layout. We also need to create both resource folders as they are not included in the default **Android project**. Here are the steps:

1. Open `activity_main.xml` and replace the contents with the following layout:

```xml
<?xml version="1.0" encoding="utf-8"?>
<LinearLayout
xmlns:android="http://schemas.android.com/apk/res/android"
    xmlns:tools="http://schemas.android.com/tools"
    android:layout_width="match_parent"
    android:layout_height="match_parent"
    android:orientation="vertical">
    <TextView
        android:id="@+id/textViewRaw"
        android:layout_width="match_parent"
        android:layout_height="0dp"
        android:layout_weight="1"
        android:gravity="center_horizontal|center_vertical"/>
    <TextView
        android:id="@+id/textViewAsset"
        android:layout_width="match_parent"
        android:layout_height="0dp"
        android:layout_weight="1"
        android:gravity="center_horizontal|center_vertical"/>
</LinearLayout>
```

2. Create the `raw` resource folder in the `res` folder. It will read as follows: `res/raw`. You can easily create it manually or let Android Studio do it for you by right-clicking on the `res` folder and selecting **New** | **Android Resource Directory**. When the Select Resource Directory dialog opens, select **raw** as the `Resource type`, as shown in this screenshot:

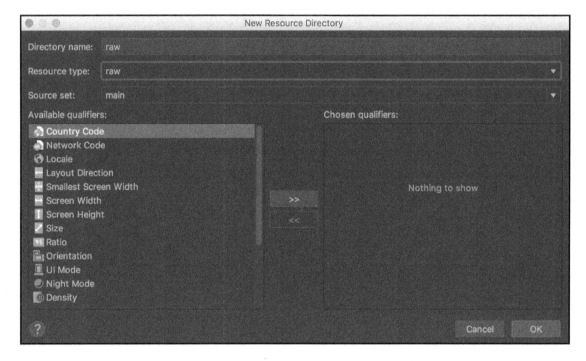

3. Create a new text file by right-clicking on the `raw` folder and select **New** | **File**. Name the file `raw_text.txt` and type some text in the file. (This text will be displayed when you run the application.)

4. Create the `asset` folder. The `asset` folder is trickier to create manually as it needs to be at the correct folder level. Fortunately, Android Studio provides a menu option that makes creating it very easy. Go to the **File** menu (or right-click on the **app** node) and select **New** | **Folder** | **Assets Folder**, as shown in this screenshot:

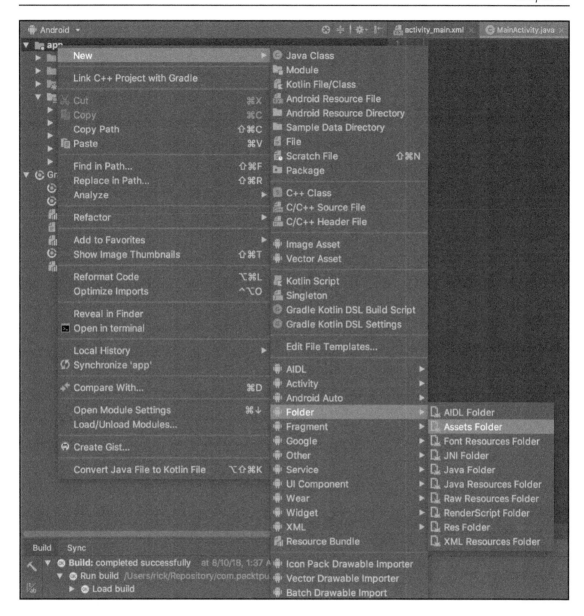

5. Create a text file in the asset folder called `asset_text.txt`. Again, whatever text you type here will be shown when you run the app. Here's how the final result should look after both text files are created:

6. Now, it's time for the code. Open `MainActivity.java` and add the following method to read the text file (which is passed into the method):

```
private String getText(InputStream inputStream) {
    StringBuilder stringBuilder = new StringBuilder();
    try {;
        if ( inputStream != null ) {
            InputStreamReader inputStreamReader = new
InputStreamReader(inputStream);
            BufferedReader bufferedReader = new
BufferedReader(inputStreamReader);
            String newLine = null;
            while ((newLine = bufferedReader.readLine()) != null )
{
                stringBuilder.append(newLine+"\n");
            }
            inputStream.close();
        }
    } catch (java.io.IOException e) {
        e.printStackTrace();
    }
    return stringBuilder.toString();
}
```

7. Finally, add the following code to the `onCreate()` method:

```
TextView textViewRaw = findViewById(R.id.textViewRaw);
textViewRaw.setText(getText(this.getResources().openRawResource(R.r
aw.raw_text)));
TextView textViewAsset = findViewById(R.id.textViewAsset);
try {
textViewAsset.setText(getText(this.getAssets().open("asset_text.txt
")));
} catch (IOException e) {
    e.printStackTrace();
}
```

8. Run the program on a device or emulator.

How it works...

To summarize, the only difference is in how we get a reference to each file. This line of code reads the `raw` resource:

```
this.getResources().openRawResource(R.raw.raw_text)
```

And this code reads the `asset` file:

```
this.getAssets().open("asset_text.txt")
```

Both calls return an `InputStream`, which the `getText()` method uses to read the file contents. It is worth noting, though, that the call to open the `asset` text file requires an additional `try`/`catch`.

As noted in the recipe introduction, resources are indexed so we have compile-time verification, which the `asset` folder does not have.

There's more...

A common approach is to include resources in your APK, but download new resources as they become available. (See the network communication in `Chapter 13`, *Telephony, Networks, and the Web*.) If new resources aren't available, you can always fall back on the resources in your APK.

See also

- Network communication recipes in Chapter 13, *Telephony, Networks, and the Web*.

Creating and using an SQLite database

In this recipe, we're going to demonstrate working with an SQLite database. If you are already familiar with SQL databases from other platforms, then much of what you know will apply. If you are new to SQLite, take a look at the reference links in the *See also* section as this recipe assumes a basic understanding of database concepts, including schemas, tables, cursors, and raw SQL.

To get you up and running with an SQLite database quickly, our example implements the basic CRUD operations. Generally, when creating a database in Android, you create a class that extends SQLiteOpenHelper, which is where your database functionality is implemented. Here is a list of the CRUD (create, read, update, and delete) functions:

- Create: insert()
- Read: query() and rawQuery()
- Update: update()
- Delete: delete()

To demonstrate a fully working database, we will create a simple Dictionary database where we'll store words and their definitions. We'll demonstrate the CRUD operations by adding new words (with their definitions) and updating existing word definitions. We'll show words in a ListView using a cursor. Pressing a word in the ListView will read the definition from the database and display it in a Toast message. A long press will delete the word.

Getting ready

Create a new project in Android Studio and call it SQLiteDatabase. Use the default **Phone & Tablet** options and select **Empty Activity** on the **Add an Activity to Mobile** dialog.

How to do it...

First, we'll create the UI, which will consist of two `EditText` fields, a button, and a
`ListView`. As we add words to the database, they will populate the `ListView`. Start
by opening `activity_main.xml` and follow these steps:

1. Replace the default XML with the following:

```xml
<?xml version="1.0" encoding="utf-8"?>
<LinearLayout
xmlns:android="http://schemas.android.com/apk/res/android"
    xmlns:app="http://schemas.android.com/apk/res-auto"
    xmlns:tools="http://schemas.android.com/tools"
    android:layout_width="match_parent"
    android:layout_height="match_parent"
    android:orientation="vertical">
    <EditText
        android:id="@+id/editTextWord"
        android:layout_width="wrap_content"
        android:layout_height="wrap_content"
        android:layout_alignParentTop="true"
        android:layout_alignParentLeft="true"
        android:layout_alignParentStart="true"
        android:hint="Word"/>
    <EditText
        android:id="@+id/editTextDefinition"
        android:layout_width="match_parent"
        android:layout_height="wrap_content"
        android:layout_below="@+id/editTextWord"
        android:layout_alignParentLeft="true"
        android:layout_alignParentStart="true"
        android:hint="Definition"/>
    <Button
        android:id="@+id/buttonAddUpdate"
        android:layout_width="wrap_content"
        android:layout_height="wrap_content"
        android:text="Save"
        android:layout_alignParentRight="true"
        android:layout_alignParentTop="true" />
    <ListView
        android:id="@+id/listView"
        android:layout_width="wrap_content"
        android:layout_height="wrap_content"
        android:layout_below="@+id/et_definition"
        android:layout_alignParentLeft="true"
        android:layout_alignParentBottom="true" />
</LinearLayout>
```

2. Add a new Java class to the project named `DictionaryDatabase`. This class extends from `SQLiteOpenHelper` and handles all the SQLite functions. Here is the class declaration:

```
public class DictionaryDatabase extends SQLiteOpenHelper {
```

3. Below the declaration, add the following constants:

```
private static final String DATABASE_NAME = "dictionary.db";
private static final String TABLE_DICTIONARY = "dictionary";

private static final String FIELD_WORD = "word";
private static final String FIELD_DEFINITION = "definition";
private static final int DATABASE_VERSION = 1;
```

4. Add the following constructor, `OnCreate()`, and `onUpgrade()` methods:

```
DictionaryDatabase(Context context) {
    super(context, DATABASE_NAME, null, DATABASE_VERSION);
}

@Override
public void onCreate(SQLiteDatabase db) {
    db.execSQL("CREATE TABLE " + TABLE_DICTIONARY +
            "(_id integer PRIMARY KEY," +
            FIELD_WORD + " TEXT, " +
            FIELD_DEFINITION + " TEXT);");
}

@Override
public void onUpgrade(SQLiteDatabase db, int oldVersion, int
newVersion) {
    //Handle database upgrade as needed
}
```

5. The following methods are responsible for creating, updating, and deleting the records:

```
public void saveRecord(String word, String definition) {
    long id = findWordID(word);
    if (id>0) {
        updateRecord(id, word,definition);
    } else {
        addRecord(word,definition);
    }
}

public long addRecord(String word, String definition) {
```

```
    SQLiteDatabase db = getWritableDatabase();

    ContentValues values = new ContentValues();
    values.put(FIELD_WORD, word);
    values.put(FIELD_DEFINITION, definition);
    return db.insert(TABLE_DICTIONARY, null, values);
}

public int updateRecord(long id, String word, String definition) {
    SQLiteDatabase db = getWritableDatabase();
    ContentValues values = new ContentValues();
    values.put("_id", id);
    values.put(FIELD_WORD, word);
    values.put(FIELD_DEFINITION, definition);
    return db.update(TABLE_DICTIONARY, values, "_id = ?", new
String[]{String.valueOf(id)});
}
public int deleteRecord(long id) {
    SQLiteDatabase db = getWritableDatabase();
    return db.delete(TABLE_DICTIONARY, "_id = ?", new
String[]{String.valueOf(id)});
}
```

6. And these methods handle reading the information from the database:

```
public long findWordID(String word) {
    long returnVal = -1;
    SQLiteDatabase db = getReadableDatabase();
    Cursor cursor = db.rawQuery(
            "SELECT _id FROM " + TABLE_DICTIONARY + " WHERE " +
FIELD_WORD + " = ?",
            new String[]{word});
    if (cursor.getCount() == 1) {
        cursor.moveToFirst();
        returnVal = cursor.getInt(0);
    }
    return returnVal;
}

public String getDefinition(long id) {
    String returnVal = "";
    SQLiteDatabase db = getReadableDatabase();
    Cursor cursor = db.rawQuery(
            "SELECT definition FROM " + TABLE_DICTIONARY + " WHERE
_id = ?",
            new String[]{String.valueOf(id)});
    if (cursor.getCount() == 1) {
        cursor.moveToFirst();
```

```
                      returnVal = cursor.getString(0);
        }
        return returnVal;
    }

    public Cursor getWordList() {
        SQLiteDatabase db = getReadableDatabase();
        String query = "SELECT _id, " + FIELD_WORD +
                " FROM " + TABLE_DICTIONARY + " ORDER BY " + FIELD_WORD
+
                " ASC";
        return db.rawQuery(query, null);
    }
```

7. With the database, class finished, open `MainActivity.java`. Add the following global variables below the class declaration:

```
EditText mEditTextWord;
EditText mEditTextDefinition;
DictionaryDatabase mDB;
ListView mListView;
```

8. Add the following method to save the fields when the button is clicked:

```
private void saveRecord() {
    mDB.saveRecord(mEditTextWord.getText().toString(),
mEditTextDefinition.getText().toString());
    mEditTextWord.setText("");
    mEditTextDefinition.setText("");
    updateWordList();
}
```

9. Add this method to populate the `ListView`:

```
private void updateWordList() {
    SimpleCursorAdapter simpleCursorAdapter = new
SimpleCursorAdapter(
            this,
            android.R.layout.simple_list_item_1,
            mDB.getWordList(),
            new String[]{"word"},
            new int[]{android.R.id.text1},
            0);
    mListView.setAdapter(simpleCursorAdapter);
}
```

10. Finally, add the following code to `onCreate()`:

```java
mDB = new DictionaryDatabase(this);
mEditTextWord = findViewById(R.id.editTextWord);
mEditTextDefinition = findViewById(R.id.editTextDefinition);
Button buttonAddUpdate = findViewById(R.id.buttonAddUpdate);
buttonAddUpdate.setOnClickListener(new View.OnClickListener() {
    @Override
    public void onClick(View v) {
        saveRecord();
    }
});

mListView = findViewById(R.id.listView);
mListView.setOnItemClickListener(new
AdapterView.OnItemClickListener() {
    @Override
    public void onItemClick(AdapterView<?> parent, View view, int
position, long id) {
        Toast.makeText(MainActivity.this, mDB.getDefinition(id),
Toast.LENGTH_SHORT).show();
    }
});
mListView.setOnItemLongClickListener(new
AdapterView.OnItemLongClickListener() {
    @Override
    public boolean onItemLongClick(AdapterView<?> parent, View
view, int position, long id) {
        Toast.makeText(MainActivity.this,
                "Records deleted = " + mDB.deleteRecord(id),
Toast.LENGTH_SHORT).show();
        updateWordList();
        return true;
    }
});
updateWordList();
```

11. Run the program on a device or emulator and try it out.

How it works...

We'll start by explaining the `DictionaryDatabase` class as that's the heart of an SQLite database. The first item to note is the constructor:

```
DictionaryDatabase(Context context) {
    super(context, DATABASE_NAME, null, DATABASE_VERSION);
}
```

Notice `DATABASE_VERSION`? Only when you make changes to your database schema do you need to increment this value.

Next is `onCreate()`, where the database is actually created. This is only called the first time the database is created, not each time the class is created. It's also worth noting the `_id` field. Android does not require tables to have a primary field, but some classes, such as the `SimpleCursorAdapter`, may require an `_id`.

We're required to implement the `onUpgrade()` callback, but as this is a new database, there's nothing to do. This method will only be called when the database version is incremented.

The `saveRecord()` method handles calling `addRecord()` or `updateRecord()`, as appropriate. Since we are going to modify the database, both methods use `getWritableDatabase()` to get an updatable database reference. A writable database requires more resources so if you don't need to make changes, get a read-only database instead.

The last method to note is `getWordList()`, which returns all the words in the database using a cursor object. We use this cursor to populate the `ListView`, which brings us to `ActivityMain.java`. The `onCreate()` method does the standard initialization we've seen before and also creates an instance of the database with the following line of code:

```
mDB = new DictionaryDatabase(this);
```

The `onCreate()` method is also where we set up the events to show the word definition (with a Toast) when an item is pressed and to delete the word on a long press. Probably the most complicated code is in `updateWordList()`.

This isn't the first time we've used an adapter, but this is the first cursor adapter, so we'll explain. We use the `SimpleCursorAdapter` to create a mapping between our field in the cursor and the `ListView` item. We use the `layout.simple_list_item_1` layout, which only includes a single text field with the ID `android.R.id.text1`. In a real application, we'd probably create a custom layout and include the definition in the `ListView` item, but we wanted to demonstrate a method to read the definition from the database.

We call `updateWordList()` in three places: during `onCreate()` to create the initial list, then again after we add/update an item, and lastly when deleting an item.

There's more...

Although this is a fully functioning example of SQLite, it is still just the basics. There are many books dedicated to SQLite for Android and they are worth checking out.

Upgrading a database

As we mentioned previously, when we increment the database version, the `onUpgrade()` method will be called. What you do here is dependent on the changes made to the database. If you changed an existing table, ideally you'll want to migrate the user data to the new format by querying the existing data and inserting it into the new format. Keep in mind that there is no guarantee the user will upgrade in consecutive order, so they could jump from version 1 to version 4, for example.

See also

- SQLite homepage: `https://www.sqlite.org/`
- SQLite database Android reference: `http://developer.android.com/reference/android/database/sqlite/SQLiteDatabase.html`

Accessing data in the background using a Loader

Any potentially long-running operations should not be done on the UI thread, as this can cause your application to be slow or become unresponsive. The Android OS will bring up the **Application Not Responding** (**ANR**) dialog when apps become unresponsive.

Since querying databases can be time-consuming, Android introduced the Loader API in Android 3.0. A Loader processes the query on a background thread and notifies the UI thread when it finishes.

The two primary benefits to Loaders are the following:

- Querying the database is (automatically) handled on a background thread
- The query auto-updates (when using a Content Provider data source)

To demonstrate a Loader, we will modify the previous SQLite database example to use a `CursorLoader` to populate `ListView`.

Getting ready

We will use the project from the previous example, *Creating and using an SQLite database*, as the base for this recipe. Create a new project in Android Studio and call it `Loader`. Use the default Phone & Tablet options and select Empty Activity on the Add an Activity to Mobile dialog. Copy the `DictionaryDatabase` class and the layout from the previous recipe. Although we will use parts of the previous `ActivityMain.java` code, we will start at the beginning in this recipe to make it easier to follow.

How to do it...

With the project set up as described in *Getting ready*, we'll continue by creating two new Java classes, and then tie it all together in `ActivityMain.java`. Here are the steps:

1. Create a new Java class called `DictionaryAdapter` that extends `CursorAdapter`. This class replaces the `SimpleCursorAdapter` used in the previous recipe. Here is the full code:

```
public class DictionaryAdapter extends CursorAdapter {
    public DictionaryAdapter(Context context, Cursor c, int flags)
    {
```

```
            super(context, c, flags);
        }

        @Override
        public View newView(Context context, Cursor cursor, ViewGroup
    parent) {
            return LayoutInflater.from(context)
    .inflate(android.R.layout.simple_list_item_1,parent, false);
        }

        @Override
        public void bindView(View view, Context context, Cursor cursor)
    {
            TextView textView = view.findViewById(android.R.id.text1);
    textView.setText(cursor.getString(getCursor().getColumnIndex("word"
    )));
        }
    }
```

2. Next, create another new Java class and call this one `DictionaryLoader`.
   Although this is the class that handles the data loading on the background
   thread, it's actually very simple:

```
    public class DictionaryLoader extends CursorLoader {
        Context mContext;
        public DictionaryLoader(Context context) {
            super(context);
            mContext = context;
        }

        @Override
        public Cursor loadInBackground() {
            DictionaryDatabase db = new DictionaryDatabase(mContext);
            return db.getWordList();
        }
    }
```

3. Next, open `ActivityMain.java`. We need to change the declaration to
   implement the `LoaderManager.LoaderCallbacks<Cursor>` interface as
   follows:

```
    public class MainActivity extends AppCompatActivity
        implements LoaderManager.LoaderCallbacks<Cursor> {
```

4. Add the adapter to the global declarations. The complete list is as follows:

```
EditText mEditTextWord;
EditText mEditTextDefinition;
DictionaryDatabase mDB;
ListView mListView;
DictionaryAdapter mAdapter;
```

5. Change `onCreate()` to use the new adapter and add a call to update the Loader after deleting a record. The final `onCreate()` method should look as follows:

```
@Override
protected void onCreate(Bundle savedInstanceState) {
    super.onCreate(savedInstanceState);
    setContentView(R.layout.activity_main);

    mDB = new DictionaryDatabase(this);

    mEditTextWord = findViewById(R.id.editTextWord);
    mEditTextDefinition = findViewById(R.id.editTextDefinition);
    Button buttonAddUpdate = findViewById(R.id.buttonAddUpdate);
    buttonAddUpdate.setOnClickListener(new View.OnClickListener() {
        @Override
        public void onClick(View v) {
            saveRecord();
        }
    });

    mListView = findViewById(R.id.listView);
    mListView.setOnItemClickListener(new
AdapterView.OnItemClickListener() {
        @Override
        public void onItemClick(AdapterView<?> parent, View view,
int position, long id) {
            Toast.makeText(MainActivity.this,
                    mDB.getDefinition(id),
                    Toast.LENGTH_SHORT).show();
        }
    });
    mListView.setOnItemLongClickListener(new
AdapterView.OnItemLongClickListener() {
        @Override
        public boolean onItemLongClick(AdapterView<?> parent, View
view, int position, long id) {
            Toast.makeText(MainActivity.this, "Records deleted = "
+ mDB.deleteRecord(id),
                    Toast.LENGTH_SHORT).show();
            getSupportLoaderManager().restartLoader(0, null,
```

```
MainActivity.this);
            return true;
        }
    });
    getSupportLoaderManager().initLoader(0, null, this);
    mAdapter = new DictionaryAdapter(this,mDB.getWordList(),0);
    mListView.setAdapter(mAdapter);
}
```

6. We no longer have the `updateWordList()` method, so change `saveRecord()` as follows:

```
private void saveRecord() {
    mDB.saveRecord(mEditTextWord.getText().toString(),
mEditTextDefinition.getText().toString());
    mEditTextWord.setText("");
    mEditTextDefinition.setText("");
    getSupportLoaderManager().restartLoader(0, null,
MainActivity.this);
}
```

7. Finally, implement these three methods for the Loader interface:

```
@Override
public Loader<Cursor> onCreateLoader(int id, Bundle args) {
    return new DictionaryLoader(this);
}

@Override
public void onLoadFinished(Loader<Cursor> loader, Cursor data) {
    mAdapter.swapCursor(data);
}

@Override
public void onLoaderReset(Loader<Cursor> loader) {
    mAdapter.swapCursor(null);
}
```

8. Run the program on a device or emulator.

How it works...

The default `CursorAdapter` requires a Content Provider URI. Since we are accessing the SQLite database directly (and not through a Content Provider), we don't have a URI to pass, so instead, we created a custom adapter by extending the `CursorAdapter` class. `DictionaryAdapter` still performs the same functionality as `SimpleCursorAdapter` from the previous recipe, namely mapping the data from the cursor to the item layout.

The next class we added was `DictionaryLoader`, which handles populating the adapter. As you can see, it's actually very simple. All it does is return the cursor from `getWordList()`. The key here is that this query is being handled in a background thread and will call the `onLoadFinished()` callback (in `MainActivity.java`) when it finishes. Fortunately, most of the heavy lifting is handled in the base class.

This takes us to `ActivityMain.java`, where we implemented the following three callbacks from the `LoaderManager.LoaderCallbacks` interface:

- `onCreateLoader()`: It's initially called in `onCreate()` with the `initLoader()` call. It's called again with the `restartLoader()` call after we make changes to the database.
- `onLoadFinished()`: It's called when the Loader `loadInBackground()` finishes.
- `onLoaderReset()`: It's called when the Loader is being recreated (such as with the `restart()` method). We set the old cursor to `null` because it will be invalidated and we don't want a reference kept around.

There's more...

As you saw in the previous example, we need to manually notify the Loader to re-query the database using `restartLoader()`. One of the benefits of using a Loader is that it can auto-update, but it requires a Content Provider as the data source. A Content Provider supports using an SQLite database as the data source and is recommended for a serious application. (See the following Content Provider link to get started.)

See also

- The *AsyncTask* recipe in `Chapter 14`, *Location and Using Geofencing*.
- Creating a Content Provider:
  http://developer.android.com/guide/topics/providers/content-provider-creating.html

- It's also worth checking out Paging and LiveData in the Android Jetpack Components: `https://developer.android.com/jetpack/`.
- The Loader (and AsyncTask) are both included in the Android SDK. A non-SDK option (and highly recommended) is RXJava for Android: `https://github.com/ReactiveX/RxAndroid`. RXJava is gaining popularity on Android and we're seeing more and more support for RXJava observables.

Accessing external storage with scoped directories in Android N

With security awareness on the rise, users are becoming more skeptical about allowing apps to have unnecessary permissions. Android N introduces a new option called Scoped Directory Access, allowing your application to request access to only the required permissions, instead of general access to all folders.

If your application requests `READ_EXTERNAL_STORAGE` and/or `WRITE_EXTERNAL_STORAGE` permission, but only needs access to a specific directory, you can use Scoped Directory access instead. This recipe will demonstrate how to request access to a specific directory, the `Music` folder in this case.

Getting ready

Create a new project in Android Studio and call it `ScopedDirectoryAccess`. In the **Target Android Device** dialog, be sure to select **API 24: Android 7.0 (Nougat)** or higher for the **Phone & Tablet** option. Select **Empty Activity** on the **Add an Activity to Mobile** dialog.

How to do it...

To initiate the user access request, we'll add a button to the layout. Start by opening `activity_main.xml` and follow these steps:

1. Replace the existing `TextView` with this button XML:

```
<Button
    android:id="@+id/button"
    android:layout_width="wrap_content"
    android:layout_height="wrap_content"
```

```
android:text="Request Access"
android:onClick="onAccessClick"
app:layout_constraintBottom_toBottomOf="parent"
app:layout_constraintLeft_toLeftOf="parent"
app:layout_constraintRight_toRightOf="parent"
app:layout_constraintTop_toTopOf="parent" />
```

2. Now, open `MainActivity.java` and add the following line of code to the class:

```
private final int REQUEST_FOLDER_MUSIC=101;
```

3. Add the method to handle the button click:

```
public void onAccessClick(View view) {
    StorageManager storageManager =
(StorageManager)getSystemService(Context.STORAGE_SERVICE);
    StorageVolume storageVolume =
storageManager.getPrimaryStorageVolume();
    Intent intent =
storageVolume.createAccessIntent(Environment.DIRECTORY_MUSIC);
    startActivityForResult(intent, REQUEST_FOLDER_MUSIC);
}
```

4. Override the `onActivityResult()` method as follows:

```
@Override
protected void onActivityResult(int requestCode, int resultCode,
Intent data) {
    super.onActivityResult(requestCode, resultCode, data);
    switch (requestCode) {
        case REQUEST_FOLDER_MUSIC:
            if (resultCode == Activity.RESULT_OK) {
getContentResolver().takePersistableUriPermission(data.getData(),
0);
            }
            break;
    }
}
```

5. You're ready to run the application on a device or emulator.

How it works...

The access request is handled by the OS, not by the app. To request access, we need to call `createAccessIntent()`, which we do with this line of code:

```
Intent intent =
storageVolume.createAccessIntent(Environment.DIRECTORY_MUSIC);
```

We call the Intent using the `startActivityForResult()` method, which we've used before. Since we are looking for a result to come back, we need to pass a unique identifier to know when the returned result callback is from our request. (The `onActivityResult()` callback method can receive callbacks for multiple requests.) If the request code matches our request, we then check whether the result code equals `Activity.RESULT_OK`, which means the user granted the permission request. We pass the result to `takePersistableUriPermission()` so we will not need to prompt the user the next time we need to access the same directory.

 Access to a directory also includes access to all sub-directories.

There's more...

For the best user experience, observe the following best practices:

1. Make sure to persist the URI after the user grants permission to avoid repeatedly requesting the same permission (as we do with `takePersistableUriPermission()`)
2. If the user denies the permission request, don't annoy your users by continuously asking

See also

- See the following link for more information on the Storage Access Framework: `http://developer.android.com/guide/topics/providers/document-provider.html`

8
Alerts and Notifications

In this chapter, we will cover the following topics:

- Lights, Action, and Sound - getting the user's attention!
- Creating a Toast with a custom layout
- Displaying a message box with AlertDialog
- Displaying a progress dialog
- Lights, Action, and Sound Redux using Notifications
- Creating a Media Player Notification
- Making a Flashlight with a Heads-Up Notification
- Notifications with Direct Reply

Introduction

Android provides many ways to notify your user, including both visual and non-visual methods. Keep in mind, notifications distract your user, so it's a good idea to be very judicious when using any notification. Users like to be in control of their device (it is theirs, after all), so give them the option to enable and disable notifications as they desire. Otherwise, your user might get annoyed and uninstall your app altogether.

We'll start by reviewing the following non-UI-based notification options:

- Flash LED
- Vibrate phone
- Play ringtone

Then, we'll move on to visual notifications, including the following:

- Toasts
- AlertDialog
- ProgressDialog
- Status Bar Notifications

The recipes that follow will show you how to implement each of these notifications in your own applications. It's worth reading the following link to understand best practices when using notifications:

Refer to **Android Notification Design Guidelines** at `http://developer.android.com/design/patterns/notifications.html`.

Lights, Action, and Sound – getting the user's attention!

Most of the recipes in this chapter use the `Notification` object to alert your users, so this recipe will show an alternative approach for when you don't actually need a notification.

As the recipe title implies, we're going to use lights, action, and sound:

- **Lights**: Normally, you'd use the LED device, but that is only available through the `Notification` object, which we'll demonstrate later in the chapter. Instead, we'll take this opportunity to use `setTorchMode()` (added in API 23-Android 6.0), to use the camera flash as a flashlight. (Note: as you'll see in the code, this feature will only work on an Android 6.0 device with a camera flash.)
- **Action**: We'll vibrate the phone.
- **Sound**: We'll use the `RingtoneManager` to play the default notification sound.

As you'll see, the code for each of these is quite simple.

As demonstrated in the following *Lights, Action, and Sound Redux using Notifications* recipe, all three options, LED, vibrate, and sounds, are available through the Notification object. The Notification object would certainly be the most appropriate method to provide alerts and reminders when the user is not actively engaged in your app. But for those times when you want to provide feedback while they are using your app, these options are available. The vibrate option is a good example; if you want to provide haptic feedback to a button press (common with keyboard apps), call the vibrate method directly.

Getting ready

Create a new project in Android Studio and call it LightsActionSound. When prompted for the API level, we need API 21 or above to compile the project. Select **Empty Activity** when prompted for the **Activity Type**.

How to do it...

We'll use three buttons to initiate each action, so start by opening activity_main.xml and perform the following steps:

1. Replace the existing layout XML with the following layout:

```
<?xml version="1.0" encoding="utf-8"?>
<RelativeLayout
xmlns:android="http://schemas.android.com/apk/res/android"
    xmlns:app="http://schemas.android.com/apk/res-auto"
    xmlns:tools="http://schemas.android.com/tools"
    android:layout_width="match_parent"
    android:layout_height="match_parent"
    tools:context=".MainActivity">
<ToggleButton
        android:id="@+id/buttonLights"
        android:layout_width="wrap_content"
        android:layout_height="wrap_content"
        android:text="Lights"
        android:layout_centerHorizontal="true"
        android:layout_above="@+id/buttonAction"
        android:onClick="clickLights" />
<Button
        android:id="@+id/buttonAction"
        android:layout_width="wrap_content"
        android:layout_height="wrap_content"
        android:text="Action"
        android:layout_centerVertical="true"
```

```
        android:layout_centerHorizontal="true"
        android:onClick="clickVibrate"/&gt;
&lt;Button
        android:id="@+id/buttonSound"
        android:layout_width="wrap_content"
        android:layout_height="wrap_content"
        android:text="Sound"
        android:layout_below="@+id/buttonAction"
        android:layout_centerHorizontal="true"
        android:onClick="clickSound"/&gt;
&lt;/RelativeLayout&gt;
```

2. Add the following permission to the Android Manifest:

```
&lt;uses-permission android:name="android.permission.VIBRATE" /&gt;
```

3. Open `ActivityMain.java` and add the following global variables:

```
private CameraManager mCameraManager;
private String mCameraId=null;
private ToggleButton mButtonLights;
```

4. Add the following method to get the Camera ID:

```
private String getCameraId() {
    try {
        String[] ids = mCameraManager.getCameraIdList();
        for (String id : ids) {
            CameraCharacteristics c =
mCameraManager.getCameraCharacteristics(id);
            Boolean flashAvailable =
c.get(CameraCharacteristics.FLASH_INFO_AVAILABLE);
            Integer facingDirection =
c.get(CameraCharacteristics.LENS_FACING);
            if (flashAvailable != null
                    && flashAvailable
                    && facingDirection != null
                    && facingDirection ==
CameraCharacteristics.LENS_FACING_BACK) {
                return id;
            }
        }
    } catch (CameraAccessException e) {
        e.printStackTrace();
    }
    return null;
}
```

5. Add the following code to the `onCreate()` method:

```
mButtonLights = findViewById(R.id.buttonLights);
if (Build.VERSION.SDK_INT &gt;= Build.VERSION_CODES.M) {
    mCameraManager = (CameraManager)
this.getSystemService(Context.CAMERA_SERVICE);
    mCameraId = getCameraId();
    if (mCameraId==null) { mButtonLights.setEnabled(false);
    } else {
        mButtonLights.setEnabled(true);
    }
} else {
    mButtonLights.setEnabled(false);
}
```

6. Now, add the code to handle each of the button clicks:

```
public void clickLights(View view) {
    if (Build.VERSION.SDK_INT &gt;= Build.VERSION_CODES.M) {
        try {
            mCameraManager.setTorchMode(mCameraId,
mButtonLights.isChecked());
        } catch (CameraAccessException e) {
            e.printStackTrace();
        }
    }
}
public void clickVibrate(View view) {
    ((Vibrator) getSystemService(VIBRATOR_SERVICE)).vibrate(1000);
}

public void clickSound(View view) {
    Uri notificationSoundUri =
RingtoneManager.getDefaultUri(RingtoneManager.TYPE_NOTIFICATION);
    Ringtone ringtone =
RingtoneManager.getRingtone(getApplicationContext(),
            notificationSoundUri);
    ringtone.play();
}
```

7. You're ready to run the application on a physical device. The code presented here will need Android 6.0 (or higher) to use the flashlight option.

How it works...

As you can see from the previous paragraphs, most of the code is related to finding and opening the camera to use the flash feature. `setTorchMode()` was introduced in API 23, which is why we have the API version check:

```
if (Build.VERSION.SDK_INT &gt;= Build.VERSION_CODES.M){}
```

This app demonstrates using the new `camera2` libraries, which were introduced in Lollipop (API 21). Both the `vibrate` and `ringtone` methods have been available since API 1.

The `getCameraId()` method is where we check for the camera. We want an outward-facing camera with a flash. If one is found, the ID is returned; otherwise, it is null. If the camera id is null, we disable the button.

To play the sound, we use the `Ringtone` object from the `RingtoneManager`. Besides being relatively easy to implement, another benefit to this method is that we can use the default notification sound, which we get with this code:

```
Uri notificationSoundUri =
RingtoneManager.getDefaultUri(RingtoneManager.TYPE_NOTIFICATION);
```

This way, if the user changes their preferred notification sound, we use it automatically.

Last is the call to vibrate the phone. This was the simplest code to use, but it does require permission, which we added to the Manifest:

```
&lt;uses-permission android:name="android.permission.VIBRATE" /&gt;
```

There's more...

In a production-level application, you wouldn't want to simply disable the button if you didn't have to. In this case, there are other means to use the camera flash as a flashlight. For additional examples on using the camera, see `Chapter 12`, *Multimedia*, where we'll see `getCameraId()` used again.

See also

- Refer to the *Lights, Action, and Sound Redux using Notifications* recipe later in this chapter to see the equivalent features using the `Notification` object
- Refer to `Chapter 12`, *Multimedia*, for examples using the new camera API and other sound options

Creating a Toast with a custom layout

We've used Toasts quite a bit already in previous chapters as they provide a quick and easy way to display information, both for user notification and for ourselves when debugging.

The previous examples have all used the simple one-line syntax, but Toasts aren't limited to this. Toasts, like most components in Android, can be customized, as we'll demonstrate in this recipe.

Android Studio offers a shortcut for making a simple Toast statement. As you start to type the Toast command, you'll see the following:

Press *Enter* to auto-complete. Then, press *Ctrl* + spacebar and you'll see the following:

When you press Enter again, it will auto-complete with the following:

```
Toast.makeText(this, "", Toast.LENGTH_SHORT).show();
```

In this recipe, we'll use the Toast Builder to change the default layout, and gravity to create a custom Toast, as shown in the following screenshot:

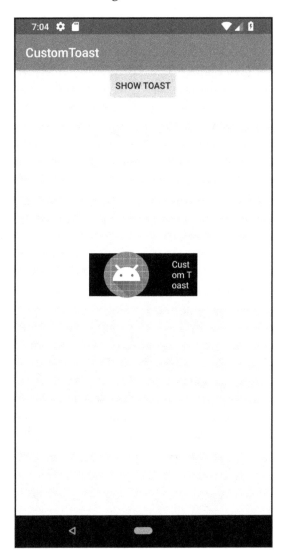

Getting ready

Create a new project in Android Studio and call it `CustomToast`. Use the default **Phone & Tablet** options and select **Empty Activity** when prompted for the **Activity Type**.

How to do it...

We're going to change the shape of the Toast to a square and create a custom layout to display an image and text message. Start by opening `activity_main.xml` and follow these steps:

1. Replace the existing <TextView> element with a <Button> as follows:

```
&lt;Button
    android:id="@+id/button"
    android:layout_width="wrap_content"
    android:layout_height="wrap_content"
    android:text="Show Toast"
    android:onClick="showToast"
    app:layout_constraintLeft_toLeftOf="parent"
    app:layout_constraintRight_toRightOf="parent"
    app:layout_constraintTop_toTopOf="parent" /&gt;
```

2. Create a new drawable resource file in the `res/drawable` folder named `border_square.xml` using the following code:

```
&lt;?xml version="1.0" encoding="utf-8"?&gt;
&lt;layer-list
xmlns:android="http://schemas.android.com/apk/res/android"&gt;
    &lt;item
        android:left="4px"
        android:top="4px"
        android:right="4px"
        android:bottom="4px"&gt;
        &lt;shape android:shape="rectangle" &gt;
            &lt;solid android:color="@android:color/black" /&gt;
            &lt;stroke android:width="5px"
android:color="@android:color/white"/&gt;
        &lt;/shape&gt;
    &lt;/item&gt;
&lt;/layer-list&gt;
```

3. Create a new layout resource file in the `res/layout` folder named `toast_custom.xml` with the following code:

```xml
<?xml version="1.0" encoding="utf-8"?>
<LinearLayout
xmlns:android="http://schemas.android.com/apk/res/android"
    android:id="@+id/toast_layout_root"
    android:layout_width="match_parent"
    android:layout_height="match_parent"
    android:orientation="horizontal"
    android:background="@drawable/border_square">
    <ImageView
        android:layout_width="wrap_content"
        android:layout_height="wrap_content"
        android:id="@+id/imageView"
        android:layout_weight="1"
        android:src="@mipmap/ic_launcher" />
    <TextView
        android:id="@android:id/message"
        android:layout_width="0dp"
        android:layout_height="match_parent"
        android:layout_weight="1"
        android:textColor="@android:color/white"
        android:padding="10dp" />
</LinearLayout>
```

4. Now, open `ActivityMain.java` and add the following method:

```java
public void showToast(View view) {
    LayoutInflater inflater = (LayoutInflater)this
            .getSystemService(Context.LAYOUT_INFLATER_SERVICE);
    View layout = inflater.inflate(R.layout.toast_custom, null);
((TextView)layout.findViewById(android.R.id.message)).setText("Cust
om Toast");
    Toast toast = new Toast(this);
    toast.setGravity(Gravity.CENTER, 0, 0);
    toast.setDuration(Toast.LENGTH_LONG);
    toast.setView(layout);
    toast.show();
}
```

5. Run the program on a device or emulator.

How it works...

This custom Toast changes the default gravity and shape, and adds an image just to show that "it can be done."

The first step is to create a new Toast layout, which we do by inflating our `custom_toast` layout. Once we have the new layout, we need to get the `TextView` so we can set our message, which we do with the standard `setText()` method. With this done, we create a Toast object and set the individual properties. We set the Toast gravity with the `setGravity()` method. The gravity determines where on the screen our Toast will display. We specify our custom layout with the `setView()` method call. And just like in the single-line variation, we display the Toast with the `show()` method.

See also

- For a Kotlin version, see the *Creating a Toast in Kotlin* recipe in `Chapter 16`, *Getting Started with Kotlin*

Displaying a message box with AlertDialog

In `Chapter 4`, *Menus*, we created a theme to make an Activity look like a dialog. In this recipe, we'll demonstrate how to create a dialog using the `AlertDialog` class. `AlertDialog` offers a Title, up to three buttons, and a list or custom layout area, as shown in the following example:

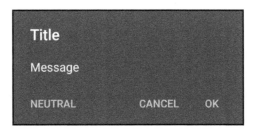

 The button arrangement can vary depending on the OS version.

Getting ready

Create a new project in Android Studio and call it `AlertDialog`. Use the default **Phone & Tablet** options and select the **Empty Activity** option when prompted for the **Activity Type**.

How to do it...

To demonstrate, we'll create a **Confirm Delete** dialog to prompt the user for confirmation after pressing the Delete button. Start by opening the `main_activity.xml` layout file and follow these steps:

1. Add the following `&lt;Button&gt;`:

```
&lt;Button
    android:id="@+id/buttonDelete"
    android:layout_width="wrap_content"
    android:layout_height="wrap_content"
    android:text="Delete"
    android:onClick="confirmDelete"
    app:layout_constraintBottom_toBottomOf="parent"
    app:layout_constraintLeft_toLeftOf="parent"
    app:layout_constraintRight_toRightOf="parent"
    app:layout_constraintTop_toTopOf="parent" /&gt;
```

2. Add the `confirmDelete()` method to `ActivityMain.java`; this is called by the button:

```
public void confirmDelete(View view) {
    AlertDialog.Builder builder = new AlertDialog.Builder(this);
    builder.setTitle("Delete")
            .setMessage("Are you sure you?")
            .setPositiveButton(android.R.string.ok, new
DialogInterface.OnClickListener() {
                public void onClick(DialogInterface dialog, int id)
{
                    Toast.makeText(MainActivity.this, "OK Pressed",
                        Toast.LENGTH_SHORT).show();
                }
            })
            .setNegativeButton(android.R.string.cancel, new
DialogInterface.OnClickListener() {
                public void onClick(DialogInterface dialog, int id)
{
                    Toast.makeText(MainActivity.this, "Cancel
Pressed",
```

```
                                    Toast.LENGTH_SHORT).show();
                    }
                });
        builder.create().show();
    }
```

3. Run the application on a device or emulator.

How it works...

This dialog is meant to serve as a simple confirmation dialog, such as confirming a delete action. Basically, just create an `AlertDialog.Builder` object and set the properties as needed. We use a Toast message to indicate the user selection. We don't even have to close the dialog; it's taken care of by the base class.

There's more...

As shown in the recipe introduction screenshot, the `AlertDialog` also has a third button, called the Neutral button, which can be set using the following method:

```
builder.setNeutralButton()
```

Add an icon

To add an icon to the dialog, use the `setIcon()` method. The following is an example:

```
.setIcon(R.mipmap.ic_launcher)
```

 Introduced in Android 4.3, the mipmap folder is a drawable folder for storing bitmaps that should not be modified/converted during APK optimization. This is the recommended location for storing app icons so the launcher can have the best available image when displaying the app icon.

Using a list

We can also create a list of items to select from with various list setting methods, including the following:

```
.setItems()
.setAdapter()
```

```
.setSingleChoiceItems()
.setMultiChoiceItems()
```

As you can see, there are also methods for single-choice (using a radio button) and multi-choice lists (using a checkbox).

> You can't use both the Message and the Lists, as `setMessage()` will take priority.

Custom layout

Finally, we can also create a custom layout, and set it using the following:

```
.setView()
```

If you use a custom layout and replace the standard buttons, you are also responsible for closing the dialog. Use `hide()` if you plan to reuse the dialog and `dismiss()` when finished to release the resources.

Displaying a progress dialog

`ProgressDialog` has been available since API 1 and is widely used. As we'll demonstrate in this recipe, it's simple to use, but keep this message in mind (posted on the Android Dialog Guidelines site at `http://developer.android.com/guide/topics/ui/dialogs.html`):

> Android includes another dialog class called ProgressDialog that shows a dialog with a progress bar. However, if you need to indicate loading or indeterminate progress, you should instead follow the design guidelines for Progress & Activity and use a ProgressBar in your layout.

This message doesn't mean `ProgressDialog` is deprecated or is bad code. It's suggesting that the use of `ProgressDialog` should be avoided since the user cannot interact with your app while the dialog is displayed. If possible, use a layout that includes a progress bar (so other views are still usable), instead of stopping everything with `ProgressDialog`.

The Google Play app provides a good example. When adding items to download, Google Play shows a progress bar, but it's not a dialog so the user can continue interacting with the app, even adding more items to download. If possible, use that approach instead.

There are times when you may not have that luxury; for example, after placing an order, the user is going to expect an order confirmation. (Even with Google Play, you still see a confirmation dialog when actually purchasing apps.) So, remember to avoid the progress dialog if possible. But, for those times when something must complete before continuing, this recipe provides an example of how to use `ProgressDialog`. The following screenshot shows `ProgressDialog` from the recipe:

Getting ready

Create a new project in Android Studio and call it `ProgressDialog`. Use the default **Phone & Tablet** options and select **Empty Activity** when prompted for the **Activity Type**.

How to do it...

1. Since this is just a demonstration of using the ProgressDialog, we will create a button to show the dialog. To simulate waiting for a server response, we will use a delayed message to dismiss the dialog. To start, open `activity_main.xml` and follow these steps:

2. Replace <TextView> with the following <Button>:

```
&lt;Button
    android:id="@+id/button"
    android:layout_width="wrap_content"
    android:layout_height="wrap_content"
    android:text="Show Dialog"
    android:onClick="startProgress"
    app:layout_constraintBottom_toBottomOf="parent"
    app:layout_constraintLeft_toLeftOf="parent"
    app:layout_constraintRight_toRightOf="parent"
    app:layout_constraintTop_toTopOf="parent" /&gt;
```

3. Open `MainActivity.java` and add the following two global variables:

```
private ProgressDialog mDialog; final int THIRTY_SECONDS=30*1000;
```

4. Add the `showDialog()` method referenced by the button click:

```
public void startProgress(View view) {
    mDialog = new ProgressDialog(this);
    mDialog.setMessage("Doing something...");
    mDialog.setCancelable(false);
    mDialog.show();
    new Handler().postDelayed(new Runnable() {
        public void run() {
            mDialog.dismiss();
        }
    }, THIRTY_SECONDS);
}
```

5. Run the program on a device or emulator. When you press the **Show Dialog** button, you'll see the dialog shown in the screen from the Introduction.

How it works...

We use the `ProgressDialog` class to display our dialog. The options should be self-explanatory, but this setting is worth nothing:

```
mDialog.setCancelable(false);
```

Normally, a dialog can be canceled using the back key, but when this is set to false, the user is stuck on the dialog until it is hidden/dismissed from the code. To simulate a delayed response from a server, we use a `Handler` and the `postDelayed()` method. After the specified milliseconds (30,000 in this case, to represent 30 seconds), the `run()` method will be called, which will dismiss our dialog.

There's more...

We used the default `ProgressDialog` settings for this recipe, which creates an indeterminate dialog indicator, for example, the continuously spinning circle. If you can measure the task at hand, such as loading files, you can use a determinate style instead. Add and run this line of code:

```
mDialog.setProgressStyle(ProgressDialog.STYLE_HORIZONTAL);
```

With `STYLE_HORIZONTAL`, you'll see the percentage dialog shown here:

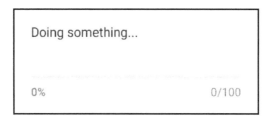

Lights, Action, and Sound Redux using Notifications

You're probably already familiar with Notifications as they've become a prominent feature (even making their way to the desktop environment) and for good reason. They provide an excellent way to raise information for your user. They provide the least intrusive option of all the alerts and notification options available.

As we saw in the first recipe, *Lights, Action, and Sound - getting the user's attention!* Lights, vibration, and sound are all very useful means of getting the user's attention. That's why the Notification object includes support for all three options, as we'll demonstrate in this recipe. Given this ability to get your user's attention, care should still be taken not to abuse your user. Otherwise, they'll likely uninstall your app. It's generally a good idea to give your users the option to enable/disable notifications and even how to present the notification: with sound or without, and so on.

Getting ready

Create a new project in Android Studio and call it LightsActionSoundRedux. Use the default **Phone & Tablet** options and select **Empty Activity** when prompted for the **Activity Type**.

How to do it...

We'll need permission to use the vibrate option, so start by opening the Android Manifest file, and follow the remaining steps:

1. Add the following permission:

```
&lt;uses-permission android:name="android.permission.VIBRATE"/&gt;
```

2. Open activity_main.xml and replace the existing <TextView> with the following button:

```
&lt;Button
    android:id="@+id/buttonSound"
    android:layout_width="wrap_content"
    android:layout_height="wrap_content"
    android:text="Lights, Action, and Sound"
    android:onClick="clickLightsActionSound"
    app:layout_constraintBottom_toBottomOf="parent"
    app:layout_constraintLeft_toLeftOf="parent"
    app:layout_constraintRight_toRightOf="parent"
    app:layout_constraintTop_toTopOf="parent" /&gt;
```

3. Now, open MainActivity.java and add the following declaration to the class:

```
final String CHANNEL_ID="notifications";
```

4. Next, add the method to handle the button click:

```
public void clickLightsActionSound(View view) {
    Uri notificationSoundUri =
RingtoneManager.getDefaultUri(RingtoneManager.TYPE_NOTIFICATION);

    if (Build.VERSION.SDK_INT &gt;= Build.VERSION_CODES.O) {
        AudioAttributes audioAttributes = new
AudioAttributes.Builder()
.setContentType(AudioAttributes.CONTENT_TYPE_SONIFICATION)
.setUsage(AudioAttributes.USAGE_NOTIFICATION_RINGTONE)
                .build();
        NotificationChannel channel = new
NotificationChannel(CHANNEL_ID,
                "Notifications",
NotificationManager.IMPORTANCE_HIGH);
        channel.setDescription("All app notifications");
        channel.setSound(notificationSoundUri, audioAttributes);
        channel.setLightColor(Color.BLUE);
        channel.enableLights(true);
        channel.enableVibration(true);
        NotificationManager notificationManager =
getSystemService(NotificationManager.class);
        notificationManager.createNotificationChannel(channel);
    }

    NotificationCompat.Builder notificationBuilder = new
            NotificationCompat.Builder(this, CHANNEL_ID)
            .setSmallIcon(R.mipmap.ic_launcher)
            .setContentTitle(getString(R.string.app_name))
            .setContentText("Lights, Action & Sound")
            .setSound(notificationSoundUri)
            .setLights(Color.BLUE, 500, 500)
            .setVibrate(new long[]{250,500,250,500,250,500})
            .setDefaults(Notification.DEFAULT_LIGHTS |
Notification.DEFAULT_VIBRATE);
    NotificationManagerCompat notificationManager =
NotificationManagerCompat.from(this);
    notificationManager.notify(0, notificationBuilder.build());
}
```

5. Run the program on a physical device to experience all the notification effects.

How it works...

We combined all three actions into a single notification, simply because we could. You don't have to use all three extra notification options or even any. Only the following are required:

```
.setSmallIcon()
.setContentText()
```

If you don't set both the icon and text, the notification will not show.

We used `NotificationCompat` to build our notification. This comes from the support library and makes it easier to be backward-compatible with older OS versions. If we request a notification feature that is not available on the user's version of OS, it will simply be ignored.

These three lines of code produce our extra notification options:

```
.setSound(notificationSoundUri)
.setLights(Color.BLUE, 500, 500)
.setVibrate(new long[]{250,500,250,500,250,500});
```

It's worth noting that we use the same sound URI with the notification as we did with the `RingtoneManager` from the earlier *Lights, Action, and Sound* recipe. The vibrate feature also required the same vibrate permission as the previous recipe, but notice the value we send is different. Instead of sending just a duration for the vibration, we are sending a vibrate pattern. The first value represents the `off` duration (in milliseconds); the next value represents the vibration `on` duration and repeats.

As you can see in the following line of code:

```
if (Build.VERSION.SDK_INT &gt;= Build.VERSION_CODES.O)
```

If the app is running on Android 8 Oreo (API 26) or greater, there are two parts to creating a notification: the notification itself along with the notification channel (or "category" as the user will see in the settings). The notification "category" feature was added to Android 8 to make it easier for the user to manage the many notifications being displayed by apps. Prior to this feature being added, notifications were either on or off for an app. The user had no way to allow only certain notification types.

If the user is running on Android 8 or greater, we need to create the channel and channel characteristics. Keep in mind, once the channel is created, the properties cannot be changed. For example, if you don't have sound enabled when you first create the channel, changing it later will have no effect. (This applies across app restarts as well.)

On devices with LED notification, you won't see the LED notification while the screen is active.

There's more...

This recipe shows the basics of a notification, but like many features on Android, options have expanded with later OS releases. (Keep in mind the following Toasts can vary in appearance based on the OS version and manufacturer.)

Adding a button to the notification using addAction()

There are several design considerations you should keep in mind when adding action buttons, as listed in the Notification Guidelines link in the chapter introduction. You can add a button (up to three) using the addAction() method on the notification builder. The following is an example of a notification with one action button:

Here's the code to create this notification:

```
NotificationCompat.Builder notificationBuilder = new
        NotificationCompat.Builder(this, CHANNEL_ID)
        .setSmallIcon(R.mipmap.ic_launcher)
        .setContentTitle("LightsActionSoundRedux")
        .setContentText("Lights, Action & Sound");
Intent activityIntent = new Intent(this, MainActivity.class);
PendingIntent pendingIntent = PendingIntent.getActivity(
        this,0,activityIntent,0);
notificationBuilder.addAction(android.R.drawable.ic_dialog_email, "Email",
        pendingIntent);
```

An `Action` requires three parameters: the image, the text, and `PendingIntent`. The first two items are for the visual display, while the third item, `PendingIntent`, is called when the user presses the button.

The previous code creates a very simple `PendingIntent`; it just launches the app. This is probably the most common intent for notifications and is often used when the user presses the notification. To set the notification intent, use the following code:

```
.setContentIntent(pendingIntent)
```

A button action would probably require more information as it should take the user to the specific item in your app. You should also create an application back-stack for the best user experience.

Expanded notifications

Expanded notifications were introduced in Android 4.1 (API 16) and are available by using the `setStyle()` method on the Notification Builder. If the user's OS does not support expanded notifications, the notification will appear as a normal notification.

The three expanded styles currently available in the `NotificationCompat` library include the following:

- InboxStyle: Large-format notifications that include a list of strings
- BigPictureStyle: Large-format notification that includes a large image attachment
- BigTextStyle: Large-format notifications that include a lot of text

Here's an example of each notification style, and the code used to create the example:

1. `InboxStyle`: Large-format notifications that include a list of strings

Here's the code for this style:

```
NotificationCompat.Builder notificationBuilder =
        new NotificationCompat.Builder(this, CHANNEL_ID)
                .setSmallIcon(R.mipmap.ic_launcher);
NotificationCompat.InboxStyle inboxStyle = new
NotificationCompat.InboxStyle();
inboxStyle.setBigContentTitle("InboxStyle - Big Content Title")
        .addLine("Line 1")
        .addLine("Line 2");
notificationBuilder.setStyle(inboxStyle);
```

2. `BigPictureStyle`: **Large-format notification that includes a large image attachment**

Check out the code for this style:

```
NotificationCompat.Builder notificationBuilder = new
NotificationCompat.Builder(this, CHANNEL_ID)
        .setSmallIcon(R.mipmap.ic_launcher)
        .setContentTitle("LightsActionSoundRedux")
        .setContentText("BigPictureStyle");
NotificationCompat.BigPictureStyle bigPictureStyle = new
NotificationCompat.BigPictureStyle();
bigPictureStyle.bigPicture(BitmapFactory.decodeResource(getResource
s(), R.mipmap.ic_launcher));
notificationBuilder.setStyle(bigPictureStyle);
```

3. `BigTextStyle` : Large-format notifications that include a lot of text

 LightsActionSoundRedux   7:58 PM
This is an example of the BigTextStyle
expanded notification.

Here's how the code for this style would look.

```
NotificationCompat.Builder notificationBuilder =
        new NotificationCompat.Builder(this, CHANNEL_ID)
        .setSmallIcon(R.mipmap.ic_launcher)
        .setContentTitle("LightsActionSoundRedux");
NotificationCompat.BigTextStyle BigTextStyle = new
NotificationCompat.BigTextStyle();
BigTextStyle.bigText("This is an example of the BigTextStyle
expanded notification.");
notificationBuilder.setStyle(BigTextStyle);
```

Lock screen notifications

Android 5.0 (API 21) and above can show notifications on the lock screen, based on the user's lock screen visibility. Use `setVisibility()` to specify the notification visibility using the following values:

- `VISIBILITY_PUBLIC`: All content can be displayed.
- `VISIBILITY_SECRET`: No content should be displayed.
- `VISIBILITY_PRIVATE`: Display the basic content (title and icon) but the rest is hidden.

See also

- See the *Creating a Media Player Notification* and *Making a Flashlight with a Heads-Up Notification* recipes for additional notification options with Android 5.0 (API 21) and greater.

Creating a Media Player Notification

This recipe is going to take a look at the new Media Player style introduced in Android 5.0 (API 21). Unlike the previous recipe, *Lights, Action, and Sound Redux using Notifications*, which used `NotificationCompat`, this recipe does not, as this style is not available in the support library.

Here's a screenshot showing how the notification will appear:

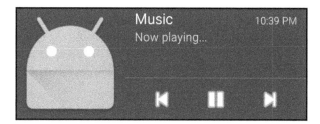

This screenshot shows an example of the Media Player Notification on a lock screen:

Getting ready

Create a new project in Android Studio and call it `MediaPlayerNotification`. In the **Target Android Devices** dialog, select **API 21: Android 5.0 (Lollipop)**, or higher, for this project. Select **Empty Activity** on the **Add an Activity to Mobile** dialog.

How to do it...

We just need a single button to call our code to send the notification. Open `activity_main.xml` and follow these steps:

1. Replace the existing <TextView> with the following button code:

```
<Button
    android:id="@+id/button"
    android:layout_width="wrap_content"
```

```
                    android:layout_height="wrap_content"
                    android:text="Show Notification"
                    android:onClick="showNotification"
                    app:layout_constraintBottom_toBottomOf="parent"
                    app:layout_constraintLeft_toLeftOf="parent"
                    app:layout_constraintRight_toRightOf="parent"
                    app:layout_constraintTop_toTopOf="parent" /&gt;
```

2. Open `MainActivity.java` and add the `showNotification()` method:

```
@SuppressWarnings("deprecated")
public void showNotification(View view) {
    Intent activityIntent = new Intent(this,MainActivity.class);
    PendingIntent pendingIntent = PendingIntent.getActivity(this,
0, activityIntent, 0);

    Log.i(this.getClass().getSimpleName(),"showNotification()" );
    Notification.Builder notificationBuilder;
    if (Build.VERSION.SDK_INT &gt;= Build.VERSION_CODES.M) {
        notificationBuilder = new Notification.Builder(this)
                .setVisibility(Notification.VISIBILITY_PUBLIC)
                .setSmallIcon(Icon.createWithResource(this,
R.mipmap.ic_launcher))
                .addAction(new Notification.Action.Builder(
                        Icon.createWithResource(this,
android.R.drawable.ic_media_previous),
                        "Previous", pendingIntent).build())
                .addAction(new Notification.Action.Builder(
                        Icon.createWithResource(this,
android.R.drawable.ic_media_pause),
                        "Pause", pendingIntent).build())
                .addAction(new Notification.Action.Builder(
                        Icon.createWithResource(this,
android.R.drawable.ic_media_next),
                        "Next", pendingIntent).build())
                .setContentTitle("Music")
                .setContentText("Now playing...")
                .setLargeIcon(Icon.createWithResource(this,
R.mipmap.ic_launcher))
                .setStyle(new
Notification.MediaStyle().setShowActionsInCompactView(1));
    } else {
        notificationBuilder = new Notification.Builder(this)
                .setVisibility(Notification.VISIBILITY_PUBLIC)
                .setSmallIcon(R.mipmap.ic_launcher)
                .addAction(new
Notification.Action.Builder(android.R.drawable.ic_media_previous,
                        "Previous", pendingIntent).build())
```

```
                    .addAction(new
Notification.Action.Builder(android.R.drawable.ic_media_pause,
                    "Pause", pendingIntent).build())
                    .addAction(new
Notification.Action.Builder(android.R.drawable.ic_media_next,
                    "Next", pendingIntent).build())
                    .setContentTitle("Music")
                    .setContentText("Now playing...")
    .setLargeIcon(BitmapFactory.decodeResource(getResources(),
R.mipmap.ic_launcher))
                    .setStyle(new
Notification.MediaStyle().setShowActionsInCompactView(1));
        }
        if (Build.VERSION.SDK_INT &gt;= Build.VERSION_CODES.O) {
            notificationBuilder.setChannelId(createChannel());
        }
        NotificationManager notificationManager =
                (NotificationManager)
this.getSystemService(Context.NOTIFICATION_SERVICE);
        notificationManager.notify(0, notificationBuilder.build());
    }
```

3. Add the following method to create the channel for Android O and later:

```
private String createChannel() {
    final String channelId = "mediaplayer";
    if (Build.VERSION.SDK_INT &gt;= Build.VERSION_CODES.O) {
        NotificationChannel channel = new
NotificationChannel(channelId, "Notifications",
                NotificationManager.IMPORTANCE_HIGH);
        channel.setDescription("All app notifications");
        channel.enableVibration(true);
        NotificationManager notificationManager =
                getSystemService(NotificationManager.class);
        notificationManager.createNotificationChannel(channel);
    }
    return channelId;
}
```

4. Run the program on a device or emulator.

How it works...

The first detail to note is that we decorate our `showNotification()` method with the following:

```
@SuppressWarnings("deprecated")
```

This tells the compiler we know we are using deprecated calls. (Without this, the compiler will flag the code.) We follow this with an API check, using this call:

```
if (Build.VERSION.SDK_INT &gt;= Build.VERSION_CODES.M)
```

The icon resource was changed in API 23, but we want this application to run on API 21 (Android 5.0) and later, so we still need to call the old methods when running on API 21 and API 22.

If the user is running on Android 6.0 (or higher), we use the new `Icon` class to create our icons; otherwise, we use the old constructor. (You'll notice the IDE shows deprecated calls with a strikethrough.) Checking the current OS version during runtime is a common strategy for remaining backward-compatible.

We create three actions using `addAction()` to handle the media player functionality. Since we don't really have a media player going, we use the same intent for all the actions, but you'll want to create separate intents in your application.

To make the notification visible on the lock screen, we need to set the visibility level to `VISIBILITY_PUBLIC`, which we do with the following call:

```
.setVisibility(Notification.VISIBILITY_PUBLIC)
```

This call is worth noting:

```
.setShowActionsInCompactView(1)
```

Just as the method name implies, this sets the actions to show when the notification is shown with a reduced layout. (See the lock screen image in the recipe introduction.)

There's more...

We only created the visual notification in this recipe. If we were creating an actual media player, we could instantiate a `MediaSession` class and pass in the session token with this call:

```
.setMediaSession(mMediaSession.getSessionToken())
```

This will allow the system to recognize the media content and react accordingly, such as updating the lock screen with the current album artwork.

See also

- **MediaSession** developer documents: https://developer.android.com/reference/android/media/sessi on/MediaSession.html
- The *Lock Screen Visibility* section in the *Lights, Action, and Sound Redux using Notifications* recipe discusses visibility options

Making a Flashlight with a Heads-Up Notification

Android 5.0-Lollipop (API 21) introduced a new type of notification called the Heads-Up Notification. Many people do not care for this new notification as it can be extremely intrusive, as it forces its way on top of other apps. (See the following screenshot.) Keep this in mind when using this type of notification. We're going to demonstrate the Heads-Up Notification with a Flashlight as this demonstrates a good use case scenario.

Here's a screenshot showing the Heads-Up Notification we'll create further on:

If you have a device running Android 6.0, you may have noticed the new Flashlight settings option. As a demonstration, we're going to create something similar in this recipe.

Getting ready

Create a new project in Android Studio and call it `FlashlightWithHeadsUp`. When prompted for the API level, we need API 23 (or higher) for this project. Select **Empty Activity** when prompted for the **Activity Type**.

How to do it...

Our activity layout will consist of just a `ToggleButton` to control the flashlight mode. We'll be using the same `setTorchMode()` code as the *Lights, Action, and Sound - getting the user's attention!* recipe presented earlier, and will add a Heads-Up Notification. We'll need permission to use the vibrate option, so start by opening the Android Manifest and following these steps:

1. Add the following permission:

    ```
    <uses-permission android:name="android.permission.VIBRATE"/>
    ```

2. Specify that we only want a single instance of `MainActivity` by adding `android:launchMode="singleInstance"` to the `<MainActivity>` element. It will look as follows:

    ```
    <activity android:name=".MainActivity"
        android:launchMode="singleInstance">
    ```

3. With the changes to `AndroidManifest` done, open the `activity_main.xml` layout and replace the existing `<TextView>` element with this `<ToggleButton>` code:

    ```
    <ToggleButton
        android:id="@+id/buttonLight"
        android:layout_width="wrap_content"
        android:layout_height="wrap_content"
        android:text="Flashlight"
        android:onClick="clickLight"
        app:layout_constraintBottom_toBottomOf="parent"
        app:layout_constraintLeft_toLeftOf="parent"
        app:layout_constraintRight_toRightOf="parent"
        app:layout_constraintTop_toTopOf="parent" />
    ```

4. Now, open `ActivityMain.java` and add the following global variables:

```
private static final String ACTION_STOP="STOP";
private CameraManager mCameraManager;
private String mCameraId=null;
private ToggleButton mButtonLight;
```

5. Add the following code to `onCreate()` to set up the camera:

```
mButtonLight = findViewById(R.id.buttonLight);
mCameraManager = (CameraManager)
this.getSystemService(Context.CAMERA_SERVICE);
mCameraId = getCameraId();
if (mCameraId==null) {
    mButtonLight.setEnabled(false);
} else {
    mButtonLight.setEnabled(true);
}
```

6. Add the following method to handle the response when the user presses the notification:

```
@Override
protected void onNewIntent(Intent intent) {
    super.onNewIntent(intent);
    if (ACTION_STOP.equals(intent.getAction())) {
        setFlashlight(false);
    }
}
```

7. Add the method to get the camera ID:

```
private String getCameraId() {
    try {
        String[] ids = mCameraManager.getCameraIdList();
        for (String id : ids) {
            CameraCharacteristics c =
mCameraManager.getCameraCharacteristics(id);
            Boolean flashAvailable =
c.get(CameraCharacteristics.FLASH_INFO_AVAILABLE);
            Integer facingDirection =
c.get(CameraCharacteristics.LENS_FACING);
            if (flashAvailable != null
                    && flashAvailable
                    && facingDirection != null
                    && facingDirection ==
CameraCharacteristics.LENS_FACING_BACK) {
                return id;
```

```
                }
            }
        } catch (CameraAccessException e) {
            e.printStackTrace();
        }
        return null;
    }
```

8. Add these two methods to handle the flashlight mode:

```
public void clickLight(View view) {
    setFlashlight(mButtonLight.isChecked());
    if (mButtonLight.isChecked()) {
        showNotification();
    }
}

private void setFlashlight(boolean enabled) {
    mButtonLight.setChecked(enabled);
    try {
        mCameraManager.setTorchMode(mCameraId, enabled);
    } catch (CameraAccessException e) {
        e.printStackTrace();
    }
}
```

9. Finally, add this method to create the notification:

```
private void showNotification() {
    final String CHANNEL_ID = "flashlight";
    if (Build.VERSION.SDK_INT &gt;= Build.VERSION_CODES.O) {
        NotificationChannel channel = new
NotificationChannel(CHANNEL_ID,
                "Notifications",
NotificationManager.IMPORTANCE_HIGH);
        channel.setDescription("All app notifications");
        channel.enableVibration(true);
        NotificationManager notificationManager =
getSystemService(NotificationManager.class);
        notificationManager.createNotificationChannel(channel);
    }

    Intent activityIntent = new Intent(this, MainActivity.class);
    activityIntent.setAction(ACTION_STOP);
    PendingIntent pendingIntent =
            PendingIntent.getActivity(this, 0, activityIntent, 0);
    final NotificationCompat.Builder notificationBuilder =
            new NotificationCompat.Builder(this, CHANNEL_ID)
```

```
                        .setContentTitle("Flashlight")
                        .setContentText("Press to turn off the flashlight")
                        .setSmallIcon(R.mipmap.ic_launcher)
            .setLargeIcon(BitmapFactory.decodeResource(getResources(),
            R.mipmap.ic_launcher))
                        .setContentIntent(pendingIntent)
                        .setVibrate(new long[]{DEFAULT_VIBRATE})
                        .setPriority(PRIORITY_MAX)
                        .setAutoCancel(true);
            NotificationManager notificationManager = (NotificationManager)
            this.getSystemService(Context.NOTIFICATION_SERVICE);
            notificationManager.notify(0, notificationBuilder.build());
        }
```

10. You're ready to run the application on a physical device. As noted previously, you'll need an Android 6.0 (or higher) device, with an outward-facing camera flash.

How it works...

Since this recipe uses the same flashlight code as *Lights, Action, and Sound - getting the user's attention!*, we'll jump to the `showNotification()` method. Most notification builder calls are the same as in previous examples, but there are two significant differences:

```
.setVibrate()
.setPriority(PRIORITY_MAX)
```

> Notifications will not be escalated to Heads-Up Notifications unless the priority is set to `HIGH` (or above) and uses either vibrate or sound.

> Note this from the Developer documentation
> at `http://developer.android.com/reference/android/app/Notificatio n.html#headsUpContentView`:

> "At its discretion, the system UI may choose to show this as a heads-up notification."

We create a `PendingIntent` as we've done previously, but here we set the action with the following:

```
activityIntent.setAction(ACTION_STOP);
```

We set the app to only allow a single instance in the `AndroidManifest` file, as we don't want to start a new instance of the app when the user presses the notification. The `PendingIntent` we created sets the action, which we check in the `onNewIntent()` callback. If the user opens the app without pressing the notification, they can still disable the flashlight with the `ToggleButton`.

There's more...

You may have noticed the following line of code:

```
.setAutoCancel(true);
```

`.setAutoCancel()` tells the OS to automatically remove the notification when the user clicks on it. This is great if the user presses the notification to turn off the light, but what happens if they use the toggle button? The light will turn off as it should, but they are left with a useless notification. To fix that, we can add a new method to cancel the notification:

```
private void cancelNotification() {
    NotificationManager notificationManager = (NotificationManager)
            this.getSystemService(Context.NOTIFICATION_SERVICE);
    notificationManager.cancelAll();
}
```

Then we call it when they press the button. Here's how `clickLight()` will look:

```
public void clickLight(View view) {
    setFlashlight(mButtonLight.isChecked());
    if (mButtonLight.isChecked()) {
        showNotification();
    } else {
        cancelNotification();
    }
}
```

See also

- Refer to the earlier *Lights, Action, and Sound - getting the user's attention!* recipe for more information on the torch API
- Refer to the earlier *Lights, Action, and Sound Redux using Notifications* recipe for more Notification examples

Notifications with Direct Reply

One of the most exciting new features introduced in Android N was inline reply, called Direct Reply. With Direct Reply, users can respond without leaving the Notification Bar!

In this recipe, we'll add the ability to create an inline reply by passing a RemoteInput to the `addRemoteInput()` method.

Getting ready

Create a new project in Android Studio and call it `DirectReply`. In the **Target Android Devices** dialog, select the **Phone & Tablet** option and choose API 24: Android Nougat 7.0 (or later) for the Minimum SDK. Select **Empty Activity** when prompted for the Activity Type.

How to do it...

Our app will consist of a single button on the main screen to initiate the initial notification. Start by opening `activity_main.xml` and follow these steps:

1. Replace the existing `TextView` with the button XML:

```
&lt;Button
    android:layout_width="wrap_content"
    android:layout_height="wrap_content"
    android:text="Send Notification"
    android:id="@+id/buttonSend"
    android:onClick="onClickSend"
    app:layout_constraintBottom_toBottomOf="parent"
    app:layout_constraintLeft_toLeftOf="parent"
    app:layout_constraintRight_toRightOf="parent"
    app:layout_constraintTop_toTopOf="parent" /&gt;
```

2. Now, open `MainActivity.java` and add the following code to the class:

```
private final String KEY_REPLY_TEXT = "KEY_REPLY_TEXT";
private final int NOTIFICATION_ID = 1;
```

3. Add the following code to the existing `onCreate()` method:

```
if (getIntent()!=null) {
    Toast.makeText(MainActivity.this, getReplyText(getIntent()),
Toast.LENGTH_SHORT).show();
}
```

4. Override the `onNewIntent()` method as follows:

```
@Override
protected void onNewIntent(Intent intent) {
    super.onNewIntent(intent);
    Toast.makeText(MainActivity.this, getReplyText(intent),
Toast.LENGTH_SHORT).show();
}
```

5. Add the following method to handle the button click:

```
public void onClickSend(View view){
    Intent activityIntent = new Intent(this,MainActivity.class);
    PendingIntent pendingIntent =
            PendingIntent.getActivity(this,0,activityIntent,0);

    RemoteInput remoteInput = new
RemoteInput.Builder(KEY_REPLY_TEXT)
            .setLabel("Reply")
            .build();

    NotificationCompat.Action action =
            new
NotificationCompat.Action.Builder(android.R.drawable.ic_menu_revert
,
                    "Reply", pendingIntent)
            .addRemoteInput(remoteInput)
            .build();

    NotificationCompat.Builder notificationBuilder =
            new NotificationCompat.Builder(this,getChannelId())
    .setSmallIcon(android.R.drawable.ic_dialog_email)
                    .setContentTitle("Reply")
                    .setContentText("Content")
                    .addAction(action);

    NotificationManagerCompat notificationManager =
NotificationManagerCompat.from(this);
    notificationManager.notify(0, notificationBuilder.build());
}
```

```
private String getChannelId() {
    final String channelId = "directreply";
    if (Build.VERSION.SDK_INT &gt;= Build.VERSION_CODES.O) {
        NotificationChannel channel = new
NotificationChannel(channelId,
                "Notifications",
NotificationManager.IMPORTANCE_DEFAULT);
        channel.setDescription("All app notifications");
        channel.enableVibration(true);
        NotificationManager notificationManager =
getSystemService(NotificationManager.class);
        notificationManager.createNotificationChannel(channel);
    }
    return channelId;
}
```

6. Add the `getReplyText()` method:

```
private CharSequence getReplyText(Intent intent) {
    Bundle notificationReply =
RemoteInput.getResultsFromIntent(intent);
    if (notificationReply != null) {
        return notificationReply.getCharSequence(KEY_REPLY_TEXT);
    }
    return null;
}
```

7. You're ready to run the application on a device or emulator.

How it works...

Adding the Inline Reply option to a notification is actually very simple. We start with a Notification object as we've done in the previous recipes. (We're using NotifcationCompat from the support library to provide greater backward compatibility.) When creating the Action, call the `addRemoteInput()` method, passing in a RemoteInput. RemoteInput is where you define they key to retrieve the user input text. After the user enters a reply, the OS calls the PendingIntent, passing the data back to your app in an Intent.
Use `RemoteInput.getResultsFromIntent()` to retrieve the user text as we did in the `getReplyText()` method.

See also

- The **Notifications Overview** guide at `https://developer.android.com/guide/topics/ui/notifiers/notifications`

Using the Touchscreen and Sensors

9

In this chapter, we will cover the following topics:

- Listening for click and long-press events
- Recognizing tap and other common gestures
- Pinch-to-zoom with multi-touch gestures
- Swipe-to-refresh
- Listing available sensors—an introduction to the Android Sensor Framework
- Reading sensor data—using Android Sensor Framework events
- Reading device orientation

Introduction

These days, mobile devices are packed with sensors, often including a gyroscope, magnetic, gravity, pressure, and/or temperature sensors, not to mention the touchscreen. This provides many new and exciting options to interact with your user. Through the sensors, you can determine three-dimensional device location and how the device is being used, such as shaking, rotation, tilt, and so on. Even the touchscreen offers many new input methods from just the simple click to gestures and multi-touch.

We'll start this chapter by exploring touchscreen interactions, starting with a simple click and long-press, then move on to detecting common gestures using the `SimpleOnGestureListener` class. Next, we'll look at multi-touch using the pinch-to-zoom gesture with `ScaleGestureDetector`.

This book is meant to offer a quick guide to adding features and functionality to your own applications. As such, the focus is on the code required but it's highly recommended that you become familiar with the design guidelines as well.

Check out the Google Gesture Design Guidelines at
`https://www.google.com/design/spec/patterns/gestures.html`.

In the latter part of this chapter, we'll look at sensor abilities in Android, using the Android Sensor Framework. We'll demonstrate how to obtain a list of all available sensors, plus how to check for a specific sensor. Once we identify a sensor, we'll demonstrate setting up a listener to read the sensor data. Finally, we'll end the chapter with a demonstration of how to determine the device orientation.

Listening for click and long-press events

Almost every application needs to recognize and respond to basic events such as clicks and long-presses. It's so basic, in most recipes we use the XML `onClick` attribute, but more advanced listeners require to be set up through code.

Android provides an Event Listener interface for receiving a single notification when certain actions occur, as shown in the following list:

- `onClick()`: It's called when a View is pressed
- `onLongClick()`: It's called when the View is long-pressed
- `onFocusChange()`: It's called when the user navigates to or from the View
- `onKey()`: It's called when a hardware key is pressed or released
- `onTouch()`: It's called when a touch event occurs

This recipe will demonstrate responding to a click event, as well as a long-press event.

Getting ready

Create a new project in Android Studio and call it `PressEvents`. Use the default **Phone & Tablet** options and select **Empty Activity** on the **Add an Activity** to **Mobile** dialog.

How to do it...

Setting up to receive basic View events is very simple. First, we will create a View; we'll use a button for our example, then set the Event Listener in the Activity's `onCreate()` method. Following are the steps:

1. Open `activity_main.xml` and replace the existing `TextView` with the following `Button`:

```
<Button
    android:id="@+id/button"
    android:layout_width="wrap_content"
    android:layout_height="wrap_content"
    android:text="Button"
    app:layout_constraintBottom_toBottomOf="parent"
    app:layout_constraintLeft_toLeftOf="parent"
    app:layout_constraintRight_toRightOf="parent"
    app:layout_constraintTop_toTopOf="parent" />
```

2. Now open `MainActivy.java` and add the following code to the existing `onCreate()` method:

```
Button button = findViewById(R.id.button);
button.setOnClickListener(new View.OnClickListener() {
    @Override
    public void onClick(View v) {
        Toast.makeText(MainActivity.this, "Click",
Toast.LENGTH_SHORT).show();
    }
});
button.setOnLongClickListener(new View.OnLongClickListener() {
    @Override
    public boolean onLongClick(View v) {
        Toast.makeText(MainActivity.this, "Long Press",
Toast.LENGTH_SHORT).show();
        return true;
    }
});
```

3. Run the application on a device or emulator and try a regular click and long-press.

How it works...

In most examples used in this book, we set up the onClick listener in XML using the following attribute:

```
android:onClick=""
```

You may notice the XML onClick() method callback requires the same method signature as the setOnClickListener.onClick() callback:

```
public void onClick(View v) {}
```

That's because Android automatically sets up the callback for us when we use the XML onClick attribute. This example also demonstrates that we can have multiple listeners on a single View.

The last point to note is that the onLongClick() method returns a Boolean, as do most of the other event listeners. true is returned to indicate the event has been handled.

There's more...

Although a button is typically used to indicate where a user should press, we could have used both setOnClickListener() and setOnLongClickListener() with any View, or even a TextView.

As mentioned in the introduction, there are other Event Listeners. You can use Android Studio's auto-complete feature to bring up a list of available listeners by typing the following:

```
button.setOn
```

As you start typing, you'll see a list of available choices with Android Studio's auto-complete list.

Recognizing tap and other common gestures

Unlike the Event Listeners described in the previous recipe, gestures require a two-step process:

    1. Gather movement data

2. Analyze the data to determine whether it matches a known gesture

Step 1 begins when the user touches the screen, which fires the `onTouchEvent()` callback with the movement data sent in a `MotionEvent` object. Fortunately, Android makes step 2, analyzing the data, easier with the `GestureDetector` class, which detects the following gestures:

- `onTouchEvent()`
- `onDown()`
- `onFling()`
- `onLongPress()`
- `onScroll()`
- `onShowPress()`
- `onDoubleTap()`
- `onDoubleTapEvent()`
- `onSingleTapConfirmed()`

This recipe will demonstrate using `GestureDetector.SimpleOnGestureListener` to recognize the touch and double tap gestures.

Getting ready

Create a new project in Android Studio and call it `CommonGestureDetector`. Use the default **Phone & Tablet** options and select **Empty Activity** when prompted for the **Activity Type**.

How to do it...

We will be using the activity itself to detect gestures, so we don't need to add any Views to the layout. Open `MainActivity.java` and perform the following steps:

1. Add the following global variable:

```
private GestureDetectorCompat mGestureDetector;
```

2. Add the following `GestureListener` class within the `MainActivity` class:

```
private class GestureListener extends
GestureDetector.SimpleOnGestureListener {
```

```
        @Override
        public boolean onSingleTapConfirmed(MotionEvent e) {
            Toast.makeText(MainActivity.this, "onSingleTapConfirmed",
Toast.LENGTH_SHORT).show();
            return super.onSingleTapConfirmed(e);
        }
        @Override
        public boolean onDoubleTap(MotionEvent e) {
            Toast.makeText(MainActivity.this, "onDoubleTap",
Toast.LENGTH_SHORT).show();
            return super.onDoubleTap(e);
        }
    }
```

3. Add the following `onTouchEvent()` method to the `MainActivity` class to handle touch event notifications:

```
public boolean onTouchEvent(MotionEvent event) {
    mGestureDetector.onTouchEvent(event);
    return super.onTouchEvent(event);
}
```

4. Lastly, add the following line of code to `onCreate()`:

```
mGestureDetector = new GestureDetectorCompat(this, new
GestureListener());
```

5. Run this application on a device or emulator.

How it works...

We're using `GestureDetectorCompat`, which is from the support library that allows gesture support on devices running Android 1.6 and later.

As mentioned in the recipe introduction, detecting gestures is a two-step process. To gather movement or gesture data, we start tracking movement with the touch event. Every time the `onTouchEvent()` is called, we send that data to the `GestureDetector`. The `GestureDetector` handles the second step, analyzing the data. Once a gesture has been detected, the appropriate callback is made. Our example handles both single and double tap gestures.

There's more...

Your application can easily add support for the remaining gestures detected by the GestureDetector simply by overriding the appropriate callback.

See also

- See the next recipe, *Pinch-to-zoom with multi-touch gestures*, for multi-touch gestures

Pinch-to-zoom with multi-touch gestures

The previous recipe used SimpleOnGestureListener to provide detection of simple, one-finger gestures. In this recipe, we'll use the SimpleOnScaleGestureListener class to detect the common multi-touch gesture "pinch to zoom".

Here are two screenshots from the application we'll create in this recipe. The first shows the icon zoomed out:

This second screenshot shows the icon zoomed in:

Getting ready

Create a new project in Android Studio and call it `MultiTouchZoom`. Use the default **Phone & Tablet** options and select **Empty Activity** when prompted for the **Activity Type**.

How to do it...

To provide a visual indication of pinch-to-zoom, we'll use an `ImageView` with the application icon. Open `activity_main.xml` and follow these steps:

1. Replace the existing `TextView` with the following `ImageView`:

```
<android.support.v7.widget.AppCompatImageView
    android:id="@+id/imageView"
    android:layout_width="wrap_content"
    android:layout_height="wrap_content"
    android:src="@mipmap/ic_launcher"
    app:layout_constraintBottom_toBottomOf="parent"
    app:layout_constraintLeft_toLeftOf="parent"
    app:layout_constraintRight_toRightOf="parent"
    app:layout_constraintTop_toTopOf="parent" />
```

2. Now, open `MainActivity.java` and add the following global variables to the class:

```
private ScaleGestureDetector mScaleGestureDetector;
private float mScaleFactor = 1.0f;
private AppCompatImageView mImageView;
```

3. Add the following `onTouchEvent()` implementation to the `MainActivity` class:

```
public boolean onTouchEvent(MotionEvent motionEvent) {
    mScaleGestureDetector.onTouchEvent(motionEvent);
    return true;
}
```

4. Add the following `ScaleListener` class to the `MainActivity` class:

```
private class ScaleListener extends
ScaleGestureDetector.SimpleOnScaleGestureListener {
    @Override
    public boolean onScale(ScaleGestureDetector
scaleGestureDetector) {
        mScaleFactor *= scaleGestureDetector.getScaleFactor();
        mScaleFactor = Math.max(0.1f, Math.min(mScaleFactor,
10.0f));
        mImageView.setScaleX(mScaleFactor);
        mImageView.setScaleY(mScaleFactor);
        return true;
    }
}
```

5. Add the following code to the existing `onCreate()` method:

```
mImageView=findViewById(R.id.imageView);
mScaleGestureDetector = new ScaleGestureDetector(this, new
ScaleListener());
```

6. To experiment with the pinch-to-zoom functionality, run the application on a device with a touchscreen.

How it works...

The `ScaleGestureDetector` does all the work by analyzing gesture data and reporting the final scale factor through the `onScale()` callback. We get the actual scale factor by calling `getScaleFactor()` on `ScaleGestureDetector`.

We use an `ImageView` with the application icon to provide a visual representation of the scaling by setting the `ImageView` scale, using the scale factor returned from `ScaleGestureDetector`. We use the following code to prevent the scaling from becoming too large or too small:

```
mScaleFactor = Math.max(0.1f, Math.min(mScaleFactor, 10.0f));
```

Swipe-to-Refresh

Pulling down a list to indicate a manual refresh is known as the Swipe-to-Refresh gesture. It's such a common feature that this functionality has been encapsulated in a single widget called `SwipeRefreshLayout`.

This recipe will add Swipe-to-Refresh functionality with a `ListView`. The following screenshot shows the refresh in action:

Getting ready

Create a new project in Android Studio and call it `SwipeToRefresh`. Use the default **Phone & Tablet** options and select **Empty Activity** on the **Add an Activity** to **Mobile** dialog.

How to do it...

First, we need to add the `SwipeRefreshLayout` widget and `ListView` to the activity layout, then we will implement the refresh listener in the Java code. Here are the detailed steps:

1. Open `activity_main.xml` and replace the existing constraint layout with the following:

```xml
<?xml version="1.0" encoding="utf-8"?>
<RelativeLayout
xmlns:android="http://schemas.android.com/apk/res/android"
    xmlns:app="http://schemas.android.com/apk/res-auto"
    xmlns:tools="http://schemas.android.com/tools"
    android:layout_width="match_parent"
    android:layout_height="match_parent"
    tools:context=".MainActivity">
    <android.support.v4.widget.SwipeRefreshLayout
        android:id="@+id/swipeRefresh"
        android:layout_width="match_parent"
        android:layout_height="match_parent">
        <ListView
            android:id="@android:id/list"
            android:layout_width="match_parent"
            android:layout_height="match_parent" />
    </android.support.v4.widget.SwipeRefreshLayout>
</RelativeLayout>
```

2. Now open `MainActivity.java` and add the following global variables to the class:

```java
SwipeRefreshLayout mSwipeRefreshLayout;
ListView mListView;
List mArrayList = new ArrayList<>();
private int mRefreshCount=0;
```

3. Add the following method to the `MainActivity` class to handle the refresh:

```java
private void refreshList() {
    mRefreshCount++;
```

```
mArrayList.add("Refresh: " + mRefreshCount);
ListAdapter countryAdapter = new ArrayAdapter<String>(this,
        android.R.layout.simple_list_item_1, mArrayList);
mListView.setAdapter(countryAdapter);
mSwipeRefreshLayout.setRefreshing(false);
}
```

4. Add the following code to the existing `onCreate()` method:

```
mSwipeRefreshLayout = findViewById(R.id.swipeRefresh);
mSwipeRefreshLayout.setOnRefreshListener(new
SwipeRefreshLayout.OnRefreshListener() {
    @Override
    public void onRefresh() {
        refreshList();
    }
});
mListView = findViewById(android.R.id.list);
final String[] countries = new String[]{"China", "France",
"Germany", "India",
        "Russia", "United Kingdom", "United States"};
mArrayList = new ArrayList<>(Arrays.asList(countries));
ListAdapter countryAdapter = new ArrayAdapter<String>(this,
        android.R.layout.simple_list_item_1, mArrayList);
mListView.setAdapter(countryAdapter);
```

5. Run the application on a device or an emulator.

How it works...

Most of the code for this recipe simulates a refresh by adding items to the ListView each time the refresh method is called. The main steps for implementing Swipe-to-Refresh include:

1. Add the SwipeRefreshLayout widget
2. Include the ListView within the SwipeRefreshLayout
3. Add the OnRefreshListener to call your refresh method
4. Call setRefreshing(false) after completing your update

That's it. The widget makes adding Swipe-to-Refresh very easy!

There's more...

Although the Swipe-to-Refresh gesture is a common feature these days, it's still good practice to include a menu item (especially for accessibility reasons). Following is a snippet of XML for the menu layout:

```xml
<menu xmlns:android="http://schemas.android.com/apk/res/android" >
    <item
        android:id="@+id/menu_refresh"
        android:showAsAction="never"
        android:title="@string/menu_refresh"/>
</menu>
```

Call your refresh method in the `onOptionsItemSelected()` callback. When performing a refresh from code, such as from the menu item event, you want to notify `SwipeRefreshLayout` of the refresh so it can update the UI. Do this with the following code:

```
SwipeRefreshLayout.setRefreshing(true);
```

This tells the `SwipeRefreshLayout` that a refresh is starting so it can display the in-progress indicator.

Listing available sensors – an introduction to the Android Sensor Framework

Android includes support for hardware sensors using the Android Sensor Framework. The framework includes the following classes and interfaces:

- `SensorManager`
- `Sensor`
- `SensorEventListener`
- `SensorEvent`

Most Android devices include hardware sensors, but they vary greatly between different manufacturers and models. If your application utilizes sensors, you have two choices:

- Specify the sensor in the Android Manifest
- Check for the sensor at runtime

To specify your application uses a sensor, include the `<uses-feature>` declaration in the Android Manifest. Here is an example requiring a compass to be available:

```
<uses-feature android:name="android.hardware.sensor.compass"
android:required="true"/>
```

If your application utilizes the compass, but does not require it to function, you should set `android:required="false"` instead; otherwise your application will not be available to install from Google Play.

Sensors are grouped into the following three categories:

- Motion sensors: Measure acceleration and rotational forces along three axes
- Environmental sensors: Measure the local environment, such as ambient air temperature and pressure, humidity, and illumination
- Position sensors: Measure the physical position of the device using position and a magnometer

The Android SDK provides support for the following sensor types:

Sensor	Detects	Use
TYPE_ACCELEROMETER	Motion detection including gravity	Used to determine shake, tilt, and so on
TYPE_AMBIENT_TEMPERATURE	Measures ambient room temperature	Used for determining local temperature
TYPE_GRAVITY	Measures the force of gravity on all three axes	Used for motion detection
TYPE_GYROSCOPE	Measures rotation on all three axes	Used to determine turn, spin, and so on
TYPE_LIGHT	Measures light level	Used for setting screen brightness
TYPE_LINEAR_ACCELERATION	Motion detection excluding gravity	Used to determine acceleration
TYPE_MAGNETIC_FIELD	Measures geomagnetic field	Used to create a compass or determine bearing
TYPE_PRESSURE	Measures air pressure	Used for barometer
TYPE_PROXIMITY	Measures objects relative to the screen	Used to determine whether the device is being held against the ear during a phone call

Sensor	Detects	Use
`TYPE_RELATIVE_HUMIDITY`	Measures relative humidity	Used to determine dew point and humidity
`TYPE_ROTATION_VECTOR`	Measures device orientation	Used to detect motion and rotation

There are two additional sensors, `TYPE_ORIENTATION` and `TYPE_TEMPERATURE`, which have been deprecated as they have been replaced by newer sensors.

This recipe will demonstrate retrieving a list of available sensors. Here is a screenshot from the Pixel 2 emulator:

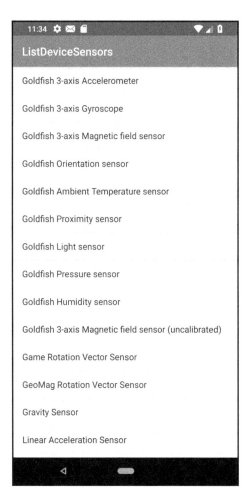

Getting ready

Create a new project in Android Studio and call it `ListDeviceSensors`. Use the default **Phone & Tablet** options and select **Empty Activity** when prompted for the **Activity Type**.

How to do it...

First, we'll query the list of sensors available, then display the results in a `ListView`. Here are the detailed steps:

1. Open `activity_main.xml` and replace the existing `TextView` with the following:

```
<ListView
    android:id="@+id/list"
    android:layout_width="match_parent"
    android:layout_height="match_parent"
    app:layout_constraintBottom_toBottomOf="parent"
    app:layout_constraintLeft_toLeftOf="parent"
    app:layout_constraintRight_toRightOf="parent"
    app:layout_constraintTop_toTopOf="parent" />
```

2. Next, open `ActivityMain.java` and add the following code to the existing `onCreate()` method:

```
ListView listView = findViewById(R.id.list);
List sensorList = new ArrayList<String>();

List<Sensor> sensors = ((SensorManager)
getSystemService(Context.SENSOR_SERVICE))
        .getSensorList(Sensor.TYPE_ALL);
for (Sensor sensor : sensors ) {
    sensorList.add(sensor.getName());
}
ListAdapter sensorAdapter = new ArrayAdapter<String>(this,
        android.R.layout.simple_list_item_1, sensorList);
listView.setAdapter(sensorAdapter);
```

3. Run the program on a device or emulator.

How it works...

The following line of code is responsible for getting the list of available sensors; the rest of the code populates the `ListView`:

```
List<Sensor> sensors = ((SensorManager) getSystemService(
      Context.SENSOR_SERVICE)).getSensorList(Sensor.TYPE_ALL);
```

Notice that we get back a list of `Sensor` objects. We only get the sensor name to display in the `ListView`, but there are other properties available as well. See the link provided in the *See also* section for a complete list.

There's more...

It's important to note a device can have multiple sensors of the same type. If you are looking for a specific sensor, you can pass in one of the constants from the table shown in the introduction. In this case, if you wanted to see all the accelerometer sensors available, you could use this call:

```
List<Sensor> sensors =
sensorManager.getSensorList(Sensor.TYPE_ACCELEROMETER);
```

If you're not looking for a list of sensors, but need to work with a specific sensor, you can check for a default sensor using this code:

```
SensorManager sensorManager =  ((SensorManager)
getSystemService(Context.SENSOR_SERVICE));
if (sensorManager.getDefaultSensor(Sensor.TYPE_ACCELEROMETER) != null){
    //Sensor is available - do something here
}
```

See also

- The **Android Developer Sensor** website at
  http://developer.android.com/reference/android/hardware/Sensor.html

Reading sensor data – using Android Sensor Framework events

The previous recipe, *Listing available sensors – an introduction to the Android Sensor Framework*, provided an introduction to the Android Sensor Framework. Now, we'll look at reading sensor data using `SensorEventListener`. The `SensorEventListener` interface only has two callbacks:

- `onSensorChanged()`
- `onAccuracyChanged()`

When the sensor has new data to report, it calls `onSensorChanged()` with a `SensorEvent` object. This recipe will demonstrate reading a light sensor, but since all the sensors use the same framework, it's very easy to adapt this example to any of the other sensors. (See the list of sensor types available in the previous recipe's introduction.)

Getting ready

Create a new project in Android Studio and call it `ReadingSensorData`. Use the default **Phone & Tablet** options and select **Empty Activity** when prompted for the **Activity Type**.

How to do it...

We'll add a `TextView` to the activity layout to display sensor data, then we'll add the `SensorEventListener` to the Java code. We'll use the `onResume()` and `onPause()` events to start and stop our Event Listener. To get started, open `activity_main.xml` and follow these steps:

1. Modify the existing `TextView` as follows:

```
<TextView
    android:id="@+id/textView"
    android:layout_width="wrap_content"
    android:layout_height="wrap_content"
    android:text="0"
    app:layout_constraintBottom_toBottomOf="parent"
    app:layout_constraintLeft_toLeftOf="parent"
    app:layout_constraintRight_toRightOf="parent"
    app:layout_constraintTop_toTopOf="parent" />
```

2. Now, open `MainActivity.java` and add the following global variable declarations:

```
private SensorManager mSensorManager;
private Sensor mSensor;
private TextView mTextView;
```

3. Implement the `SensorListener` class in the `MainActivity` class as follows:

```
private SensorEventListener mSensorListener = new
SensorEventListener() {
    @Override
    public void onSensorChanged(SensorEvent event) {
        mTextView.setText(String.valueOf(event.values[0]));
    }
    @Override
    public void onAccuracyChanged(Sensor sensor, int accuracy) {
        //Nothing to do
    }
};
```

4. We'll register and unregister sensor events in `onResume()` and `onPause()` as follows:

```
@Override
protected void onResume() {
    super.onResume();
    mSensorManager.registerListener(mSensorListener, mSensor,
SensorManager.SENSOR_DELAY_NORMAL);
}

@Override
protected void onPause() {
    super.onPause();
    mSensorManager.unregisterListener(mSensorListener);
}
```

5. Add the following code to `onCreate()`:

```
mTextView = (TextView)findViewById(R.id.textView);
mSensorManager = (SensorManager)
getSystemService(Context.SENSOR_SERVICE);
mSensor = mSensorManager.getDefaultSensor(Sensor.TYPE_LIGHT);
```

6. You can now run the application on a physical device to see the raw data from the light sensor.

How it works...

Using the Android Sensor Framework starts with obtaining the sensor, which we do in `onCreate()`. Here, we call `getDefaultSensor()`, requesting `TYPE_LIGHT`. We register the listener in `onResume()` and unregister it again in `onPause()` to reduce battery consumption. We pass in our `mSensorListener` object when we call `registerListener()`.

In our case, we are only looking for sensor data, which is sent in the `onSensorChanged()` callback. When the sensor changes, we update the `TextView` with the sensor data.

There's more...

Now that you've worked with one sensor, you know how to work with all sensors, as they all use the same framework. Of course, what you do with the data will vary greatly, depending on the type of data you're reading. Environment sensors, as shown here, return a single value, but position and motion sensors can also return additional elements, indicated as follows.

Environment sensors

Android supports the following four environment sensors:

- Humidity
- Light
- Pressure
- Temperature

Environment sensors are generally easier to work with since the data returned is in a single element and doesn't usually require calibration or filtering. We used a light sensor (`Sensor.TYPE_LIGHT`) for this recipe since most devices include a light sensor to control screen brightness.

Position sensors

Position sensors include:

- Geomagnetic Field
- Proximity

The following sensor types use the Geomagnetic field:

- TYPE_GAME_ROTATION_VECTOR
- TYPE_GEOMAGNETIC_ROTATION_VECTOR
- TYPE_MAGNETIC_FIELD
- TYPE_MAGNETIC_FIELD_UNCALIBRATED

These sensors return three values in the onSensorChanged() event, except for TYPE_MAGNETIC_FIELD_UNCALIBRATED, which sends six values.

A third sensor, the Orientation sensor, has been deprecated, and you are now recommended to use getRotation() and getRotationMatrix() to calculate orientation changes. (For device orientation, such as Portrait and Landscape modes, see the next recipe: *Reading device orientation*.)

Motion sensors

Motion sensors include the following:

- Accelerometer
- Gyroscope
- Gravity
- Linear acceleration
- Rotation vector

These include the following sensor types:

- TYPE_ACCELEROMETE
- TYPE_GRAVITY
- TYPE_GYROSCOPE
- TYPE_GYROSCOPE_UNCALIBRATED
- TYPE_LINEAR_ACCELERATION
- TYPE_ROTATION_VECTOR
- TYPE_SIGNIFICANT_MOTION
- TYPE_STEP_COUNTER
- TYPE_STEP_DETECTOR

These sensors also include three data elements, with the exception of the last three. `TYPE_SIGNIFICANT_MOTION` and `TYPE_STEP_DETECTOR` indicate an event, while `TYPE_STEP_COUNTER` returns the number of steps since last boot (while the sensor was active).

See also

- The *Listing available sensors - an introduction to the Android Sensor Framework* recipe
- The *Creating a Compass using sensor data and RotateAnimation* recipe in `Chapter 10`, *Graphics and Animation*
- For device orientation, see the next recipe: *Reading device orientation*
- See the GPS and Location recipe in `Chapter 14`, *Location and Using Geofencing*

Reading device orientation

Although the Android framework will automatically load new resources (such as the layout) upon orientation changes, there are times when you may wish to disable this behavior. If you wish to be notified of an orientation change instead of Android handling it automatically, add the following attribute to the Activity in the Android Manifest:

```
android:configChanges="keyboardHidden|orientation|screenSize"
```

When any of the following configuration changes occur, the system will notify you through the `onConfigurationChanged()` method instead of handling it automatically:

- `keyboardHidden`
- `orientation`
- `screenSize`

The `onConfigurationChanged()` signature is as follows:

```
onConfigurationChanged (Configuration newConfig)
```

You'll find the new orientation in `newConfig.orientation`.

Disabling the automatic configuration change (which causes the layout to be reloaded and state information to be reset) should not be used as a replacement for properly saving state information. Your application can still be interrupted or stopped altogether at any time and killed by the system. (See *Saving an activity's state* in `Chapter 1`, *Activities*, for how to properly save a state.)

This recipe will demonstrate how to determine the current device orientation.

Getting ready

Create a new project in Android Studio and call it `GetDeviceOrientation`. Use the default **Phone & Tablet** options and select **Empty Activity** when prompted for the **Activity Type**.

How to do it...

We'll add a button to the layout to check the orientation on demand. Start by opening `activity_main.xml` and follow these steps:

1. Replace the existing `TextView` with the following `Button`:

```
<Button
    android:layout_width="wrap_content"
    android:layout_height="wrap_content"
    android:text="Check Orientation"
    android:id="@+id/button"
    android:onClick="checkOrientation"
    app:layout_constraintBottom_toBottomOf="parent"
    app:layout_constraintLeft_toLeftOf="parent"
    app:layout_constraintRight_toRightOf="parent"
    app:layout_constraintTop_toTopOf="parent" />
```

2. Add the following method to handle the button click:

```
public void checkOrientation(View view){
    int orientation = getResources()
            .getConfiguration().orientation;
    switch (orientation) {
        case Configuration.ORIENTATION_LANDSCAPE:
            Toast.makeText(MainActivity.this,
"ORIENTATION_LANDSCAPE",
                    Toast.LENGTH_SHORT).show();
```

```
                    break;
              case Configuration.ORIENTATION_PORTRAIT:
                  Toast.makeText(MainActivity.this,
        "ORIENTATION_PORTRAIT",
                          Toast.LENGTH_SHORT).show();
                    break;
              case Configuration.ORIENTATION_UNDEFINED:
                  Toast.makeText(MainActivity.this,
        "ORIENTATION_UNDEFINED",
                          Toast.LENGTH_SHORT).show();
                    break;
          }
      }
```

3. Run the application on a device or emulator.

Use *Ctrl + F11* to rotate the emulator.

How it works...

All we need to do to get the current orientation is call this line of code:

```
getResources().getConfiguration().orientation
```

The orientation is returned as an `int`, which we compare to one of three possible values, as demonstrated.

There's more...

Another scenario where you may need to know the current orientation is when working with camera data, pictures, and/or videos. In this case, you need to get the device orientation as and when required.

Getting current device rotation

Often, the image may be rotated according to the device orientation or to compensate for the current orientation. In this scenario, there's another option available to get the rotation:

```
int rotation = getWindowManager().getDefaultDisplay().getRotation();
```

In the preceding line of code, `rotation` will be one of the following values:

- `Surface.ROTATION_0`
- `Surface.ROTATION_90`
- `Surface.ROTATION_180`
- `Surface.ROTATION_270`

 The rotation value will be from its normal orientation. For example, when using a table with a normal orientation of landscape, if a picture is taken in portrait orientation the value will be `ROTATION_90` or `ROTATION_270`.

See also

- The *Saving an activity's state* recipe in `Chapter 1`, *Activities*
- Refer to the following developer link for more information on the Configuration class:
  `http://developer.android.com/reference/android/content/res/Configuration.html`
- Refer to the following link for more information on the `getRotation()` method: `http://developer.android.com/reference/android/view/Display.html#getRotation()`

Graphics and Animation

10

In this chapter, we will cover the following topics:

- Scaling down large images to avoid Out of Memory exceptions
- A transition animation: Defining scenes and applying a transition
- Creating a Compass using sensor data and RotateAnimation
- Creating a slideshow with ViewPager
- Creating a Card Flip Animation with Fragments
- Creating a Zoom Animation with a Custom Transition
- Displaying an animated image (GIF/WebP) with the new ImageDecoder library
- Creating a circle image with the new ImageDecoder

Introduction

Animations can be both visually appealing and functional, as demonstrated with the simple button press. The graphical representation of the button press brings the app alive, plus it provides a functional value by giving the user a visual response to the event.

The Android Framework provides several animation systems to make it easier to include animations in your own application. They include the following:

- **View Animation** (the original animation system): It usually requires less code but has limited animation options
- **Property Animation**: It's a more flexible system, allowing the animation of any property of any object
- **Drawable Animation**: It uses drawable resources to create frame-by-frame animations (like a movie)

The Property Animation system was introduced in Android 3.0, and it is usually preferred over the View Animation because of the flexibility. The main drawbacks to the View Animation include the following:

- Limited aspects of what can be animated, such as scale and rotation
- Can only animate the contents of the view; it cannot change where on the screen the view is drawn (so it cannot animate moving a ball across the screen)
- Can only animate View objects

Here is a simple example demonstrating a View Animation to "blink" a view (a simple simulation of a button press):

```
Animation blink =AnimationUtils.loadAnimation(this,R.anim.blink);
view.startAnimation(blink);
```

Here are the contents for the `blink.xml` resource file, located in the `res/anim` folder:

```
<?xml version="1.0" encoding="utf-8"?>
<set xmlns:android="http://schemas.android.com/apk/res/android">
    <alpha android:fromAlpha="1.0"
        android:toAlpha="0.0"
        android:background="#000000"
        android:interpolator="@android:anim/linear_interpolator"
        android:duration="100"
        android:repeatMode="restart"
        android:repeatCount="0"/>
</set>
```

As you can see, it's very simple to create this animation, so if the View Animation accomplishes your goal, use it. When it doesn't meet your needs, turn to the Property Animation system. We'll demonstrate Property Animation using the new `objectAnimator` in the *Creating a Card Flip Animation with Fragments* and *Creating a Zoom Animation with a Custom Transition* recipes.

The *A transition animation – defining scenes and applying a transition* recipe will provide additional information on the Android Transition Framework, which we will use in many of the recipes.

 The Interpolator is a function that defines the rate of change for an animation.

`Interpolators` will be mentioned in several recipes in this chapter, as well as in the previous blink example. The Interpolator defines how the transition is calculated. A Linear Interpolator will calculate the change evenly over a set duration, whereas an `AccelerateInterpolator` function would create faster movement for the duration. Here is the full list of `Interpolators` available, along with the XML identifier:

- AccelerateDecelerateInterpolator
  (`@android:anim/accelerate_decelerate_interpolator`)
- AccelerateInterpolator (`@android:anim/accelerate_interpolator`)
- AnticipateInterpolator (`@android:anim/anticipate_interpolator`)
- AnticipateOvershootInterpolator
  (`@android:anim/anticipate_overshoot_interpolator`)
- BounceInterpolator (`@android:anim/bounce_interpolator`)
- CycleInterpolator (`@android:anim/cycle_interpolator`)
- DecelerateInterpolator (`@android:anim/decelerate_interpolator`)
- LinearInterpolator (`@android:anim/linear_interpolator`)
- OvershootInterpolator (`@android:anim/overshoot_interpolator`)

Although animations don't generally require much memory, the graphic resources often do. Many of the images you may want to work with often exceed the available device memory. In the first recipe of this chapter, *Scaling down large images to avoid Out of Memory exceptions*, we'll discuss how to subsample (or scale down) images.

Scaling down large images to avoid Out of Memory exceptions

Working with images can be very memory intensive, often resulting in your application crashing with an *Out of Memory* exception. This is especially true with pictures taken with the device camera, as they often have a much higher resolution than the device itself.

Loading a higher resolution image than the UI supports doesn't provide any visual benefit to the user. In this example, we'll demonstrate how to take smaller samples of the image for display. We'll use `BitmapFactory` to first check the image size, then load a scaled-down image.

Here's a screenshot from this recipe showing a thumbnail of a very large image:

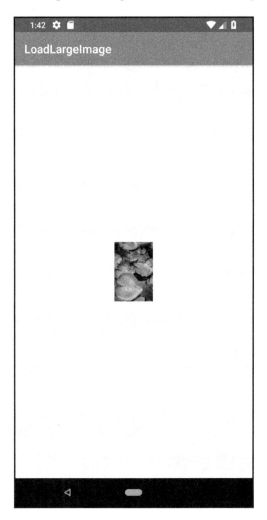

Getting ready

Create a new project in Android Studio and call it LoadLargeImage. Use the default **Phone & Tablet** options and select **Empty Activity** when prompted for the **Activity Type**.

We'll need a large image for this recipe. We turned to Unsplash.com to download a free image, (`https://unsplash.com`), although any large (multi-megabyte) image will do.

How to do it...

As mentioned in *Getting ready*, we need a large image to demonstrate the scaling. Once you have the image, follow these steps:

1. Copy the image to your `res/drawable` folder.

2. Open `activity_main.xml` and replace the existing `TextView` with the following `ImageView`:

```
<android.support.v7.widget.AppCompatImageView
    android:id="@+id/imageViewThumbnail"
    android:layout_width="100dp"
    android:layout_height="100dp"
    app:layout_constraintBottom_toBottomOf="parent"
    app:layout_constraintLeft_toLeftOf="parent"
    app:layout_constraintRight_toRightOf="parent"
    app:layout_constraintTop_toTopOf="parent" />
```

3. Now, open `MainActivity.java` and add this method, which we'll explain shortly:

```
public Bitmap loadSampledResource(int imageID, int targetHeight,
int targetWidth) {
    final BitmapFactory.Options options = new
BitmapFactory.Options();
    options.inJustDecodeBounds = true;
    BitmapFactory.decodeResource(getResources(), imageID, options);
    final int originalHeight = options.outHeight;
    final int originalWidth = options.outWidth;
    int inSampleSize = 1;
    while ((originalHeight / (inSampleSize *2)) > targetHeight
            && (originalWidth / (inSampleSize *2)) > targetWidth) {
        inSampleSize *= 2;
    }
    options.inSampleSize = inSampleSize;
    options.inJustDecodeBounds = false;
    return BitmapFactory.decodeResource(getResources(), imageID,
options);
}
```

4. Add the following code to the existing `onCreate()` method:

```
AppCompatImageView imageView =
findViewById(R.id.imageViewThumbnail);
imageView.setImageBitmap(
loadSampledResource(R.drawable.miguel_henriques_789508_unsplash,
100, 100));
```

5. Run the application on a device or emulator.

How it works...

The purpose of the `loadSampledResource()` method is to load a smaller image, to reduce the memory consumption of the image. If we attempted to load the original full-size image (see the previous *Getting ready* section), the app would require over 3 MB of RAM to load. That's more memory than most devices can handle (at the moment anyway), and even if it could be loaded completely, it would provide no visual benefit to our thumbnail view.

To avoid an `Out of Memory` situation, we use the `inSampleSize` property of `BitmapFactory.Options` to reduce, or subsample, the image. (If we set the `inSampleSize=2`, it will reduce the image by half. If we use `inSampleSize=4`, it will reduce the image by one quarter) To calculate `inSampleSize`, first, we need to know the image size. We can use the `inJustDecodeBounds` property as follows:

```
options.inJustDecodeBounds = true;
```

This tells `BitmapFactory` to get the image dimensions without actually storing the image contents. Once we have the image size, we calculate the sample using this code:

```
while ((originalHeight / (inSampleSize *2)) > targetHeight
        && (originalWidth / (inSampleSize *2)) > targetWidth) {
    inSampleSize *= 2;
}
```

The purpose of this code is to determine the largest sample size that does not reduce the image below the target dimensions. To do that, we double the sample size and check whether the size exceeds the target size dimensions. If it doesn't, we save the doubled sample size and repeat. Once the reduced size falls below the target dimensions, we use the last saved `inSampleSize`.

From the `inSampleSize` documentation (link in the following *See also* section), note that the decoder uses a final value based on powers of 2, so any other value will be rounded down to the nearest power of 2.

Once we have the sample size, we set the `inSampleSize` property and set `inJustDecodeBounds` to `false`, to load normally. Here is the code:

```
options.inSampleSize = inSampleSize;
options.inJustDecodeBounds = false;
```

It's important to note that this recipe illustrates the concept of applying the task to your own application. Loading and processing images can be a long operation, which can cause your application to stop responding. This is not a good thing and could cause Android to show the **Application Not Responding (ANR)** dialog. It is recommended to perform long tasks on a background thread to keep your UI thread responsive. The `AsyncTask` class is available for doing background network processing, but there are many other libraries available as well (links at the end of the recipe).

There's more...

It's important to note that the `targetHeight` and `targetWidth` parameters we pass to the `loadSampledResource()` method do not actually set the image size. If you run the application using the same size image we used (4,000 x 6,000), the sample size will be 32, resulting in a loaded image size of 187 x 125.

If your layout needs a specific size of image, either set the size in the layout file, or you can modify the image size directly using the Bitmap class.

See also

- Developer Docs: BitmapFactory.inSampleSize() at
  `https://developer.android.com/reference/android/graphics/BitmapFactory.Options.html#inSampleSize`
- Refer to Glide at `https://github.com/bumptech/glide`
- Refer to Picasso from Square at `https://square.github.io/picasso/`
- Refer to Fresco from Facebook at `https://github.com/facebook/fresco`
- Check the *AsyncTask* task in `Chapter 15`, *Getting Your App Ready for the Play Store*, for processing long-running operations on a background thread.

A transition animation – defining scenes and applying a transition

The Android Transition Framework offers the following:

- **Group-level animations**: Animation applies to all views in a hierarchy
- **Transition-based animation**: Animation based on starting and ending property change
- **Built-in animations**: Some common transition effects, such as fade-in/out and movement
- **Resource file support**: Save animation values to a resource (XML) file to load during runtime
- **Lifecycle callbacks**: Receive callback notifications during the animation

A transition animation consists of the following:

- **Starting Scene**: The view (or `ViewGroup`) at the start of the animation
- **Transition**: The change type (see later on)
- **Ending Scene**: The ending view (or `ViewGroup`)
- **Transitions**: Android provides built-in support for the following three transitions:
    - **AutoTransition (default transition)**: Fade out, move, resize, then fade in (in that order)
    - **Fade**: Fade in, fade out (default), or both (specify order)
    - **ChangeBounds**: Move and resize

The Transition Framework will automatically create the frames needed to animate from the start to end scenes.

The following are some known limitations of the Transition Framework when working with the following classes:

- **SurfaceView**: Animations may not appear correct since the `SurfaceView` animations are performed on a non-UI thread, so they may be out of sync with the application
- **TextView**: Animating text-size changes may not work correctly resulting in the text jumping to the final state

- **AdapterView**: Classes that extend `AdapterView`, such as `ListView` and `GridView`, may hang
- **TextureView**: Some transitions may not work

This recipe provides a quick tutorial on using the transition animation system. We'll start by defining the scenes and transition resources, then applying the transition, which creates the animation. The following steps will walk you through creating the resources in XML, as they are generally recommended. Resources can also be created through code, which we'll discuss in the *There's more* section.

Getting ready

Create a new project in Android Studio and call it `TransitionAnimation`. In the **Target Android Devices** dialog, select the **Phone & Tablet** option and choose API 19 (or above) for the **Minimum SDK**. Select **Empty Activity** when prompted for the **Activity Type**.

How to do it...

Here are the steps to create the resource files and apply the transition animation:

1. Replace the existing `activity.main.xml` layout with the following XML:

```xml
<?xml version="1.0" encoding="utf-8"?>
<RelativeLayout
xmlns:android="http://schemas.android.com/apk/res/android"
    xmlns:tools="http://schemas.android.com/tools"
    android:id="@+id/layout"
    android:layout_width="match_parent"
    android:layout_height="match_parent">
    <TextView
        android:layout_width="wrap_content"
        android:layout_height="wrap_content"
        android:text="Top"
        android:id="@+id/textViewTop"
        android:layout_alignParentTop="true"
        android:layout_centerHorizontal="true" />
    <TextView
        android:layout_width="wrap_content"
        android:layout_height="wrap_content"
        android:text="Bottom"
        android:id="@+id/textViewBottom"
        android:layout_alignParentBottom="true"
        android:layout_centerHorizontal="true" />
```

```
    <Button
        android:layout_width="wrap_content"
        android:layout_height="wrap_content"
        android:text="Go"
        android:id="@+id/button"
        android:layout_centerInParent="true"
        android:onClick="goAnimate"/>
</RelativeLayout>
```

2. Create a new layout file called `activity_main_end.xml` using the following XML:

```xml
<?xml version="1.0" encoding="utf-8"?>
<RelativeLayout
xmlns:android="http://schemas.android.com/apk/res/android"
    xmlns:tools="http://schemas.android.com/tools"
    android:id="@+id/layout"
    android:layout_width="match_parent"
    android:layout_height="match_parent">
    <TextView
        android:layout_width="wrap_content"
        android:layout_height="wrap_content"
        android:text="Bottom"
        android:id="@+id/textViewBottom"
        android:layout_alignParentTop="true"
        android:layout_centerHorizontal="true" />
    <TextView
        android:layout_width="wrap_content"
        android:layout_height="wrap_content"
        android:text="Top"
        android:id="@+id/textViewTop"
        android:layout_alignParentBottom="true"
        android:layout_centerHorizontal="true" />
    <Button
        android:layout_width="wrap_content"
        android:layout_height="wrap_content"
        android:text="Go"
        android:id="@+id/button"
        android:layout_centerInParent="true"/>
</RelativeLayout>
```

3. Make a new transition resource directory (**File** | **New** | **Android resource directory** and choose **Transition** as the **Resource type**).

4. Create a new file in the `res/transition` folder called `transition_move.xml` using the following XML:

```xml
<?xml version="1.0" encoding="utf-8"?>
<changeBounds xmlns:android=
    "http://schemas.android.com/apk/res/android" />
```

5. Add the `goAnimate()` method using the following code:

```java
public void goAnimate(View view) {
    ViewGroup root = findViewById(R.id.layout);
    Scene scene = Scene.getSceneForLayout(root,
R.layout.activity_main_end, this);
    Transition transition = TransitionInflater.from(this)
            .inflateTransition(R.transition.transition_move);
    TransitionManager.go(scene, transition);
}
```

6. You're ready to run the application on a device or emulator.

How it works...

You probably find the code itself rather simple. As outlined in the recipe introduction, we just need to create the starting and ending scenes and set the transition type. Here's a detailed breakdown of the code:

- Creating the start Scene: The following line of code will load the Start Scene:

```java
ViewGroup root = findViewById(R.id.layout);
```

- Creating the transition: The following line of code will create the transition:

```java
Transition transition = TransitionInflater.from(this)
            .inflateTransition(R.transition.transition_move);
```

- Defining the ending scene: The following line of code will define the ending scene:

```java
Scene scene = Scene.getSceneForLayout(root,
R.layout.activity_main_end, this);
```

- Starting the transition: The following line of code will start the transition:

```java
TransitionManager.go(scene, transition);
```

Although simple, most of the work for this recipe was in creating the necessary resource files.

There's more...

Now, we'll take a look at creating this same transition animation with a code-only solution (although we'll still use the initial `activity_main.xml` layout file):

```
ViewGroup root = findViewById(R.id.layout);
Scene scene = new Scene(root);

Transition transition = new ChangeBounds();
TransitionManager.beginDelayedTransition(root, transition);

TextView textViewTop = findViewById(R.id.textViewTop);
RelativeLayout.LayoutParams params =
(RelativeLayout.LayoutParams)textViewTop.getLayoutParams();
params.addRule(RelativeLayout.ALIGN_PARENT_BOTTOM, 1);
params.addRule(RelativeLayout.ALIGN_PARENT_TOP, 0);
textViewTop.setLayoutParams(params);

TextView textViewBottom = findViewById(R.id.textViewBottom);
params = (RelativeLayout.LayoutParams) textViewBottom.getLayoutParams();
params.addRule(RelativeLayout.ALIGN_PARENT_BOTTOM, 0);
params.addRule(RelativeLayout.ALIGN_PARENT_TOP, 1);
textViewBottom.setLayoutParams(params);

TransitionManager.go(scene);
```

We still need the starting and ending scene along with the transition; the only difference is how we create the resources. In the previous code, we created the Start Scene using the current layout.

Before we start modifying the layout through code, we call the `beginDelayedTransition()` method of `TransitionManager` with the transition type. `TransitionManager` will track the changes for the ending scene. When we call the `go()` method, `TransitionManager` automatically animates the change.

See also

- Refer to the Animation resources web page at
  https://developer.android.com/guide/topics/resources/animation-resourc e.html

Creating a Compass using sensor data and RotateAnimation

In the previous chapter, we demonstrated reading sensor data from the physical device sensors. In that recipe, we used the Light Sensor since the data from Environment Sensors generally doesn't require any extra processing. Although it's easy to get the magnetic field strength data, the numbers themselves don't have much meaning and certainly don't create an appealing display.

In this recipe, we'll demonstrate getting the magnetic field data along with the accelerometer data to calculate magnetic north. We'll use `SensorManager.getRotationMatrix` to animate the compass while responding to the device movement. Here's a screenshot of our compass application on a physical device:

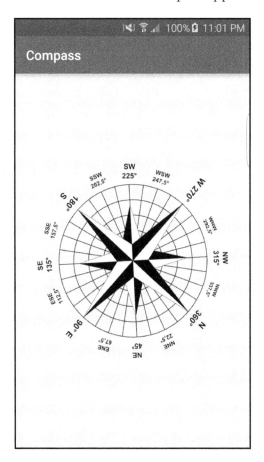

Getting ready

Create a new project in Android Studio and call it `Compass`. Use the default **Phone & Tablet** options and select **Empty Activity** when prompted for the **Activity Type**.

We will need an image for the compass indicator. There's an image on www.Pixabay.Com that will work for us at this link:

`https://pixabay.com/en/geography-map-compass-rose-plot-42608/`.

Although not required, this image has a transparent background, which looks better when rotating the image.

How to do it...

As mentioned in the previous *Getting ready* section, we'll need an image for the compass. You can download the one previously linked, or use any image you prefer, then follow these steps:

1. Copy your image to the `res/drawable` folder and name it `compass.png`.
2. Open `activity_main.xml` and replace the existing `TextView` with the following `ImageView`:

```
<android.support.v7.widget.AppCompatImageView
    android:id="@+id/imageViewCompass"
    android:layout_width="wrap_content"
    android:layout_height="wrap_content"
    android:layout_centerInParent="true"
    android:src="@drawable/compass"
    app:layout_constraintBottom_toBottomOf="parent"
    app:layout_constraintLeft_toLeftOf="parent"
    app:layout_constraintRight_toRightOf="parent"
    app:layout_constraintTop_toTopOf="parent" />
```

3. Now, open `MainActivity.java` and add the following global variable declarations:

```
private SensorManager mSensorManager;
private Sensor mMagnetometer;
private Sensor mAccelerometer;
private AppCompatImageView mImageViewCompass;
private float[] mGravityValues=new float[3];
private float[] mAccelerationValues=new float[3];
private float[] mRotationMatrix=new float[9];
private float mLastDirectionInDegrees = 0f;
```

4. Add the following `SensorEventListener` class to the `MainActivity` class:

```
private SensorEventListener mSensorListener = new
SensorEventListener() {
    @Override
    public void onSensorChanged(SensorEvent event) {
        calculateCompassDirection(event);
    }

    @Override
    public void onAccuracyChanged(Sensor sensor, int
            accuracy) {
        //Nothing to do
    }
};
```

5. Override `onResume()` and `onPause()` as follows:

```
@Override
protected void onResume() {
    super.onResume();
    mSensorManager.registerListener(mSensorListener, mMagnetometer,
            SensorManager.SENSOR_DELAY_FASTEST);
    mSensorManager.registerListener(mSensorListener,
mAccelerometer,
            SensorManager.SENSOR_DELAY_FASTEST);
}

@Override
protected void onPause() {
    super.onPause();
    mSensorManager.unregisterListener(mSensorListener);
}
```

6. Add the following code to the existing `onCreate()` method:

```
mImageViewCompass = findViewById(R.id.imageViewCompass);
mSensorManager = (SensorManager)
getSystemService(Context.SENSOR_SERVICE);
mMagnetometer =
mSensorManager.getDefaultSensor(Sensor.TYPE_MAGNETIC_FIELD);
mAccelerometer =
mSensorManager.getDefaultSensor(Sensor.TYPE_ACCELEROMETER);
```

7. The final code does the actual calculations and animation:

```
private void calculateCompassDirection(SensorEvent event) {
    switch (event.sensor.getType()) {
        case Sensor.TYPE_ACCELEROMETER:
            mAccelerationValues = event.values.clone();
            break;
        case Sensor.TYPE_MAGNETIC_FIELD:
            mGravityValues = event.values.clone();
            break;
    }
    boolean success =
SensorManager.getRotationMatrix(mRotationMatrix, null,
            mAccelerationValues, mGravityValues);
    if (success) {
        float[] orientationValues = new float[3];
        SensorManager.getOrientation(mRotationMatrix,
orientationValues);
        float azimuth = (float) Math.toDegrees(-
orientationValues[0]);
        RotateAnimation rotateAnimation = new
RotateAnimation(mLastDirectionInDegrees, azimuth,
                Animation.RELATIVE_TO_SELF, 0.5f,
                Animation.RELATIVE_TO_SELF, 0.5f);
        rotateAnimation.setDuration(50);
        rotateAnimation.setFillAfter(true);
        mImageViewCompass.startAnimation(rotateAnimation);
        mLastDirectionInDegrees = azimuth;
    }
}
```

8. You're ready to run the application. Although you can run this application on an emulator, without an accelerometer and magnetometer, you won't see the compass move.

How it works...

Since we've already covered reading sensor data in the *Reading sensor data – using the Android Sensor Framework* section (in the previous chapter), we won't repeat explaining the sensor framework, and, instead, jump right to the `calculateCompassDirection()` method.

We call this method directly from the `onSensorChanged()` callback. Since we used the same class to handle the sensor callbacks for both the Magnetometer and Accelerometer, we first check which sensor is being reported in `SensorEvent`. Then, we call `SensorManager.getRotationMatrix()`, passing in the last sensor data. If the calculation is successful, it returns `RotationMatrix`, which we use to call the `SensorManager.getOrientation()` method. Note that `getOrientation()` will return the following data in the `orientationValues` array:

- **Azimuth**: `value [0]`
- **Pitch**: `value [1]`
- **Roll**: `value [2]`

The azimuth is reported in radians, in the opposite direction, so we reverse the sign and convert it to degrees using `Math.toDegrees()`. The azimuth represents the direction of North, so we use it in our `RotateAnimation`.

With the math already done by `SensorManager`, the actual compass animation is very simple. We create `RotateAnimation` using the previous direction and the new direction. We use the `Animation.RELATIVE_TO_SELF` flag and 0.5f (or 50%) to set the center of the image as the rotation point. Before calling `startAnimation()` to update the compass, we set the animation duration using `setDuration()` and `setFillAfter(true)`. (Using `true` indicates we want the image to be left "as is" after the animation completes; otherwise, the image would reset back to the original image.) Finally, we save the azimuth for the next sensor update.

There's more...

It's worth taking some time to experiment with the `RotationAnimation` settings and the sensor update timing. In our call to register the sensor listener, we use `SensorManager.SENSOR_DELAY_FASTEST` along with 50 milliseconds for `setDuration()` to create a fast animation. You could also try using a slower sensor update and a slower animation, and compare the results.

See also

- *Reading sensor data - using the Android Sensor Framework* in the previous chapter for details on reading sensor data
- Refer to the **getRotationMatrix()** Developer Document at
  `http://developer.android.com/reference/android/hardware/SensorManager.html#getRotationMatrix(float[], float[], float[], float[])`
- Refer to the **getOrientation()** Developer Document at
  `http://developer.android.com/reference/android/hardware/SensorManager.html#getOrientation(float[], float[])`
- Refer to the **RotateAnimation** Developer Document at
  `http://developer.android.com/reference/android/view/animation/RotateAnimation.html`

Creating a slideshow with ViewPager

This recipe will show you how to create a slideshow using the `ViewPager` class. Here is a screenshot showing a transition from one picture to another:

Getting ready

Create a new project in Android Studio and call it `SlideShow`. Use the default **Phone & Tablet** options and select **Empty Activity** when prompted for the **Activity Type**.

We need four images for the slideshow.

How to do it...

We'll create a Fragment to display each image for our slideshow, then set up `ViewPager` in the Main Activity. Here are the steps:

1. Copy four images to the `/res/drawable` folder and name them `slide_0` through `slide_3`, keeping the original file extensions.

2. Create a new layout file called `fragment_slide.xml` using the following XML:

```xml
<?xml version="1.0" encoding="utf-8"?>
<LinearLayout
xmlns:android="http://schemas.android.com/apk/res/android"
    android:orientation="vertical"
    android:layout_width="match_parent"
    android:layout_height="match_parent">
    <android.support.v7.widget.AppCompatImageView
        android:layout_width="wrap_content"
        android:layout_height="wrap_content"
        android:id="@+id/imageView"
        android:layout_gravity="center_horizontal" />
</LinearLayout>
```

3. Now, create a new Java class called `SlideFragment.java`. It will extend `Fragment` as follows:

```java
public class SlideFragment extends Fragment {
```

   • Import from the support library, resulting in the following import:

```java
import android.support.v4.app.Fragment;
```

4. Add the following global declaration:

```java
private int mImageResourceID;
```

5. Add the following empty, default fragment constructor:

```java
public SlideFragment() {}
```

6. Add the following method to save the image resource ID:

```
public void setImage(int resourceID) {
    mImageResourceID=resourceID;
}
```

7. Override `onCreateView()` as follows:

```
@Override
public View onCreateView(LayoutInflater inflater, ViewGroup
container, Bundle savedInstanceState){
    ViewGroup rootView = (ViewGroup)
inflater.inflate(R.layout.fragment_slide, container, false);
    AppCompatImageView imageView =
rootView.findViewById(R.id.imageView);
    imageView.setImageResource(mImageResourceID);
    return rootView;
}
```

8. Our main activity will display just a `ViewPager`. Open `activity_main.xml` and replace the file contents with the following:

```
<android.support.v4.view.ViewPager
    xmlns:android="http://schemas.android.com/apk/res/android"
    android:id="@+id/viewPager"
    android:layout_width="match_parent"
    android:layout_height="match_parent" />
```

9. Now, open `MainActivity.java` and add the following global declarations:

```
private final int PAGE_COUNT=4;
private ViewPager mViewPager;
private PagerAdapter mPagerAdapter;
```

- Use the following imports:

```
import android.support.v4.view.PagerAdapter;
import android.support.v4.view.ViewPager;
```

10. Create the following subclass within the `MainActivity` class:

```
private class SlideAdapter extends FragmentStatePagerAdapter {
    public SlideAdapter(FragmentManager fm) {
        super(fm);
    }
    @Override
    public Fragment getItem(int position) {
        SlideFragment slideFragment = new SlideFragment();
```

```
                switch (position) {
                    case 0:
                        slideFragment.setImage(R.drawable.slide_0);
                        break;
                    case 1:
                        slideFragment.setImage(R.drawable.slide_1);
                        break;
                    case 2:
                        slideFragment.setImage(R.drawable.slide_2);
                        break;
                    case 3:
                        slideFragment.setImage(R.drawable.slide_3);
                        break;
                }
                return slideFragment;
            }
            @Override
            public int getCount() {
                return PAGE_COUNT;
            }
        }
    }
```

- Use the following imports:

```
        import android.support.v4.app.Fragment;
        import android.support.v4.app.FragmentManager;
        import android.support.v4.app.FragmentStatePagerAdapter;
```

11. Override `onBackPressed()` in the `MainActivity` class as follows:

```
    @Override
    public void onBackPressed() {
        if (mViewPager.getCurrentItem() == 0) {
            super.onBackPressed();
        } else {
            mViewPager.setCurrentItem(mViewPager.getCurrentItem() - 1);
        }
    }
```

12. Add the following code to the `onCreate()` method:

```
    mViewPager = findViewById(R.id.viewPager);
    mPagerAdapter = new SlideAdapter(getSupportFragmentManager());
    mViewPager.setAdapter(mPagerAdapter);
```

13. Run the application on a device or emulator.

How it works...

The first step is to create a fragment. Since we're doing a slideshow, all we need is `ImageViewer`. We also change `MainActivity` to extend `FragmentActivity` to load the fragments into `ViewPager`.

`ViewPager` uses `FragmentStatePagerAdapter` as the source for the fragments to transition. We create `SlideAdapter` to handle the two callbacks from the `FragmentStatePagerAdapter` class:

- `getCount()`
- `getItem()`

Furthermore, `getCount()` simply returns the number of pages we have in our slideshow, and `getItem()` returns the actual fragment to display. This is where we specify the image we want to display. As you can see, it would be very easy to add to or change the slideshow.

Handling the *Backspace* key isn't a requirement for `ViewPager`, but it does provide a better user experience. However, `onBackPressed()` decrements the current page until it reaches the first page, then it sends the *Back* key to the superclass, which exits the application.

There's more...

As you can see from the example, `ViewPager` takes care of most of the work, including handling the transition animations. We can customize the transition if we want, by implementing the `transformPage()` callback on the `ViewPager.PageTransformer` interface. (See the next recipe for a custom animation.)

Creating a Setup Wizard

The `ViewPager` can also be used to create a Setup Wizard. Instead of creating a single fragment to display an image, create a fragment for each step of your wizard and return the appropriate fragment in the `getItem()` callback.

See also

- Refer to the **Android ViewPager Documentation** at
  `http://developer.android.com/reference/android/support/v4/view/ViewPag`
  `er.html`
- Refer to the *Creating a custom Zoom Animation* recipe for an example of creating a custom animation

Creating a Card Flip Animation with Fragments

The card flip is a common animation that we will demonstrate using fragment transitions. We'll use two different images, one for the front and one for the back, to create the card flip effect. We'll need four animation resources, two for the front and two for the back transitions, which we will define in XML using `objectAnimator`.

Here's a screenshot of the application we'll build showing the Card Flip Animation in action:

Getting ready

Create a new project in Android Studio and call it `CardFlip`. Use the default **Phone & Tablet** options and select **Empty Activity** when prompted for the **Activity Type**.

For the front and back images of the playing card, we found the following images on `www.pixabay.com`:

- https://pixabay.com/en/ace-hearts-playing-cards-poker-28357/
- https://pixabay.com/en/card-game-deck-of-cards-card-game-48978/

How to do it...

We'll need two fragments: one for the front of the card and the other for the back. Each fragment will define the image for the card. Then, we'll need four animation files for the full card flip effect. Here are the steps to set up the project structure correctly and to create the resources needed:

1. Once you have front and back images for the cards, copy them to the `res/drawable` folder as `card_front.jpg` and `card_back.jpg` (keep the original file extension of your images if different).

2. Create an animator resource directory: `res/animator`. (In Android Studio, go to **File | New | Android resource directory**. When the **New Android Resource** dialog displays, choose `animator` in the **Resource Type** drop-down list.)

3. Create `card_flip_left_enter.xml` in `res/animator` using the following XML:

```xml
<?xml version="1.0" encoding="utf-8"?>
<set xmlns:android="http://schemas.android.com/apk/res/android">
    <objectAnimator
        android:valueFrom="1.0"
        android:valueTo="0.0"
        android:propertyName="alpha"
        android:duration="0" />
    <objectAnimator
        android:valueFrom="-180"
        android:valueTo="0"
        android:propertyName="rotationY"
        android:interpolator="@android:interpolator/accelerate_decelerate"
        android:duration="@integer/card_flip_duration_full"/>
    <objectAnimator
        android:valueFrom="0.0"
        android:valueTo="1.0"
```

```
            android:propertyName="alpha"
            android:startOffset="@integer/card_flip_duration_half"
            android:duration="1" />
    </set>
```

4. Create `card_flip_left_exit.xml` in `res/animator` using the following XML:

```xml
<?xml version="1.0" encoding="utf-8"?>
<set xmlns:android="http://schemas.android.com/apk/res/android">
    <objectAnimator
        android:valueFrom="0"
        android:valueTo="180"
        android:propertyName="rotationY"
        android:interpolator="@android:interpolator/accelerate_decelerate"
        android:duration="@integer/card_flip_duration_full"/>
    <objectAnimator
        android:valueFrom="1.0"
        android:valueTo="0.0"
        android:propertyName="alpha"
        android:startOffset="@integer/card_flip_duration_half"
        android:duration="1" />
    </set>
```

5. Create `card_flip_right_enter.xml` in `res/animator` using the following XML:

```xml
<?xml version="1.0" encoding="utf-8"?>
<set xmlns:android="http://schemas.android.com/apk/res/android">
    <objectAnimator
        android:valueFrom="1.0"
        android:valueTo="0.0"
        android:propertyName="alpha"
        android:duration="0" />
    <objectAnimator
        android:valueFrom="180"
        android:valueTo="0"
        android:propertyName="rotationY"
        android:interpolator="@android:interpolator/accelerate_decelerate"
        android:duration="@integer/card_flip_duration_full" />
    <objectAnimator
        android:valueFrom="0.0"
        android:valueTo="1.0"
        android:propertyName="alpha"
        android:startOffset="@integer/card_flip_duration_half"
        android:duration="1" />
    </set>
```

6. Create `card_flip_right_exit.xml` in `res/animator` using the following XML:

```xml
<?xml version="1.0" encoding="utf-8"?>
<set xmlns:android="http://schemas.android.com/apk/res/android">
    <objectAnimator
        android:valueFrom="0"
        android:valueTo="-180"
        android:propertyName="rotationY"
        android:interpolator="@android:interpolator/accelerate_decelerate"
        android:duration="@integer/card_flip_duration_full" />
    <objectAnimator
        android:valueFrom="1.0"
        android:valueTo="0.0"
        android:propertyName="alpha"
        android:startOffset="@integer/card_flip_duration_half"
        android:duration="1" />
</set>
```

7. Create a new resource file in `res/values` called `timing.xml` using the following XML:

```xml
<?xml version="1.0" encoding="utf-8"?>
<resources>
    <integer name="card_flip_duration_full">1000</integer>
    <integer name="card_flip_duration_half">500</integer>
</resources>
```

8. Create a new file in `res/layout` called `fragment_card_front.xml` using the following XML:

```xml
<?xml version="1.0" encoding="utf-8"?>
<android.support.v7.widget.AppCompatImageView
    xmlns:android="http://schemas.android.com/apk/res/android"
    android:layout_width="match_parent"
    android:layout_height="match_parent"
    android:src="@drawable/card_front"
    android:scaleType="centerCrop" />
```

9. Create a new file in `res/layout` called `fragment_card_back.xml` using the following XML:

```xml
<?xml version="1.0" encoding="utf-8"?>
<android.support.v7.widget.AppCompatImageView
    xmlns:android="http://schemas.android.com/apk/res/android"
    android:layout_width="match_parent"
    android:layout_height="match_parent"
    android:src="@drawable/card_back"
    android:scaleType="centerCrop" />
```

10. Create a new Java class called `CardFrontFragment` using the following code:

```java
public class CardFrontFragment extends Fragment {
    @Override
    public View onCreateView(LayoutInflater inflater, ViewGroup container,
                             Bundle savedInstanceState) {
        return inflater.inflate(R.layout.fragment_card_front,
container, false);
    }
}
```

11. Create a new Java class called `CardBackFragment` using the following code:

```java
public class CardBackFragment extends Fragment {
    @Override
    public View onCreateView(LayoutInflater inflater, ViewGroup container,
                             Bundle savedInstanceState) {
        return inflater.inflate(R.layout.fragment_card_back,
container, false);
    }
}
```

12. Replace the existing `activity_main.xml` file with the following XML:

```xml
<?xml version="1.0" encoding="utf-8"?>
<FrameLayout
    xmlns:android="http://schemas.android.com/apk/res/android"
    android:id="@+id/container"
    android:layout_width="match_parent"
    android:layout_height="match_parent" />
```

13. Open `MainActivity.java` and add the following global declaration:

```
boolean mShowingBack = false;
```

14. Add the following code to the existing `onCreate()` method:

```
FrameLayout frameLayout = findViewById(R.id.container);
frameLayout.setOnClickListener(new View.OnClickListener() {
    @Override
    public void onClick(View v) {
        flipCard();
    }
});

if (savedInstanceState == null) {
    getSupportFragmentManager()
            .beginTransaction()
            .add(R.id.container, new CardFrontFragment())
            .commit();
}
```

15. Add the following method, which handles the actual fragment transition:

```
void flipCard() {
    if (mShowingBack) {
        mShowingBack = false;
        getSupportFragmentManager().popBackStack();
    } else {
        mShowingBack = true;
        getSupportFragmentManager()
                .beginTransaction()
                .setCustomAnimations(
                        R.animator.card_flip_right_enter,
                        R.animator.card_flip_right_exit,
                        R.animator.card_flip_left_enter,
                        R.animator.card_flip_left_exit)
                .replace(R.id.container, new CardBackFragment())
                .addToBackStack(null)
                .commit();
    }
}
```

16. You're ready to run the application on a device or emulator.

How it works...

Most of the effort to create the card flip is in setting up the resources. Since we want a front and back view of the card, we create two fragments with the appropriate images. We call the `flipCard()` method when the card is pressed. The actual animation is handled by `setCustomAnimations()`. This is where we pass in the four animation resources we defined in the XML. As you can see, Android makes it very easy.

It's important to note that we did not use the Support Library Fragment Manager, as the support library does not support `objectAnimator`. If you want support pre-Android 3.0, you'll need to include the old anim resources and check the OS version at runtime, or create the animation resources in code. (See the next recipe.)

See also

- See the next recipe, *Creating a Zoom Animation with a Custom Transition*, for an example of animation resources created in code
- Refer to the **Integer Resource Type** web page at `https://developer.android.com/guide/topics/resources/more-resources.html#Integer`

Creating a Zoom Animation with a Custom Transition

The previous recipe, *Creating a Card Flip Animation with Fragments*, demonstrated a transition animation using animation resource files. In this recipe, we will create a zoom effect using animation resources created in code. The application shows a thumbnail image, then expands to an enlarged image when pressed.

The following image contains three screenshots showing the zoom animation in action:

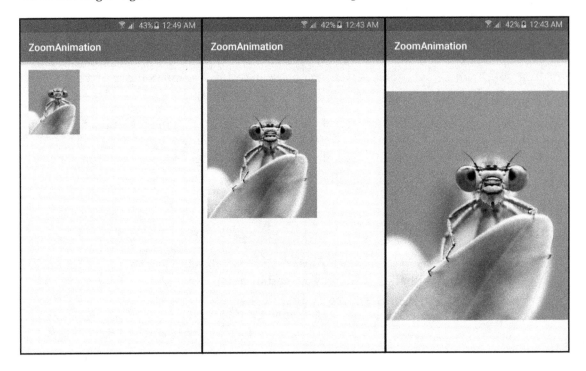

Getting ready

Create a new project in Android Studio and call it ZoomAnimation. Use the default **Phone & Tablet** options and select **Empty Activity** when prompted for the **Activity Type**.

For the image needed for this recipe, we downloaded a picture from www.pixabay.com to include in the project source files, but you can use any image.

How to do it...

Once you have your image ready, follow these steps:

1. Copy your image to the res/drawable folder and name it image.jpg (if not a JPEG image, keep the original file extension).

2. Now, open `activity_main.xml` and replace the existing XML with the following:

```xml
<?xml version="1.0" encoding="utf-8"?>
<FrameLayout
xmlns:android="http://schemas.android.com/apk/res/android"
    android:id="@+id/frameLayout"
    android:layout_width="match_parent"
    android:layout_height="match_parent">
    <LinearLayout
        android:layout_width="match_parent"
        android:layout_height="wrap_content"
        android:orientation="vertical"
        android:padding="16dp">
        <android.support.v7.widget.AppCompatImageButton
            android:id="@+id/imageViewThumbnail"
            android:layout_width="wrap_content"
            android:layout_height="wrap_content"
            android:scaleType="centerCrop"
            android:background="@android:color/transparent"/>
    </LinearLayout>
    <android.support.v7.widget.AppCompatImageView
        android:id="@+id/imageViewExpanded"
        android:layout_width="match_parent"
        android:layout_height="match_parent"
        android:visibility="invisible" />
</FrameLayout>
```

3. Now, open `MainActivity.java` and declare the following global variables:

```java
private Animator mCurrentAnimator;
private AppCompatImageView mImageViewExpanded;
```

4. Add the `loadSampledResource()` method we created in the *Scaling down large images to avoid Out of Memory exceptions* recipe to scale the image:

```java
private Bitmap loadSampledResource(int imageID, int targetHeight,
int targetWidth) {
    final BitmapFactory.Options options = new
BitmapFactory.Options();
    options.inJustDecodeBounds = true;
    BitmapFactory.decodeResource(getResources(), imageID, options);
    final int originalHeight = options.outHeight;
    final int originalWidth = options.outWidth;
    int inSampleSize = 1;
    while ((originalHeight / (inSampleSize *2)) > targetHeight
            && (originalWidth / (inSampleSize *2))
            > targetWidth) {
```

```
            inSampleSize *= 2;
        }
    options.inSampleSize =inSampleSize;
    options.inJustDecodeBounds = false;
    return (BitmapFactory.decodeResource(getResources(), imageID,
options));
    }
```

5. Add the following code to the `onCreate()` method:

```
final AppCompatImageButton imageViewThumbnail =
findViewById(R.id.imageViewThumbnail);
imageViewThumbnail.setImageBitmap(loadSampledResource(R.drawable.im
age, 100, 100));
imageViewThumbnail.setOnClickListener(new View.OnClickListener() {
    @Override
    public void onClick(View view) {
        zoomFromThumbnail(imageViewThumbnail);
    }
});
mImageViewExpanded = findViewById(R.id.imageViewExpanded);
mImageViewExpanded.setOnClickListener(new View.OnClickListener() {
    @Override
    public void onClick(View v) {
        mImageViewExpanded.setVisibility(View.GONE);
        mImageViewExpanded.setImageBitmap(null);
        imageViewThumbnail.setVisibility(View.VISIBLE);
    }
});
```

6. Add the following `zoomFromThumbnail()` method, which handles the actual animation and is explained later:

```
private void zoomFromThumbnail(final AppCompatImageButton
imageViewThumb) {
    if (mCurrentAnimator != null) {
        mCurrentAnimator.cancel();
    }

    final Rect startBounds = new Rect();
    final Rect finalBounds = new Rect();
    final Point globalOffset = new Point();

    imageViewThumb.getGlobalVisibleRect(startBounds);
findViewById(R.id.frameLayout).getGlobalVisibleRect(finalBounds,
globalOffset);
    mImageViewExpanded.setImageBitmap(
            loadSampledResource(R.drawable.image,
```

```
finalBounds.height(), finalBounds.width()));

    startBounds.offset(-globalOffset.x, -globalOffset.y);
    finalBounds.offset(-globalOffset.x, -globalOffset.y);

    float startScale;
    if ((float) finalBounds.width() / finalBounds.height() >
            (float) startBounds.width() / startBounds.height()) {
        startScale = (float) startBounds.height() /
finalBounds.height();
        float startWidth = startScale * finalBounds.width();
        float deltaWidth = (startWidth - startBounds.width()) / 2;
        startBounds.left -= deltaWidth;
        startBounds.right += deltaWidth;
    } else {
        startScale = (float) startBounds.width() /
finalBounds.width();
        float startHeight = startScale * finalBounds.height();
        float deltaHeight = (startHeight - startBounds.height()) /
2;
        startBounds.top -= deltaHeight;
        startBounds.bottom += deltaHeight;
    }

    imageViewThumb.setVisibility(View.GONE);
    mImageViewExpanded.setVisibility(View.VISIBLE);
    mImageViewExpanded.setPivotX(0f);
    mImageViewExpanded.setPivotY(0f);

    AnimatorSet animatorSet = new AnimatorSet();
    animatorSet.play(ObjectAnimator.ofFloat(mImageViewExpanded,
View.X,
            startBounds.left, finalBounds.left))
            .with(ObjectAnimator.ofFloat(mImageViewExpanded,
View.Y,
                    startBounds.top, finalBounds.top))
            .with(ObjectAnimator.ofFloat(mImageViewExpanded,
View.SCALE_X, startScale, 1f))
            .with(ObjectAnimator.ofFloat(mImageViewExpanded,
View.SCALE_Y, startScale, 1f));
    animatorSet.setDuration(1000);
    animatorSet.setInterpolator(new DecelerateInterpolator());
    animatorSet.addListener(new AnimatorListenerAdapter() {
        @Override
        public void onAnimationEnd(Animator animation) {
            mCurrentAnimator = null;
        }
```

```
            @Override
            public void onAnimationCancel(Animator animation) {
                mCurrentAnimator = null;
            }
        });
        animatorSet.start();
        mCurrentAnimator = animatorSet;
    }
```

7. Run the application on a device or emulator.

How it works...

First, take a look at the layout file we used. There are two parts: the `LinearLayout` with the `ImageView` thumbnail, and the expanded `ImageView`. We control the visibility of both views as the images are clicked. We set the starting thumbnail image using the same `loadSampledResource()` as discussed in the *Scaling down large images to avoid Out of Memory exceptions* recipe.

However, `zoomFromThumbnail()` is where the real work is being done for this demonstration. There's a lot of code, which breaks down as follows.

First, we store the current animation in `mCurrentAnimator`, so we can cancel if the animation is currently running.

Next, we get the starting position of the image using the `getGlobalVisibleRect()` method. This returns the screen position of the view. When we get the visible bounds of expanded `ImageView`, we also get `GlobalOffset` of the view to offset the coordinates from app coordinates to screen coordinates.

With the starting bounds set, the next step is to calculate the ending bounds. We want to keep the same aspect ratio for the final image to prevent it from being skewed. We need to calculate how the bounds need to be adjusted to keep the aspect ratio within the expanded `ImageView`. The screenshot shown in the introduction shows how this image was sized, but this will vary by image and device.

With the starting and ending bounds calculated, we can now create the animation. Actually, four animations, in this case, one animation for each point of the rectangle, as shown in this code:

```
animatorSet.play(ObjectAnimator.ofFloat(mImageViewExpanded, View.X,
        startBounds.left, finalBounds.left))
        .with(ObjectAnimator.ofFloat(mImageViewExpanded, View.Y,
```

```
                        startBounds.top, finalBounds.top))
            .with(ObjectAnimator.ofFloat(mImageViewExpanded, View.SCALE_X,
    startScale, 1f))
            .with(ObjectAnimator.ofFloat(mImageViewExpanded, View.SCALE_Y,
    startScale, 1f));
```

These two lines of code control the animation timing:

```
animatorSet.setDuration(1000);
animatorSet.setInterpolator(new AccelerateInterpolator());
```

The `setDuration()` method tells the animator object how long it should take to animate the translations set previously. However, `setInterpolator()` governs how the translation is made. (The Interpolator was mentioned in the *Introduction*, and a link is provided in the *See also* section of this recipe.) After starting the animation with the `start()` method, we save the current animation to the `mCurrentAnimator` variable, so the animation can be canceled, if needed. We create an `AnimatorListenerAdapter` to respond to the animation events and clear the `mCurrentAnimator` variable upon completion.

There's more...

When the user presses the expanded image, the application just hides the expanded `ImageView` and sets the thumbnail as `visible`. We could create a reverse zoom animation in the `mImageViewExpanded` click event using the expanded bounds as the starting point, then returning to the thumbnail bounds. (It would probably be easier to create the `mImageViewExpanded` event in `zoomFromThumbnail()` to avoid having to duplicate calculating the start and stop bounds again.)

Getting the default animation duration

Our code used 1,000 milliseconds when setting the duration with `setDuration()`. We purposely used a long duration to make it easier to view the animation. We can get the default Android animation duration using the following code:

```
getResources().getInteger(android.R.integer.config_shortAnimTime)
```

See also

- See the first recipe, *Scaling down large images to avoid Out of Memory exceptions*, for a detailed explanation of the `loadSampledResource()` method
- Refer to the **Interpolator Developer Document** at `http://developer.android.com/reference/android/view/animation/Interpolator.html`

Displaying animated image (GIF/WebP) with the new ImageDecoder library

Android P (API 28) introduces a new library called ImageDecoder, which will be deprecating the BitmapFactory class. This new image library promises to make it easier to work with not just bitmaps, but several other file formats not supported in the old BitmapFactory class, such as GIF and WebP animated images.

At the time of writing, it is only available on devices running Android P (or later) and is not available in the support library, but according to this issue on the Google issue tracker, there are plans to add ImageDecoder to the support library: `https://issuetracker.google.com/issues/78041382`.

When, or if, that happens, the previous examples will be updated to use this new library instead. For now, we'll take a look at new functionality, and that is native support for displaying GIF images.

Getting ready

Create a new project in Android Studio and call it `AnimatedImage`. In the Target Android Devices dialog, make sure to select API 28 (or greater) for the **Phone & Tablet** option. Select **Empty Activity** when prompted for the **Activity Type**. In the **Configure Activity** dialog (shown next), deselect the **Backwards Compatibility** option since this feature is not yet available in the support library:

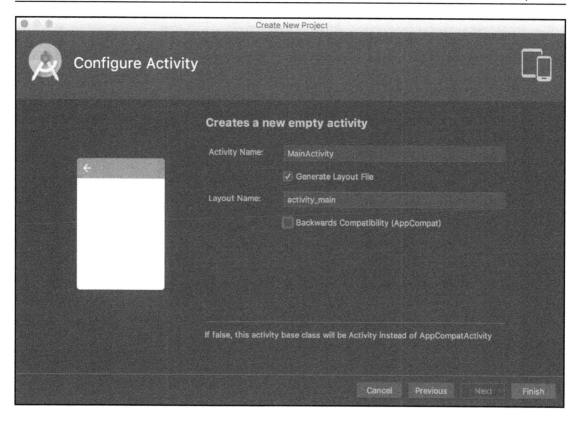

We'll also need a GIF image. We turned to Giphy.com for a royalty-free image, which you can see in the downloadable project files.

How to do it...

Once you have your GIF image, follow these steps:

1. Copy your image to the res/drawable folder. Our file is named giphy.gif but you can use your own filename instead.

2. Open activity_main.xml and replace the existing TextView with the following ImageView:

```
<ImageView
    android:id="@+id/imageView"
    android:layout_width="wrap_content"
    android:layout_height="wrap_content"
    app:layout_constraintBottom_toBottomOf="parent"
```

```
app:layout_constraintLeft_toLeftOf="parent"
app:layout_constraintRight_toRightOf="parent"
app:layout_constraintTop_toTopOf="parent" />
```

3. Open `MainActivity.java` and add the following line of code to the existing `onCreate()` method:

```
loadGif();
```

4. Finally, add the loadGif method as follows:

```
private void loadGif() {
    try {
        ImageDecoder.Source source =
ImageDecoder.createSource(getResources(),
                R.drawable.giphy);
        Drawable decodedAnimation =
ImageDecoder.decodeDrawable(source);

        ImageView imageView = findViewById(R.id.imageView);
        imageView.setImageDrawable(decodedAnimation);

        if (decodedAnimation instanceof AnimatedImageDrawable) {
            ((AnimatedImageDrawable) decodedAnimation).start();
        }
    } catch (IOException e) {
        e.printStackTrace();
    }
}
```

5. Run your app on a device or emulator running at least Android P.

If you do not see the animated image when running this code, try disabling hardware acceleration in the Android Manifest. Add the following to either the `<application>` node or the `<activity>` node: `android:hardwareAccelerated="false"`.

How it works...

As you can see in the preceding code, the `ImageDecoder` library has made it very simple to display a GIF. First, you have to define your source image. Currently, the `createSource()` method can read an image from the following sources:

- Resources (drawable) folder
- Assets folder

- ContentResolver (URI)
- Byte buffer
- File

(This could change in the final Android P release.)

In our code, we copied the image to the drawable folder. If we had copied it to the assets folder instead, the code would have been as follows:

```
ImageDecoder.Source source = ImageDecoder.createSource(getAssets(),
"giphy.gif");
```

With the image source defined, we just have to call `decodeDrawable()` to decode the image and set the drawable for the ImageView. Once the drawable is set, the final key to the animated image is to call the `start()` method. If the decoded image is of type `AnimatedDrawable` (which it will be if we loaded a valid GIF), we then call the start method to activate the animation.

See also

- The `ImageDecoder` documentation: `https://developer.android.com/reference/android/graphics/ImageDecoder`
- See the next recipe for more examples of using the ImageDecoder library

Creating a circle image with the new ImageDecoder

As mentioned in the previous recipe, the ImageDecoder library is a new library introduced in Android P and promises many new and exciting features not available before with the BitmapFactory class. One of those features is the ability to apply effects to the image with a post processor. A post processor is a new helper class allowing you to add custom processing (or manipulation) to an image after it is loaded. Custom processing might include adding a tint to the image, drawing (such as stamps) on top of the image, adding a frame, or in our example making the image round.

In our example, we start with a rectangle image (downloaded from Pixabay.com, which you can see here: `https://pixabay.com/en/wallpaper-background-eclipse-1492818/`.) We then apply a post processor to create a rounded image, as you can see in this screenshot:

This is another exciting new feature available in the ImageDecoder library because until now, developers usually turned to third-party libraries. Although many of these libraries are still going to be very useful, especially for handling image loading in lists; for something as simple as creating a rounded image, say, for a profile picture, there is now an easy native solution.

Getting ready

Create a new project in Android Studio and call it `CircleImage`. In the Target Android Devices dialog, make sure to select API 28 (or greater) for the **Phone & Tablet** option. Select **Empty Activity** when prompted for the **Activity Type**. In the **Configure Activity** dialog (shown next), deselect the **Backwards Compatibility** option since this feature is not yet available in the support library.

How to do it...

Once you have your GIF image, follow these steps:

1. Copy an image to the `res/drawable` folder. (This example uses an image named stars.jpg. Use your image name instead.) If it's smaller than the size of our circle created here, you'll need to use a smaller radius.

2. Open `activity_main.xml` and replace the existing `TextView` with the following `ImageView`:

```xml
<ImageView
    android:id="@+id/imageView"
    android:layout_width="wrap_content"
    android:layout_height="wrap_content"
    app:layout_constraintBottom_toBottomOf="parent"
    app:layout_constraintLeft_toLeftOf="parent"
    app:layout_constraintRight_toRightOf="parent"
    app:layout_constraintTop_toTopOf="parent" />
```

3. Open `MainActivity.java` and add the following code to the class declaration:

```java
PostProcessor mCirclePostProcessor = new PostProcessor() {
    @Override
    public int onPostProcess(Canvas canvas) {
        Path path = new Path();
        path.setFillType(Path.FillType.INVERSE_EVEN_ODD);
        int width = canvas.getWidth();
        int height = canvas.getHeight();
        path.addCircle(width/2,height/2,600, Path.Direction.CW);
        Paint paint = new Paint();
        paint.setAntiAlias(true);
        paint.setColor(Color.TRANSPARENT);
        paint.setXfermode(new
PorterDuffXfermode(PorterDuff.Mode.SRC));
        canvas.drawPath(path, paint);
```

```
            return PixelFormat.TRANSLUCENT;
    }
};
```

4. Add the following line of code to the existing `onCreate()` method:

```
loadImage();
```

5. The last code to add is the following `loadImage()` method:

```
private void loadImage() {
    ImageDecoder.Source source =
ImageDecoder.createSource(getResources(),
            R.drawable.stars);

    ImageDecoder.OnHeaderDecodedListener listener =
            new ImageDecoder.OnHeaderDecodedListener() {
        public void onHeaderDecoded(ImageDecoder decoder,
ImageDecoder.ImageInfo info,
                                    ImageDecoder.Source source) {
            decoder.setPostProcessor(mCirclePostProcessor);
        }
    };
    try {
        Drawable drawable = ImageDecoder.decodeDrawable(source,
listener);
        ImageView imageView = findViewById(R.id.imageView);
        imageView.setImageDrawable(drawable);
    } catch (IOException e) {
        e.printStackTrace();
    }
}
```

6. Run the app on a device or emulator running at least Android P.

How it works...

We start off with the same XML layout as the previous recipe. And if we omitted adding the post processor, we'd get a standard rectangle image. To see for yourself, comment the following line of code in `OnHeaderDecodedListener`:

```
decoder.setPostProcessor(mCirclePostProcessor);
```

The core of the work being done here is in `PostProcessor` created in step 3. Although there are a several lines of code, what's being done is pretty simple. It just creates a circle (using the dimensions we specified) and clears everything out (by setting the color to `TRANSPARENT`) not in our circle.

The key is setting the post processor, which can only be done in the `onHeaderDecoded()` callback. This is why we first create the `OnHeaderDecodedListener` so we can get a reference to the decoder.

There's more...

What if you wanted rounded corners instead of a circle image? With one simple change in the `Path` created for the post processor, you could have that effect instead. Instead of the `addCircle()` call when creating the `Path`, use this line of code instead:

```
path.addRoundRect(0, 0, width, height, 250, 250, Path.Direction.CW);
```

The value of 250 used creates a very rounded corner, so experiment to get the amount of rounding desired. Take a look at the reference links in *See also* for more information on the post processor and `Path`.

See also

- The `PostProcessor` reference documentation: `https://developer.android.com/reference/android/graphics/PostProcessor`
- The `Path` reference documentation: `https://developer.android.com/reference/android/graphics/Path`

A First Look at OpenGL ES

11

In this chapter, we will cover the following topics:

- Setting up the OpenGL ES environment
- Drawing shapes on GLSurfaceView
- Applying the projection and camera view while drawing
- Moving the triangle with rotation
- Rotating the triangle with user input

Introduction

As we saw in the previous chapter, Android offers many tools for handling graphics and animations. Although the canvas and drawable objects are designed for custom drawing, when you need high-performance graphics, especially 3D gaming graphics, Android also supports OpenGL ES. **Open Graphics Library for Embedded Systems** (**OpenGL ES**), is targeted at embedded systems. (Embedded systems include consoles and phones.)

This chapter is meant to serve as an introduction to using OpenGL ES on Android. As usual, we'll provide the steps and explain how things work, but we aren't going to be digging into the math or technical details of OpenGL. If you are already familiar with OpenGL ES from other platforms, such as iOS, this chapter should get you up and running quickly. If you are new to OpenGL, hopefully these recipes will help you decide whether this is an area you want to pursue.

Android supports the following versions of OpenGL:

- **OpenGL ES 1.0**: Android 1.0
- **OpenGL ES 2.0**: Introduced in Android 2.2 (API 8)
- **OpenGL ES 3.0**: Introduced in Android 4.3 (API 18)
- **OpenGL ES 3.1**: Introduced in Android 5.0 (API 21)

The recipes in this chapter are introductory and target OpenGL ES 2.0 and higher. OpenGL ES 2.0 is available for nearly all devices currently available. Unlike OpenGL ES 2.0 and lower, OpenGL 3.0 and higher require driver implementation from the hardware manufacturer. This means that, even if your application is running on Android 5.0, OpenGL 3.0 and higher may not be available. Therefore, it's a good programming practice to check the available OpenGL versions at runtime. Alternatively, if your application requires 3.0 and higher features, you can add a <uses-feature/> element to your Android manifest. (We'll discuss this in the first recipe that follows.)

Unlike the other chapters in this book, this chapter is written more as a tutorial, with each recipe building on lessons learned from the previous recipe. The *Getting ready* section of each recipe will clarify the prerequisites.

Setting up the OpenGL ES environment

Our first recipe will start by showing the steps to set up an activity to use an OpenGL GLSurfaceView. Similar to the canvas, the GLSurfaceView is where you will do your OpenGL drawing. As this is the starting point, the other recipes will refer to this recipe as the base step when they need a GLSurfaceView created.

Getting ready

Create a new project in Android Studio and call it SetupOpenGL. Use the default **Phone & Tablet** options and select **Empty Activity** when prompted for **Activity Type**.

How to do it...

We'll start by indicating the application's use of OpenGL in the Android Manifest, and then we'll add the OpenGL classes to the activity. Here are the steps:

1. Open the Android Manifest and add the following XML:

    ```
    <uses-feature android:glEsVersion="0x00020000"
    android:required="true" />
    ```

2. Open MainActivity.java and add the following global variables:

    ```
    private GLSurfaceView mGLSurfaceView;
    ```

3. Add the following inner class to the MainActivity class:

```
class GLRenderer implements GLSurfaceView.Renderer {
    public void onSurfaceCreated(GL10 unused, EGLConfig config) {
        GLES20.glClearColor(0.5f, 0.5f, 0.5f, 1.0f);
    }
    public void onDrawFrame(GL10 unused) {
        GLES20.glClear(GLES20.GL_COLOR_BUFFER_BIT);
    }
    public void onSurfaceChanged(GL10 unused, int width, int
height) {
        GLES20.glViewport(0, 0, width, height);
    }
}
```

4. Add another inner class to the MainActivity class:

```
class CustomGLSurfaceView extends GLSurfaceView {

    private final GLRenderer mGLRenderer;

    public CustomGLSurfaceView(Context context){
        super(context);
        setEGLContextClientVersion(2);
        mGLRenderer = new GLRenderer();
        setRenderer(mGLRenderer);
    }
}
```

5. Modify the existing onCreate() method as follows:

```
@Override
protected void onCreate(Bundle savedInstanceState) {
    super.onCreate(savedInstanceState);
    mGLSurfaceView = new CustomGLSurfaceView(this);
    setContentView(mGLSurfaceView);
}
```

6. You're ready to run the application on a device or emulator.

How it works...

If you ran the preceding application, you saw the activity created and the background set to gray. Since these are the basic steps for setting up OpenGL, you'll be reusing this code for the other recipes in this chapter as well. The following explains the process detail.

Declaring OpenGL in the Android Manifest

We start by declaring our requirement to use OpenGL ES version 2.0 in the Android Manifest with the following line:

```
<uses-feature android:glEsVersion="0x00020000" android:required="true" />
```

If we were using version 3.0, we would use this:

```
<uses-feature android:glEsVersion="0x00030000" android:required="true" />
```

For version 3.1, use this:

```
<uses-feature android:glEsVersion="0x00030001" android:required="true" />
```

Extending the GLSurfaceView class

Create a custom OpenGL `SurfaceView` class by extending `GLSurfaceView`, as we do in this code:

```
class CustomGLSurfaceView extends GLSurfaceView {

    private final GLRenderer mGLRenderer;

    public CustomGLSurfaceView(Context context){
        super(context);
        setEGLContextClientVersion(2);
        mGLRenderer = new GLRenderer();
        setRenderer(mGLRenderer);
    }
}
```

Here, we instantiate an OpenGL rendered class and pass it to the `GLSurfaceView` class with the `setRenderer()` method. The OpenGL `SurfaceView` provides a surface for our OpenGL drawing, similar to the `Canvas` and `SurfaceView` objects. The actual drawing is done in the `Renderer`, which we'll create next.

Creating an OpenGL rendered class

The last step is to create the `GLSurfaceView.Renderer` class and implement the following three callbacks:

- `onSurfaceCreated()`
- `onDrawFrame()`

- onSurfaceChanged()

Following is the code:

```
class GLRenderer implements GLSurfaceView.Renderer {
    public void onSurfaceCreated(GL10 unused, EGLConfig config) {
        GLES20.glClearColor(0.5f, 0.5f, 0.5f, 1.0f);
    }
    public void onDrawFrame(GL10 unused) {
        GLES20.glClear(GLES20.GL_COLOR_BUFFER_BIT);
    }
    public void onSurfaceChanged(GL10 unused, int width, int height) {
        GLES20.glViewport(0, 0, width, height);
    }
}
```

Right now, all we're doing with this class is setting up the callbacks and clearing the screen using the color we specify with `glClearColor()` (gray in this case).

There's more...

With the OpenGL environment set up, we'll continue to the next recipe where we'll actually draw on the view.

Drawing shapes on GLSurfaceView

The previous recipe set up the activity to use OpenGL. This recipe will continue by showing how to draw on `OpenGLSurfaceView`.

First, we need to define the shape. With OpenGL, it is important to realize that the order in which the vertices of a shape are defined is very important, as they determine the front (face) and back of the shape. It's customary (and the default behavior) to define vertices counterclockwise. (Although this behavior can be changed, it requires additional code and is not standard practice.)

It's also important to understand the OpenGL screen coordinate system, as it differs from the Android canvas. The default coordinate system defines (0, 0, 0) as the center of the screen. The four edge points are as follows:

- **Top left**: (-1.0, 1.0, 0)
- **Top right**: (1.0, 1.0, 0)

- **Bottom left**: (−1.0, −1.0, 0)
- **Bottom right**: (1.0, −1.0, 0)

The Z axis comes straight out of the screen or straight behind.

We're going to create a `Triangle` class since it is the base shape. In OpenGL, you generally use a collection of triangles to create objects. To draw a shape with OpenGL, we need to define the following:

- **Vertex shader**: This is to draw the shape
- **Fragment shader**: This is to color the shape
- **Program**: This is an OpenGL ES object for the preceding shaders

The shaders are defined using **OpenGL Shading Language** (**GLSL**), and then compiled and added to the OpenGL program object.

Following are two screenshots showing the triangle in portrait orientation:

Here is the same image when the orientation is rotated to landscape:

Getting ready

Create a new project in Android Studio and call it `ShapesWithOpenGL`. Use the default **Phone & Tablet** options and select **Empty Activity** when prompted for **Activity Type**.

This recipe uses the OpenGL environment created in the previous recipe, *Setting up the Open GL environment*. Refer to the previous recipe if you have not already completed those steps.

How to do it...

As indicated previously, we'll be using the OpenGL environment created in the previous recipe. The steps that follow will walk you through creating a class for the triangle shape and drawing it on the GLSurfaceView:

1. Create a new Java class called `Triangle`.

2. Add the following global declarations to the `Triangle` class:

```
private final String vertexShaderCode = "attribute vec4 vPosition;"
    +
```

```
                        "void main() {" +
                        "  gl_Position = vPosition;" +
                        "}";

    private final String fragmentShaderCode = "precision mediump
float;" +
                        "uniform vec4 vColor;" +
                        "void main() {" +
                        "  gl_FragColor = vColor;" +
                        "}";

    final int COORDS_PER_VERTEX = 3;
    float triangleCoords[] = {
            0.0f,  0.66f, 0.0f,
            -0.5f, -0.33f, 0.0f,
            0.5f, -0.33f, 0.0f
    };

    float color[] = { 0.63f, 0.76f, 0.22f, 1.0f };

    private final int mProgram;
    private FloatBuffer vertexBuffer;
    private int mPositionHandle;
    private int mColorHandle;
    private final int vertexCount = triangleCoords.length /
COORDS_PER_VERTEX;
    private final int vertexStride = COORDS_PER_VERTEX * 4;
```

3. Add the following `loadShader()` method to the `Triangle` class:

```
    public int loadShader(int type, String shaderCode){
        int shader = GLES20.glCreateShader(type);
        GLES20.glShaderSource(shader, shaderCode);
        GLES20.glCompileShader(shader);
        return shader;
    }
```

4. Add the `Triangle` constructor, as shown here:

```
    public Triangle() {
        int vertexShader = loadShader(
                GLES20.GL_VERTEX_SHADER,
                vertexShaderCode);
        int fragmentShader = loadShader(
                GLES20.GL_FRAGMENT_SHADER,
                fragmentShaderCode);
        mProgram = GLES20.glCreateProgram();
        GLES20.glAttachShader(mProgram, vertexShader);
```

```
GLES20.glAttachShader(mProgram, fragmentShader);
GLES20.glLinkProgram(mProgram);

ByteBuffer bb = ByteBuffer.allocateDirect(
        triangleCoords.length * 4);
bb.order(ByteOrder.nativeOrder());

vertexBuffer = bb.asFloatBuffer();
vertexBuffer.put(triangleCoords);
vertexBuffer.position(0);
}
```

5. Add the `draw()` method as follows:

```
public void draw() {
    GLES20.glUseProgram(mProgram);
    mPositionHandle = GLES20.glGetAttribLocation(mProgram,
"vPosition");
    GLES20.glEnableVertexAttribArray(mPositionHandle);
    GLES20.glVertexAttribPointer(mPositionHandle,
            COORDS_PER_VERTEX,
            GLES20.GL_FLOAT, false,
            vertexStride, vertexBuffer);
    mColorHandle = GLES20.glGetUniformLocation(mProgram,
"vColor");
    GLES20.glUniform4fv(mColorHandle, 1, color, 0);
    GLES20.glDrawArrays(GLES20.GL_TRIANGLES, 0, vertexCount);
    GLES20.glDisableVertexAttribArray(mPositionHandle);
}
```

6. Now, open `MainActivity.java` and add a `Triangle` variable to the
`GLRenderer` class as follows:

```
private Triangle mTriangle;
```

7. Initialize the `Triangle` variable in the `onSurfaceCreated()` callback as
follows:

```
mTriangle = new Triangle();
```

8. In the `onDrawFrame()` callback, call the `Triangle` `draw()` method after glClear
is called:

```
mTriangle.draw();
```

9. You're ready to run the application on a device or emulator.

How it works...

As mentioned in the introduction, to draw with OpenGL we first have to define the shaders, which we do with the following code:

```
private final String vertexShaderCode = "attribute vec4 vPosition;" +
    "void main() {" +
    "  gl_Position = vPosition;" +
    "}";

private final String fragmentShaderCode = "precision mediump float;" +
    "uniform vec4 vColor;" +
    "void main() {" +
    "  gl_FragColor = vColor;" +
    "}";
```

Since this is uncompiled **OpenGL Shading Language (OpenGLSL)**, the next step is to compile and attach it to our OpenGL object, which we do with the following two OpenGL ES methods:

- `glAttachShader()`
- `glLinkProgram()`

After setting up the shaders, we create `ByteBuffer` to store the triangle vertices, which are defined in `triangleCoords`. The `draw()` method is where the actual drawing occurs using the GLES20 library calls, which is called from the `onDrawFrame()` callback.

There's more...

From the screenshots in the introduction, you may have noticed that the triangles in the portrait and landscape do not look identical to each other. As you can see from the code, we make no distinction in terms of orientation when drawing. We'll explain why this is happening and show how to correct this issue in the next recipe.

See also

For more information on the OpenGL Shading Language, refer to the following link: https://www.opengl.org/documentation/glsl/.

Applying the projection and camera view while drawing

As we saw in the previous recipe, when we draw our shape on the screen, the shape is skewed by the screen orientation. The reason for this is because, by default, OpenGL assumes a perfectly square screen. As we mentioned before, the default screen coordinates for the top right are (1, 1, 0) and (-1, -1, 0) for the bottom left.

Since most device screens are not perfectly square, we need to map the display coordinates to match our physical device. In OpenGL, we do this with *projection*. This recipe will show how to use projection to match the GLSurfaceView coordinates with the device coordinates. Along with the projection, we'll also show how to set the Camera View. Following is a screenshot showing the final result:

Getting ready

Create a new project in Android Studio and call it `ProjectionAndCamera`. Use the default **Phone & Tablet** options and select **Empty Activity** when prompted for **Activity Type**.

This recipe builds on the previous recipe, *Drawing shapes on GLSurfaceView*. If you don't already have the previous recipe, start there before starting these steps.

How to do it...

As stated previously, this recipe will build on the previous recipe, so complete those steps before starting. We will be modifying the previous code to add the projection and camera view to the drawing calculations. Here are the steps:

1. Open the `Triangle` class and add the following global declaration to the existing declarations:

   ```
   private int mMVPMatrixHandle;
   ```

2. Add a matrix variable to `vertexShaderCode` and use it in the position calculation. Here is the final result:

   ```
   private final String vertexShaderCode = "attribute vec4 vPosition;"
   +
               "uniform mat4 uMVPMatrix;" +
               "void main() {" +
               "  gl_Position = uMVPMatrix * vPosition;" +
               "}";
   ```

3. Change the `draw()` method to pass in a matrix parameter as follows:

   ```
   public void draw(float[] mvpMatrix) {
   ```

4. To use the transformation matrix, add the following code to the `draw()` method just before the `GLES20.glDrawArrays()` method:

```
mMVPMatrixHandle = GLES20.glGetUniformLocation(mProgram,
"uMVPMatrix");
GLES20.glUniformMatrix4fv(mMVPMatrixHandle, 1, false, mvpMatrix,
0);
```

5. Open `MainActivity.java` and add the following class variables to the `GLRenderer` class:

```
private final float[] mMVPMatrix = new float[16];
private final float[] mProjectionMatrix = new float[16];
private final float[] mViewMatrix = new float[16];
```

6. Modify the `onSurfaceChanged()` callback to calculate the position matrix as follows:

```
public void onSurfaceChanged(GL10 unused, int width, int height) {
    GLES20.glViewport(0, 0, width, height);
    float ratio = (float) width / height;
    Matrix.frustumM(mProjectionMatrix, 0, -ratio, ratio, -1, 1, 3,
7);
}
```

7. Modify the `onDrawFrame()` callback to calculate the Camera View as follows:

```
public void onDrawFrame(GL10 unused) {
    Matrix.setLookAtM(mViewMatrix, 0, 0, 0, -3, 0f, 0f, 0f, 0f,
        1.0f, 0.0f);    Matrix.multiplyMM(mMVPMatrix, 0,
mProjectionMatrix, 0,
        mViewMatrix, 0);
    GLES20.glClear(GLES20.GL_COLOR_BUFFER_BIT);
    mTriangle.draw(mMVPMatrix);
}
```

8. You're ready to run the application on a device or emulator.

How it works...

First, we modify the `vertexShaderCode` to include a matrix variable. We calculate the matrix in the `onSurfaceChanged()` callback using the height and width, which are passed in as parameters. We pass the transformation matrix to the `draw()` method to use it when calculating the position to draw.

Before we call the `draw()` method, we calculate the camera view. These two lines of code calculate the camera view:

```
Matrix.setLookAtM(mViewMatrix, 0, 0, 0, -3, 0f, 0f, 0f, 0f, 1.0f, 0.0f);
Matrix.multiplyMM(mMVPMatrix, 0, mProjectionMatrix, 0, mViewMatrix, 0);
```

Without this code, there would actually be no triangle drawn as the camera perspective would not "see" our vertices. (This goes back to our discussion on how the order of the vertices dictates the front and back of the image.)

When you run the program now, you'll see the output shown in the *Introduction*. Notice that we now have an equilateral triangle (all sides equal), even when the display is rotated.

There's more...

In the next recipe, we will start showing the power of OpenGL by rotating the triangle.

Moving the triangle with rotation

What we've demonstrated so far with OpenGL would probably be easier using the traditional canvas or drawable objects. This recipe will show a bit of the power of OpenGL by rotating the triangle. Not that we can't create movement with the other drawing methods, but how easily can we do this with OpenGL?

This recipe will demonstrate how to rotate the triangle, as the following screenshot shows:

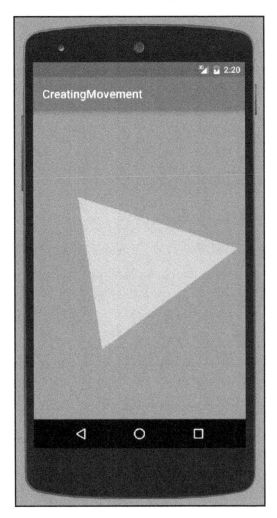

Getting ready

Create a new project in Android Studio and call it CreatingMovement. Use the default **Phone & Tablet** options and select **Empty Activity** when prompted for **Activity Type**.

This recipe builds on the previous recipe, *Applying the projection and camera view while drawing*. Refer to the previous recipe if you have not already completed those steps.

How to do it...

Since we are continuing from the previous recipe, we have very little work to do. Open MainActivity.java and follow these steps:

1. Add a Matrix to the GLRendered class:

   ```
   private float[] mRotationMatrix = new float[16];
   ```

2. In the onDrawFrame() callback, replace the existing mTriangle.draw(mMVPMatrix); statement with the following code:

   ```
   float[] tempMatrix = new float[16];
   long time = SystemClock.uptimeMillis() % 4000L;
   float angle = 0.090f * ((int) time);
   Matrix.setRotateM(mRotationMatrix, 0, angle, 0, 0, -1.0f);
   Matrix.multiplyMM(tempMatrix, 0, mMVPMatrix, 0, mRotationMatrix,
   0);
   mTriangle.draw(tempMatrix);
   ```

3. You're ready to run the application on a device or emulator.

How it works...

We're using the Matrix.setRotateM() method to calculate a new rotation matrix based on the angle we pass in. For this example, we're using the system uptime to calculate an angle. We can use whatever method we want to derive an angle, such as a sensor reading or touch events.

There's more...

Using the system clock provides the added benefit of creating continuous movement, which certainly looks better for demonstration purposes. The next recipe will demonstrate how to use user input to derive an angle for rotating the triangle.

The render mode

OpenGL offers a `setRenderMode()` option to draw only when the view is dirty. This can be enabled by adding the following code to the `CustomGLSurfaceView()` constructor just below the `setRenderer()` call:

```
setRenderMode(GLSurfaceView.RENDERMODE_WHEN_DIRTY);
```

This will cause the display to update just once, then wait until we request an update with `requestRender()`.

Rotating the triangle with user input

The previous example demonstrated rotating the triangle based on the system clock. This created a continuously rotating triangle, depending on the render mode we used. But what if you wanted to respond to the input from the user?

In this recipe, we'll show how to respond to user input by overriding the `onTouchEvent()` callback from `GLSurfaceView`. We'll still rotate the triangle using the `Matrix.setRotateM()` method, but instead of deriving an angle from the system time, we'll calculate an angle based on the touch location.

Here's a screenshot showing this recipe running on a physical device (to highlight the touch, the **Show touches** developer option is enabled):

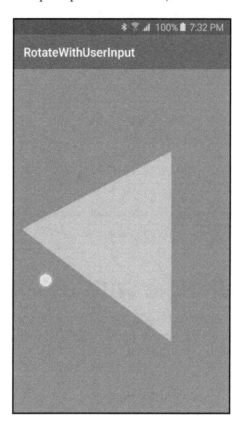

Getting ready

Create a new project in Android Studio and call it RotateWithUserInput. Use the default **Phone & Tablet** options and select **Empty Activity** when prompted for **Activity Type**.

This recipe demonstrates an alternative approach to the previous recipe and therefore will be based on the *Applying the projection and camera view while drawing* (the same starting point as the previous recipe.)

How to do it...

As stated previously, we will continue, not from the previous recipe, but from the *Applying the projection and camera view while drawing* recipe. Open `MainActivity.java` and follow these steps:

1. Add the following global variables to the `MainActivity` class:

```
private float mCenterX=0;
private float mCenterY=0;
```

2. Add the following code to the `GLRendered` class:

```
private float[] mRotationMatrix = new float[16];
public volatile float mAngle;
public void setAngle(float angle) {
    mAngle = angle;
}
```

3. In the same class, modify the `onDrawFrame()` method by replacing the existing `mTriangle.draw(mMVPMatrix);` statement with the following code:

```
float[] tempMatrix = new float[16];
Matrix.setRotateM(mRotationMatrix, 0, mAngle, 0, 0, -1.0f);
Matrix.multiplyMM(tempMatrix, 0, mMVPMatrix, 0, mRotationMatrix,
0);
mTriangle.draw(tempMatrix);
```

4. Add the following code to the `onSurfaceChanged()` callback:

```
mCenterX=width/2;
mCenterY=height/2;
```

5. Add the following code to the `CustomGLSurfaceView` constructor, which is below `setRenderer()`:

```
setRenderMode(GLSurfaceView.RENDERMODE_WHEN_DIRTY);
```

6. Add the following `onTouchEvent()` to the `CustomGLSurfaceView` class:

```
@Override
public boolean onTouchEvent(MotionEvent e) {
    float x = e.getX();
    float y = e.getY();
    switch (e.getAction()) {
        case MotionEvent.ACTION_MOVE:
            double angleRadians = Math.atan2(y-mCenterY,x-
```

```
            mCenterX);
                        mGLRenderer.setAngle((float)Math.toDegrees
                                (-angleRadians));
                        requestRender();
                }
            return true;
        }
```

7. You're ready to run the application on a device or emulator.

How it works...

The obvious difference between this example and the previous recipe lies in how we derive the angle to pass to the `Matrix.setRotateM()` call. We also changed the `GLSurfaceView` render mode using `setRenderMode()` to only draw on request. We made the request using `requestRender()` after calculating a new angle in the `onTouchEvent()` callback.

We also demonstrated the importance of deriving our own `GLSurfaceView` class. Without our `CustomGLSurfaceView` class, we would not have a way to override the `onTouchEvent` callback or any other callbacks from `GLSurfaceView`.

There's more...

This concludes the OpenGL ES recipes, but we've only just touched upon the power of OpenGL. If you're serious about learning OpenGL, see the links in the next section and check out one of the many books written on OpenGL. There are also many frameworks available, both 2D and 3D, for graphics and game development.

See also

- **OpenGL**: The Industry Standard for High-Performance Graphics: https://www.opengl.org/
- **OpenGL ES**: The Standard for Embedded Accelerated 3D Graphics: https://www.khronos.org/opengles/
- **Unreal Engine**: Android Quick Start: https://docs.unrealengine.com/latest/INT/Platforms/Android/GettingStarted/index.html
- **libGDX**: Cross-platform Java game development framework based on OpenGL: https://github.com/libgdx/libgdx

12
Multimedia

In this chapter, we will cover the following topics:

- Playing sound effects with `SoundPool`
- Playing audio with `MediaPlayer`
- Responding to hardware media controls in your app
- Taking a photo with the default camera app
- Taking a picture using the Camera2 API

Introduction

Now that we've explored graphics and animations in the previous chapters, it's time to look at the sound options available in Android. The two most popular options to play sound are the following:

- `SoundPool`: This is for short sound clips
- `MediaPlayer`: This is designed for larger sound files (such as music) and video files

The first two recipes will look at using these libraries. We'll also look at how to use hardware related to sound, such as the volume controls and media playback controls (play, pause, next and previous, often available on headphones).

The rest of the chapter will focus on using the camera, both indirectly through Intents (to pass the camera request to the default camera application) and directly using the camera APIs. We'll show a complete example using the Camera2 APIs released with Android 5.0 Lollipop (API 21).

Playing sound effects with SoundPool

When you need sound effects in your application, SoundPool is usually a good starting point.

SoundPool is interesting in that it allows us to create special effects with our sounds by changing the play rate and by allowing multiple sounds to play simultaneously.

Popular audio file types supported include:

- 3GPP (.3gp)
- 3GPP (.3gp)
- FLAC (.flac)
- MP3 (.mp3)
- MIDI Type 0 and 1 (.mid, .xmf, and .mxmf)
- Ogg (.ogg)
- WAVE (.wav)

See the Supported Media Formats link for a complete list, including network protocols.

As is common in Android, new releases to the OS bring changes to the APIs. SoundPool is no exception and the original SoundPool constructor was deprecated in Lollipop (API 21). Rather than setting our minimum API to 21 or relying on deprecated code (which may stop working at some point), we'll implement both the old and the new approach and check the OS version at runtime to use the appropriate method.

This recipe will demonstrate how to play sound effects using the Android SoundPool library. To demonstrate playing sounds simultaneously, we'll create two buttons, and each will play a sound when pressed.

Getting ready

Create a new project in Android Studio and call it SoundPool. Use the default **Phone & Tablet** options, and select **Empty Activity** when prompted for **Activity Type**.

To demonstrate playing sounds simultaneously, we need at least two audio files in the project. We went to SoundBible.com (`http://soundbible.com/royalty-free-sounds-5.html`) and found two royalty-free, public-domain sounds to include in the downloaded project files.

The first sound is a longer playing sound: `http://soundbible.com/2032-Water.html`

The second sound is shorter: `http://soundbible.com/1615-Metal-Drop.html`

How to do it...

As explained before, we'll need two audio files to include in the project. Once you have your sound files ready, follow these steps:

1. Create a new raw folder (**File | New | Android resource directory**) and choose **raw** in the **Resource** type drop-down.
2. Copy your sound files to `res/raw` as `sound_1` and `sound_2`. (Keep their original extensions.)
3. Open `activity_main.xml` and replace the existing `TextView` with the following buttons:

```
<Button
    android:id="@+id/button1"
    android:layout_width="wrap_content"
    android:layout_height="wrap_content"
    android:text="Button"
    android:onClick="playSound1"/>
<Button
    android:id="@+id/button2"
    android:layout_width="wrap_content"
    android:layout_height="wrap_content"
    android:text="Button"
    android:onClick="playSound2"
    app:layout_constraintTop_toBottomOf="@+id/button1"/>
```

4. Now, open `ActivityMain.java` and add the following global variables:

```
HashMap<Integer, Integer> mHashMap= null;
SoundPool mSoundPool;
```

5. Modify the existing onCreate() method as follows:

```
final Button button1 = findViewById(R.id.button1);
button1.setEnabled(false);
final Button button2 = findViewById(R.id.button2);
button2.setEnabled(false);

if (Build.VERSION.SDK_INT >= Build.VERSION_CODES.LOLLIPOP) {
    createSoundPoolNew();
} else {
    createSoundPoolOld();
}
mSoundPool.setOnLoadCompleteListener(new
SoundPool.OnLoadCompleteListener() {
    @Override
    public void onLoadComplete(SoundPool soundPool, int sampleId,
int status) {
        button1.setEnabled(true);
        button2.setEnabled(true);
    }
});
mHashMap = new HashMap<>();
mHashMap.put(1, mSoundPool.load(this, R.raw.sound_1, 1));
mHashMap.put(2, mSoundPool.load(this, R.raw.sound_2, 1));
```

6. Add the createSoundPoolNew() method:

```
@TargetApi(Build.VERSION_CODES.LOLLIPOP)
private void createSoundPoolNew() {
    AudioAttributes audioAttributes = new AudioAttributes.Builder()
            .setUsage(AudioAttributes.USAGE_MEDIA)
.setContentType(AudioAttributes.CONTENT_TYPE_SONIFICATION)
            .build();
    mSoundPool = new SoundPool.Builder()
            .setAudioAttributes(audioAttributes)
            .setMaxStreams(2)
            .build();
}
```

7. Add the createSoundPoolOld() method:

```
@SuppressWarnings("deprecation")
private void createSoundPoolOld(){
    mSoundPool = new SoundPool(2, AudioManager.STREAM_MUSIC, 0);
}
```

8. Add the button `onClick()` methods:

```
public void playSound1(View view){
    mSoundPool.play(mHashMap.get(1), 0.1f, 0.1f, 1, 0, 1.0f);
}
public void playSound2(View view){
    mSoundPool.play(mHashMap.get(2), 0.9f, 0.9f, 1, 1, 1.0f);
}
```

9. Override the `onStop()` callback as follows:

```
@Override
protected void onStop() {
    mSoundPool.release();
    super.onStop();
}
```

10. Run the application on a device or emulator.

How it works...

The first detail to notice is how we construct the object itself. As we mentioned in the introduction, the `SoundPool` constructor was changed in Lollipop (API 21). The old constructor was deprecated in favor of using `SoundPool.Builder()`. With a constantly changing environment such as Android, changes in the API are very common, so it's a good idea to learn how to work with the changes. As you can see, it's not difficult in this case. We just check the current OS version and call the appropriate method. It is worth noting the two method annotations. The first specifies the target API:

`@TargetApi(Build.VERSION_CODES.LOLLIPOP)`

And the second suppresses the deprecation warning:

`@SuppressWarnings("deprecation")`

After creating `SoundPool`, we set a `setOnLoadCompleteListener()` listener. Enabling the buttons is mostly for demonstration purposes to illustrate that `SoundPool` needs to load sound resources before they are available.

The final point to make on using `SoundPool` is the call to `play()`. We need to pass in the `soundID`, which was returned when we loaded the sound using `load()`. `play()` gives us a few options, including sound volume (left and right), loop count, and playback rate. To demonstrate its flexibility, we play the first sound (which is longer) at a lower volume to create more of a background effect with the running water. The second sound plays at a higher volume and we play it twice.

There's more...

If you only need a basic sound effect, such as a click, you can use the `AudioManager` `playSoundEffect()` method. Here's an example:

```
AudioManager audioManager =(AudioManager)
this.getSystemService(Context.AUDIO_SERVICE);
audioManager.playSoundEffect(SoundEffectConstants.CLICK);
```

You can only specify a sound from the `SoundEffectConstants`; you cannot use your own sound files.

See also

- `SoundPool` Developer
  Docs: https://developer.android.com/reference/android/media/SoundPool.html

- `AudioManager` Developer
  Docs: https://developer.android.com/reference/android/media/AudioManager.html

Playing audio with MediaPlayer

MediaPlayer is probably one of the most important classes for adding multimedia capability to your applications. It supports the following media sources:

- Project resources
- Local files
- External resources (such as URLs, including streaming)

MediaPlayer supports the following popular audio files:

- 3GPP (`.3gp`)
- 3GPP (`.3gp`)
- FLAC (`.flac`)
- MP3 (`.mp3`)
- MIDI Type 0 and 1 (`.mid`, `.xmf`, and `.mxmf`)
- Ogg (`.ogg`)
- WAVE (`.wav`)

And it supports these popular file types:

- 3GPP (`.3gp`)
- Matroska (`.mkv`)
- WebM (`.webm`)
- MPEG-4 (`.mp4`, `.m4a`)

See the Supported Media Formats link for a complete list, including network protocols.

This recipe will demonstrate how to set up `MediaPlayer` in your app to play a sound included with your project. (For a complete review of the full capability offered by `MediaPlayer`, see the Developer Docs link at the end of this recipe.)

Getting ready

Create a new project in Android Studio and call it `MediaPlayer`. Use the default **Phone & Tablet** options and select **Empty Activity** when prompted for **Activity Type**.

We will also need a sound for this recipe and will use the same longer playing "water" sound used in the previous recipe:

`http://soundbible.com/2032-Water.html`

How to do it...

As explained previously, we'll need a sound file to include in the project. Once you have your sound file ready, follow these steps:

1. Create a new raw folder (**File** | **New** | **Android resource directory**) and chose **raw** in the **Resource** type dropdown.
2. Copy your sound file to `res/raw` as `sound_1`. (Keep the original extension.)
3. Open `activity_main.xml` and replace the existing `TextView` with the following buttons:

```xml
<Button
    android:id="@+id/buttonPlay"
    android:layout_width="100dp"
    android:layout_height="wrap_content"
    android:text="Play"
    android:onClick="buttonPlay" />
<Button
    android:text="Pause"
    android:layout_width="100dp"
    android:layout_height="wrap_content"
    android:id="@+id/buttonPause"
    android:onClick="buttonPause"
    app:layout_constraintTop_toBottomOf="@+id/buttonPlay"/>
<Button
    android:text="Stop"
    android:layout_width="100dp"
    android:layout_height="wrap_content"
    android:id="@+id/buttonStop"
    android:onClick="buttonStop"
    app:layout_constraintTop_toBottomOf="@+id/buttonPause"/>
```

4. Now, open `ActivityMain.java` and add the following global variable:

```java
MediaPlayer mMediaPlayer;
```

5. Add the buttonPlay() method:

```
public void buttonPlay(View view){
    if (mMediaPlayer==null) {
        mMediaPlayer = MediaPlayer.create(this, R.raw.sound_1);
        mMediaPlayer.setLooping(true);
        mMediaPlayer.start();
    } else  {
        mMediaPlayer.start();
    }
}
```

6. Add the buttonPause() method:

```
public void buttonPause(View view){
    if (mMediaPlayer!=null && mMediaPlayer.isPlaying()) {
        mMediaPlayer.pause();
    }
}
```

7. Add the buttonStop() method:

```
public void buttonStop(View view){
    if (mMediaPlayer!=null) {
        mMediaPlayer.stop();
        mMediaPlayer.release();
        mMediaPlayer = null;
    }
}
```

8. Finally, override the onStop() callback with the following code:

```
@Override
protected void onStop() {
    super.onStop();
    if (mMediaPlayer!=null) {
        mMediaPlayer.release();
        mMediaPlayer = null;
    }
}
```

9. You're ready to run the application on a device or emulator.

How it works...

The code here is pretty straightforward. We create MediaPlayer with our sound and start playing the sound. The buttons will replay, pause, and stop accordingly.

Even this basic example illustrates one very important concept regarding MediaPlayer, and that is the state. If you're making serious use of MediaPlayer, review the link provided later for detailed information.

There's more...

To make our demonstration easier to follow, we use the UI thread for all our operations. For this example, using a short audio file included with the project, we aren't likely to experience any UI delays. In general, it's a good idea to use a background thread when preparing MediaPlayer. To make this common task easier, MediaPlayer already includes an asynchronous prepare method called prepareAsync(). The following code will create an OnPreparedListener() listener and use the prepareAsync() method:

```
mMediaPlayer = new MediaPlayer();
mMediaPlayer.setOnPreparedListener(new MediaPlayer.OnPreparedListener() {
    @Override
    public void onPrepared(MediaPlayer mp) {
        mMediaPlayer.start();
    }
});
try {
    mMediaPlayer.setDataSource(/*URI, URL or path here*/));
} catch (IOException e) {
    e.printStackTrace();
}
mMediaPlayer.prepareAsync();
```

Playing music in the background

Our example is meant to play audio when the application is in the foreground, and will release the MediaPlayer resources in the onStop() callback. What if you are creating a music player and want to play music in the background, even when the user is using another application? In that scenario, you'll want to use MediaPlayer in a service, instead of an activity. You'll use the MediaPlayer library the same way; you'll just need to pass information (such as sound selection) from the UI to your service.

Note that since a service runs in the same UI thread as the activities, you still do not want to perform potentially blocking operations in a service. MediaPlayer does handle background threads to prevent blocking your UI thread; otherwise, you would want to perform threading yourself. (See `Chapter 15`, *Getting Your App Ready for the Play Store* for more information on threading and options.)

Using hardware volume keys to control your app's audio volume

If you want the volume controls to control the volume in your app, use the `setVolumeControlStream()` method to specify your application's audio stream, as follows:

```
setVolumeControlStream(AudioManager.STREAM_MUSIC);
```

See the `AudioManager` link below for other streaming options.

See also

- Supported media formats:
  https://developer.android.com/guide/appendix/media-formats.html
- `MediaPlayer`
  developer docs: http://developer.android.com/reference/android/media/MediaPlayer.html
- `AudioManager`
  developer docs: https://developer.android.com/reference/android/media/AudioManager.html

Responding to hardware media controls in your app

Having your app respond to media controls (like on headphones), such as Play, Pause, Skip, and so on, is a nice touch your users will appreciate. Android makes this possible through the media library. As with the *Playing sound effects with SoundPool* recipe earlier, the Lollipop release changed how this is done. Unlike the `SoundPool` example, this recipe is able to take advantage of another approach, the compatibility library.

This recipe will show you how to set up `MediaSession` to respond to the hardware buttons, which will work on Lollipop and later, as well as previous Lollipop versions using the `MediaSessionCompat` library. (The compatibility library will take care of checking the OS version and using the correct API calls automatically.)

Getting ready

Create a new project in Android Studio and call it `HardwareMediaControls`. Use the default **Phone & Tablet** options and select **Empty Activity** on the **Add an Activity** to **Mobile** dialog.

How to do it...

We'll just be using Toast messages to respond to the hardware events and therefore will not need to make any changes to the activity layout. The first step is to add the V13 support library to the project. Start by opening `build.gradle (Module: app)` and perform the following steps:

1. Add the following library to the dependency section:

   ```
   implementation 'com.android.support:support-v13:28.0.0-rc02'
   ```

2. Next, open `ActivityMain.java` and add the following `mMediaSessionCallback` to the class declaration:

   ```
   MediaSessionCompat.Callback mMediaSessionCallback = new
   MediaSessionCompat.Callback() {
       @Override
       public void onPlay() {
           super.onPlay();
           Toast.makeText(MainActivity.this, "onPlay()",
   Toast.LENGTH_SHORT).show();
       }
       @Override
       public void onPause() {
           super.onPause();
           Toast.makeText(MainActivity.this, "onPause()",
   Toast.LENGTH_SHORT).show();
       }
       @Override
       public void onSkipToNext() {
           super.onSkipToNext();
           Toast.makeText(MainActivity.this, "onSkipToNext()",
   Toast.LENGTH_SHORT).show();
   ```

```
        }
        @Override
        public void onSkipToPrevious() {
            super.onSkipToPrevious();
            Toast.makeText(MainActivity.this, "onSkipToPrevious()",
Toast.LENGTH_SHORT).show();
        }
};
```

3. Add the following code to the existing `onCreate()` callback:

```
MediaSessionCompat mediaSession =
        new MediaSessionCompat(this,
getApplication().getPackageName());
mediaSession.setCallback(mMediaSessionCallback);
mediaSession.setFlags(MediaSessionCompat.FLAG_HANDLES_MEDIA_BUTTONS
);
mediaSession.setActive(true);
PlaybackStateCompat state = new PlaybackStateCompat.Builder()
        .setActions(PlaybackStateCompat.ACTION_PLAY |
                PlaybackStateCompat.ACTION_PLAY_PAUSE |
                PlaybackStateCompat.ACTION_PAUSE |
                PlaybackStateCompat.ACTION_SKIP_TO_NEXT |
PlaybackStateCompat.ACTION_SKIP_TO_PREVIOUS).build();
mediaSession.setPlaybackState(state);
```

4. Run the application on a device or emulator with media controls (such as headphones) to see the Toast messages.

How it works...

There are four steps to setting this up:

1. Create a `MediaSession.Callback` and attach it to `MediaSession`
2. Set the `MediaSession` flags to indicate we want media buttons
3. Set `SessionState` to active
4. Set `PlayBackState` with the actions we're going to handle

Steps 4 and 1 work together as the callback will only get the events set in the `PlayBackState`.

Since we're not actually controlling any playback in this recipe, we just demonstrate how to respond to the hardware events. You'll want to implement actual functionality in `PlayBackState` and include a call to `setState()` after the `setActions()` call.

This is a very nice example of how the changes to the API can make things easier. And since the new `MediaSession` and `PlaybackState` were rolled into the `Compatibility` library, we can take advantage of these new APIs on older versions of the OS.

There's more...

With all the variety of hardware available on the market, how can your app check what is being used?

Checking the hardware type

If you want your app to respond differently based on the current output hardware, you can use `AudioManager` to check. The following is an example:

```
AudioManager audioManager =(AudioManager)
this.getSystemService(Context.AUDIO_SERVICE);
if (audioManager.isBluetoothA2dpOn()) {
    // Adjust output for Bluetooth.
} else if (audioManager.isSpeakerphoneOn()) {
    // Adjust output for Speakerphone.
} else if (audioManager.isWiredHeadsetOn()) {
    //Only checks if a wired headset is plugged in
    //May not be the audio output
} else {
    // Regular speakers?
}
```

See also

- `MediaSession` developer docs:
  https://developer.android.com/reference/android/media/session/MediaSession.html

- `MediaSessionCompat` developer docs:
  https://developer.android.com/reference/android/support/v4/media/session/MediaSessionCompat.html

- `PlaybackState` developer docs:
  https://developer.android.com/reference/android/support/v4/media/session/PlaybackStateCompat.html

- `PlaybackStateCompat` developer docs:
  https://developer.android.com/reference/android/support/v4/media/sessi
  on/PlaybackStateCompat.html

Taking a photo with the default camera app

If your application needs an image from the camera, but is not a camera replacement app, it may be better to allow the default camera app to take the picture. This also respects your user's preferred camera application.

When you take a photo, unless it is specific to your application, it's considered good practice to make the photo publicly available. (This allows it to be included in the user's photo gallery.) This recipe will demonstrate using the default photo application to click a picture, save it to the public folder, and display the image.

Getting ready

Create a new project in Android Studio and call it `UsingTheDefaultCameraApp`. Use the default **Phone & Tablet** options and select **Empty Activity** on the **Add an Activity** to **Mobile** dialog.

How to do it...

We're going to create a layout with an ImageView and button. The button will create an Intent to launch the default Camera app. When the camera app is done, our app will get a callback. We'll check the result and display the picture if available. Start by opening the Android Manifest and follow these steps:

1. Add the following permission:

   ```
   <uses-permission
     android:name="android.permission.READ_EXTERNAL_STORAGE" />
   ```

2. Open `activity_main.xml` and replace the existing TextView with the following views:

   ```
   <android.support.v7.widget.AppCompatImageView
     android:id="@+id/imageView"
     android:layout_width="wrap_content"
     android:layout_height="wrap_content"
     android:src="@mipmap/ic_launcher"
     app:layout_constraintTop_toTopOf="parent"
   ```

```
app:layout_constraintLeft_toLeftOf="parent"
app:layout_constraintRight_toRightOf="parent" />
<android.support.v7.widget.AppCompatButton
android:id="@+id/button"
android:layout_width="wrap_content"
android:layout_height="wrap_content"
android:text="Take Picture"
android:onClick="takePicture"
app:layout_constraintBottom_toBottomOf="parent"
app:layout_constraintLeft_toLeftOf="parent"
app:layout_constraintRight_toRightOf="parent"/>
```

3. Open `MainActivity.java` and add the following global variables to the `MainActivity` class:

```
final int PHOTO_RESULT=1;
private Uri mLastPhotoURI=null;
```

4. Add the following method to create the URI for the photo:

```
private Uri createFileURI() {
    String timeStamp = new SimpleDateFormat("yyyyMMdd_HHmmss")
            .format(System.currentTimeMillis());
    String fileName = "PHOTO_" + timeStamp + ".jpg";
    return Uri.fromFile(new File(Environment
.getExternalStoragePublicDirectory(Environment.DIRECTORY_PICTURES),
fileName));
}
```

5. Add the following method to handle the button click:

```
public void takePicture(View view) {
    Intent takePictureIntent = new
Intent(MediaStore.ACTION_IMAGE_CAPTURE);
    if (takePictureIntent.resolveActivity(getPackageManager()) !=
null) {
        mLastPhotoURI = createFileURI();
        takePictureIntent.putExtra(MediaStore.EXTRA_OUTPUT,
mLastPhotoURI);
        startActivityForResult(takePictureIntent, PHOTO_RESULT);
    }
}
```

6. Add a new method to override `onActivityResult()` as follows:

```
@Override
protected void onActivityResult(int requestCode, int resultCode,
Intent data) {
```

```
        if (requestCode == PHOTO_RESULT && resultCode == RESULT_OK ) {
            AppCompatImageView imageView =
findViewById(R.id.imageView);
imageView.setImageBitmap(BitmapFactory.decodeFile(mLastPhotoURI.get
Path()));
        }
    }
```

7. Add the following code to the end of the existing `onCreate()` method:

```
StrictMode.VmPolicy.Builder builder = new
StrictMode.VmPolicy.Builder();
StrictMode.setVmPolicy(builder.build());

if (ContextCompat.checkSelfPermission(this,
Manifest.permission.READ_EXTERNAL_STORAGE)
        != PackageManager.PERMISSION_GRANTED ) {
    ActivityCompat.requestPermissions(this,
            new String[]
{Manifest.permission.READ_EXTERNAL_STORAGE},0);
    }
```

8. You're ready to run the application on a device or emulator.

How it works...

There are two parts to working with the default camera app. The first is to set up the Intent to launch the app. We create the Intent using `MediaStore.ACTION_IMAGE_CAPTURE` to indicate we want a photo app. We verify a default app exists by checking the results from `resolveActivity()`. As long as it's not null, we know an application is available to handle the Intent. (Otherwise, our app will crash.) We create a filename and add it to the Intent with `putExtra(MediaStore.EXTRA_OUTPUT, mLastPhotoURI)`.

When we get the callback in `onActivityResult()`, we first make sure it's `PHOTO_RESULT` and `RESULT_OK` (the user could have cancelled), then we load the photo in ImageView. You might be wondering what the `StrictMode` calls are for in `onCreate()`. Basically, those lines of code disable an additional security check made by the OS. If we don't disable StrictMode, the app will crash when creating the file URI with a `FileUriExposedException` exception. For a production app, one solution would be to create a FileProvider as we did in the *Accessing External Storage with Scoped Directories* recipe from `Chapter 7`, *Data Storage*. Refer to the *See also* section for other options.

There's more...

If you don't care where the picture is stored, you can call the Intent without using the `MediaStore.EXTRA_OUTPUT` extra. If you don't specify the output file, `onActivityResult()` will include a thumbnail of the image in the data Intent. The following is how you can display the thumbnail:

```
if (data != null) {
    imageView.setImageBitmap((Bitmap) data.getExtras().get("data"));
}
```

Here's the code to load the full resolution image, using the URI returned in the data Intent:

```
if (data != null) {
    try {
        imageView.setImageBitmap(
            MediaStore.Images.Media. getBitmap(getContentResolver(),
            Uri.parse(data.toUri(Intent.URI_ALLOW_UNSAFE))));
    } catch (IOException e) {
        e.printStackTrace();
    }
}
```

Calling the default video app

It's the same process if you want to call the default video capture application. Just change the Intent in step 5, as follows:

```
Intent takeVideoIntent = new Intent(MediaStore.ACTION_VIDEO_CAPTURE);
```

You can get the URI to the video in `onActivityResult()`, as follows:

```
Uri videoUri = intent.getData();
```

See also

- The *Scaling down large images to avoid Out of Memory exceptions* recipe in `Chapter 10`, *Graphics and Animation*
- The *Accessing External Storage with Scoped Directories* recipe in `Chapter 7`, *Data Storage*

Taking a picture using the Camera2 API

The previous recipe demonstrated how to use an Intent to call the default photo application. If you only need a quick photo, the Intent is probably the ideal solution. If not, and you need more control over the camera, this recipe will show you how to use the camera directly with the Camera2 API.

Now that 85% of devices are using Android 5.0 or later, this recipe focuses only on the Camera2 API. (Google has already deprecated the original Camera API.)

Getting ready

Create a new project in Android Studio and call it Camera2API. In the **Target Android Devices** dialog, select the **Phone & Tablet** option and choose **API 21: Android 5.0 (Lollipop)**, or later, for the minimum SDK. Select Empty Activity on the Add an Activity to Mobile dialog.

How to do it...

As you'll see, there's a lot of code for this recipe. Start by opening the Android Manifest and following these steps:

1. Add the following two permissions:

   ```xml
   <uses-permission android:name="android.permission.CAMERA" />
   <uses-permission
   android:name="android.permission.WRITE_EXTERNAL_STORAGE" />
   ```

2. Now, open `activity_main.xml` and replace the existing TextView with the following views:

   ```xml
   <TextureView
       android:id="@+id/textureView"
       android:layout_width="match_parent"
       android:layout_height="match_parent"
       app:layout_constraintTop_toTopOf="parent"
       app:layout_constraintBottom_toTopOf="@+id/button"
       app:layout_constraintLeft_toLeftOf="parent"
       app:layout_constraintRight_toRightOf="parent" />
   <android.support.v7.widget.AppCompatButton
       android:id="@+id/button"
       android:layout_width="wrap_content"
       android:layout_height="wrap_content"
   ```

```
            android:text="Take Picture"
            android:onClick="takePictureClick"
            app:layout_constraintBottom_toBottomOf="parent"
            app:layout_constraintLeft_toLeftOf="parent"
            app:layout_constraintRight_toRightOf="parent"/>
```

3. Now, open `MainActivity.java` and add the following global variables to the `MainActivity` class:

```
    private CameraDevice mCameraDevice = null;
    private CaptureRequest.Builder mCaptureRequestBuilder = null;
    private CameraCaptureSession mCameraCaptureSession  = null;
    private TextureView mTextureView = null;
    private Size mPreviewSize = null;
```

4. Add the following `Comparator` class to the `MainActivity` class:

```
    static class CompareSizesByArea implements Comparator<Size> {
        @Override
        public int compare(Size lhs, Size rhs) {
            return Long.signum((long) lhs.getWidth() * lhs.getHeight()
                    - (long) rhs.getWidth() * rhs.getHeight());
        }
    }
```

5. Add the following `CameraCaptureSession.StateCallback`:

```
    private CameraCaptureSession.StateCallback mPreviewStateCallback =
    new CameraCaptureSession.StateCallback() {
        @Override
        public void onConfigured(CameraCaptureSession session) {
            startPreview(session);
        }
        @Override
        public void onConfigureFailed(CameraCaptureSession session) {}
    };
```

6. Add the following `SurfaceTextureListener`:

```
    private TextureView.SurfaceTextureListener mSurfaceTextureListener
    =
            new TextureView.SurfaceTextureListener() {
                @Override
                public void onSurfaceTextureUpdated(SurfaceTexture
                surface)
                {
                }
                @Override
```

```
            public void onSurfaceTextureSizeChanged(
                    SurfaceTexture surface, int width, int height)
    {

            }
            @Override
            public boolean onSurfaceTextureDestroyed(SurfaceTexture
            surface) {
                return false;
            }
            @Override
            public void onSurfaceTextureAvailable(
                    SurfaceTexture surface, int width, int height)
    {

                openCamera();
            }
        };
```

7. Add `CameraDevice.StateCallback` as follows:

```
    private CameraDevice.StateCallback mStateCallback = new
    CameraDevice.StateCallback() {
        @Override
        public void onOpened(CameraDevice camera) {
            mCameraDevice = camera;
            SurfaceTexture texture = mTextureView.getSurfaceTexture();
            if (texture == null) {
                return;
            }
            texture.setDefaultBufferSize(mPreviewSize.getWidth(),
            mPreviewSize.getHeight());
            Surface surface = new Surface(texture);
            try {
                mCaptureRequestBuilder = mCameraDevice
            .createCaptureRequest(CameraDevice.TEMPLATE_PREVIEW);
            } catch (CameraAccessException e){
                e.printStackTrace();
            }
            mCaptureRequestBuilder.addTarget(surface);
            try {
                mCameraDevice.createCaptureSession(Arrays
                        .asList(surface), mPreviewStateCallback, null);
            } catch (CameraAccessException e) {
                e.printStackTrace();
            }
        }
        @Override
        public void onError(CameraDevice camera, int error) {}
        @Override
```

```
    public void onDisconnected(CameraDevice camera) {}
};
```

8. Add the following `CaptureCallback` class to receive the capture completed event:

```
final CameraCaptureSession.CaptureCallback mCaptureCallback =
        new CameraCaptureSession.CaptureCallback() {
    @Override
    public void onCaptureCompleted(CameraCaptureSession session,
     CaptureRequest request,
     TotalCaptureResult result) {
        super.onCaptureCompleted(session, request, result);
        Toast.makeText(MainActivity.this, "Picture Saved",
        Toast.LENGTH_SHORT).show();
        startPreview(session);
    }
};
```

9. Add the following code to the existing `onCreate()` callback:

```
mTextureView = findViewById(R.id.textureView);
mTextureView.setSurfaceTextureListener(mSurfaceTextureListener);

if(ActivityCompat.checkSelfPermission(this,
Manifest.permission.CAMERA)
        != PackageManager.PERMISSION_GRANTED) {
    ActivityCompat.requestPermissions(this, new
String[]{Manifest.permission.CAMERA}, 1);
}
```

10. Add the following methods to override `onPause()` and `onResume()`:

```
@Override
protected void onPause() {
    super.onPause();
    if (mCameraDevice != null) {
        mCameraDevice.close();
        mCameraDevice = null;
    }
}
@Override
public void onResume() {
    super.onResume();
    if (mTextureView.isAvailable()) {
        openCamera();
    } else {
```

```
            mTextureView.setSurfaceTextureListener(
                mSurfaceTextureListener);
        }
    }
```

11. Add the `openCamera()` method:

```
    private void openCamera() {
        CameraManager manager = (CameraManager)
    getSystemService(CAMERA_SERVICE);
        try{
            String cameraId = manager.getCameraIdList()[0];
            CameraCharacteristics characteristics =
    manager.getCameraCharacteristics(cameraId);
            StreamConfigurationMap map = characteristics
    .get(CameraCharacteristics.SCALER_STREAM_CONFIGURATION_MAP);
            mPreviewSize = map.getOutputSizes(SurfaceTexture.class)
    [0];
            manager.openCamera(cameraId, mStateCallback, null);
        } catch(CameraAccessException e) {
            e.printStackTrace();
        } catch (SecurityException e) {
            e.printStackTrace();
        }
    }
```

12. Add the `startPreview()` method:

```
    private void startPreview(CameraCaptureSession session) {
        mCameraCaptureSession = session;
        mCaptureRequestBuilder.set(CaptureRequest.CONTROL_MODE,
        CameraMetadata.CONTROL_MODE_AUTO);
        HandlerThread backgroundThread = new
        HandlerThread("CameraPreview");
        backgroundThread.start();
        Handler backgroundHandler = new Handler(backgroundThread.
        getLooper());
        try {
            mCameraCaptureSession
    .setRepeatingRequest(mCaptureRequestBuilder.build(),
        null, backgroundHandler);
        } catch (CameraAccessException e) {
            e.printStackTrace();
        }
    }
```

13. Add the `getPictureFile()` method:

```
private File getPictureFile() {
    String timeStamp = new SimpleDateFormat("yyyyMMdd_HHmmss")
            .format(System.currentTimeMillis());
    String fileName = "PHOTO_" + timeStamp + ".jpg";
    return new File(Environment
.getExternalStoragePublicDirectory(Environment.DIRECTORY_PICTURES),
fileName);
}
```

14. Add the following method to save the image file:

```
private void saveImage(ImageReader reader) {
    Image image = null;
    try {
        image = reader.acquireLatestImage();
        ByteBuffer buffer = image.getPlanes()[0].getBuffer();
        byte[] bytes = new byte[buffer.capacity()];
        buffer.get(bytes);
        OutputStream output = new
FileOutputStream(getPictureFile());
        output.write(bytes);
        output.close();
    } catch (FileNotFoundException e) {
        e.printStackTrace();
    } catch (IOException e) {
        e.printStackTrace();
    } finally {
        if (image != null) {
            image.close();
        }
    }
}
```

15. Add the following method to handle the button click:

```
public void takePictureClick(View view) {
    if (null == mCameraDevice) {
        return;
    }
    takePicture();
}
```

16. Add the final code to actually set up the camera and take the picture:

```
private void takePicture() {
    CameraManager manager = (CameraManager)
getSystemService(Context.CAMERA_SERVICE);
    try {
        CameraCharacteristics characteristics = manager
                .getCameraCharacteristics(mCameraDevice.getId());
        StreamConfigurationMap configurationMap = characteristics
        .get(CameraCharacteristics.SCALER_STREAM_CONFIGURATION_MAP);
        if (configurationMap == null) return;
        Size largest =
Collections.max(Arrays.asList(configurationMap
                .getOutputSizes(ImageFormat.JPEG)), new
        CompareSizesByArea());
        ImageReader reader = ImageReader
                .newInstance(largest.getWidth(),
largest.getHeight(),
        ImageFormat.JPEG, 1);
        List<Surface> outputSurfaces = new ArrayList<>(2);
        outputSurfaces.add(reader.getSurface());
        outputSurfaces.add(new
        Surface(mTextureView.getSurfaceTexture()));
        final CaptureRequest.Builder captureBuilder = mCameraDevice
        .createCaptureRequest(CameraDevice.TEMPLATE_STILL_CAPTURE);
        captureBuilder.addTarget(reader.getSurface());
        captureBuilder.set(CaptureRequest.CONTROL_MODE,
        CameraMetadata.CONTROL_MODE_AUTO);
        ImageReader.OnImageAvailableListener readerListener =
                new ImageReader.OnImageAvailableListener() {
            @Override
            public void onImageAvailable(ImageReader reader) {
                saveImage(reader);
            }
        };
        HandlerThread thread = new HandlerThread("CameraPicture");
        thread.start();
        final Handler backgroundHandler = new
        Handler(thread.getLooper());
        reader.setOnImageAvailableListener(readerListener,
        backgroundHandler);
        mCameraDevice.createCaptureSession(outputSurfaces,
                new CameraCaptureSession.StateCallback() {
                    @Override
                    public void onConfigured(CameraCaptureSession
                    session) {
                        try {
                            session.capture(captureBuilder.build(),
```

```
                                    mCaptureCallback,
                    backgroundHandler);
                        } catch (CameraAccessException e) {
                            e.printStackTrace();
                        }
                    }
                    @Override
                    public void
        onConfigureFailed(CameraCaptureSession
                        session) { }
                    }, backgroundHandler);
            } catch (CameraAccessException e) {
                e.printStackTrace();
            }
        }
```

17. Run the application on a device or emulator with a camera.

How it works...

As you can see, there are a lot of steps for this recipe, but at a high level, it's pretty simple:

- Set up the camera preview
- Capture the image

Now, we'll look at each in detail.

Setting up the camera preview

Here's a rundown on how the code sets up the preview:

1. First, we set up the TextureView.SurfaceTextureListener with the setSurfaceTextureListener() method in onCreate()

2. When we get the onSurfaceTextureAvailable() callback, we open the camera

3. We pass our CameraDevice.StateCallback class to the openCamera() method, which eventually calls the onOpened() callback

4. onOpened() gets the surface for the preview by calling getSurfaceTexture() and passes it to the CameraDevice by calling createCaptureSession()

5. Finally, when CameraCaptureSession.StateCallback onConfigured() is called, we start the preview with the setRepeatingRequest() method

Capturing the image

Even though the `takePicture()` method may appear to be procedural, capturing an image also involves several classes and relies on callbacks. Here's a breakdown of how the code works:

1. The process starts when the Take Picture button is clicked.
2. Then the code queries the camera to find the largest available image size
3. Then an ImageReader is created.
4. Next, the code sets up `OnImageAvailableListener`, and saves the image in the `onImageAvailable()` callback.
5. Then it creates `CaptureRequest.Builder` and includes the `ImageReader` surface.
6. Next it creates `CameraCaptureSession.CaptureCallback`, which defines the `onCaptureCompleted()` callback. When the capture is complete, it restarts the preview.
7. Finally, the `createCaptureSession()` method is called, creating a `CameraCaptureSession.StateCallback`. This is where the `capture()` method is called, passing in the `CameraCaptureSession.CaptureCallback` created earlier.

There's more...

We've just created the base code to demonstrate a working Camera application. There are many areas for improvement. First, you should handle the device orientation, for both the preview and when saving the images. (See the following links.) Also, with Android 6.0 (API 23) having over 60% of the market share, your apps should already be using the new permission model. Instead of just checking for an exception as we do in the `openCamera()` method, it would be better to check for the required permission.

See also

- Camera2 API Developer Docs
  `https://developer.android.com/reference/android/hardware/camera2/packa ge-summary.html`
- For examples on detecting the current device orientation, refer to `Chapter 9`, *Using the Touchscreen and Sensors*
- The *The Android 6.0 Runtime Permission Model* recipe in `Chapter 15`, *Getting your app ready for the Play Store*

13
Telephony, Networks, and the Web

In this chapter, we will cover the following topics:

- How to make a phone call
- Monitoring phone call events
- How to send SMS (text) messages
- Receiving SMS messages
- Displaying a web page in your application
- Checking online status and connection type
- Phone number blocking API

Introduction

We'll start this chapter by looking at telephony functionality with *How to make a phone call*. After exploring how to make a call, we'll look at how to monitor a phone call with monitoring phone call events. We'll move on to SMS messaging in the How to send SMS messages section, and then we'll cover receiving SMS messages in the Receiving SMS messages section.

We'll then explore `WebView` for adding browser functionality to your app. At its basic level, `WebView` is a basic HTML viewer. We'll show how you can extend a `WebViewClient` class and modify the settings through `WebSettings` to create full browser functionality, including JavaScript and Zoom features.

The last recipe of this chapter will explore a new API (added in Android 7.0 Nougat) for blocking phone numbers at the OS level.

How to make a phone call

As we've seen in previous recipes, we can call the default applications simply by using an Intent. There are two Intents for phone calls:

- ACTION_DIAL: Uses the default phone application to make the phone call (no permission required)
- CALL_PHONE: Bypasses the UI to directly dial the number (requires permission)

Here's the code to set and call the Intent for using the default Phone app:

```
Intent intent = new Intent(Intent.ACTION_DIAL);
intent.setData(Uri.parse("tel:" + number));
startActivity(intent);
```

Since your application is not doing the dialing and the user must press the Dial button, your app does not need any dialing permissions. The recipe that follows will show you how to place a call directly, bypassing the Dialer app.

Getting ready

Create a new project in Android Studio and call it DialPhone. Use the default **Phone & Tablet** option and select **Empty Activity** when prompted for **Activity Type**.

How to do it...

First, we need to add the appropriate permission to make the call. Then, we need to add a button to call our Dial method. Start by opening the Android Manifest and follow these steps:

1. Add the following permission:

   ```
   <uses-permission android:name="android.permission.CALL_PHONE"/>
   ```

2. Open activity_main.xml and replace the existing TextView with the following button:

   ```
   <Button
       android:id="@+id/button"
       android:layout_width="wrap_content"
       android:layout_height="wrap_content"
       android:text="Dial"
   ```

```
android:onClick="dialPhone"
app:layout_constraintBottom_toBottomOf="parent"
app:layout_constraintLeft_toLeftOf="parent"
app:layout_constraintRight_toRightOf="parent"
app:layout_constraintTop_toTopOf="parent" />
```

3. Add this method, which will check whether your app has been granted the CALL_PHONE permission:

```
private boolean checkPermission(String permission) {
    int permissionCheck = ContextCompat.checkSelfPermission(this,
permission);
    return (permissionCheck == PackageManager.PERMISSION_GRANTED);
}
```

4. Add the code to dial the number:

```
public void dialPhone(View view){
    if (checkPermission(Manifest.permission.CALL_PHONE)) {
        Intent intent = new Intent(Intent.ACTION_CALL);
        intent.setData(Uri.parse("tel:0123456789"));
        startActivity(intent);
    } else {
        ActivityCompat.requestPermissions(this, new String[]
{Manifest.permission.CALL_PHONE},1);
    }
}
```

5. Before running this on your device, be sure to replace 0123456789 with a valid number.

How it works...

As we discussed in the introduction, using the CALL_PHONE Intent requires the appropriate permission. We add the required permission to the manifest in step 1 and use the method in step 3 to verify the permission before actually calling the Intent in step 4. Starting with Android 6.0 Marshmallow (API 23), permissions are no longer granted during installation. Therefore, we check whether the application has permission before attempting to dial.

See also

- Refer to *The Android 6.0 Runtime Permission Model* recipe in `Chapter 15`, *Getting Your App Ready for the Play Store*, for more information on the new runtime permissions

Monitoring phone call events

In the previous recipe, we demonstrated how to make a phone call, both with an Intent to call the default application, as well as by directly dialing the number with no UI.

What if you want to be notified when the calls ends? This is where it gets a bit more complicated, as you'll need to monitor the Telephony events and track the phone state. In this recipe, we'll demonstrate how to create a `PhoneStateListener` to read phone state events.

Getting ready

Create a new project in Android Studio and call it `PhoneStateListener`. Use the default **Phone & Tablet options** and select **Empty Activity** in the **Add an Activity** to **Mobile** dialog.

Although it's not required, you can use the previous recipe to initiate a phone call. Otherwise, use the default dialer and/or watch the events from an incoming call.

How to do it...

We only need a single `TextView` on the layout to display the event information. Open the `activity_main.xml` file and follow these steps:

1. Add or modify the `TextView` as follows:

```
<TextView
    android:id="@+id/textView"
    android:layout_width="wrap_content"
    android:layout_height="wrap_content"
    app:layout_constraintLeft_toLeftOf="parent"
    app:layout_constraintTop_toTopOf="parent" />
```

2. Add the following permission to the Android Manifest:

```
<uses-permission
    android:name="android.permission.READ_PHONE_STATE"/>
```

3. Open `MainActivity.java` and add the following `PhoneStateListener` class to the `MainActivity` class:

```
PhoneStateListener mPhoneStateListener = new PhoneStateListener() {
    @Override
    public void onCallStateChanged(int state, String number) {
        String phoneState = number;
        switch (state) {
            case TelephonyManager.CALL_STATE_IDLE:
                phoneState += "CALL_STATE_IDLE\n";
                break;
            case TelephonyManager.CALL_STATE_RINGING:
                phoneState += "CALL_STATE_RINGING\n";
                break;
            case TelephonyManager.CALL_STATE_OFFHOOK:
                phoneState += "CALL_STATE_OFFHOOK\n";
                break;
        }
        TextView textView = findViewById(R.id.textView);
        textView.append(phoneState);
    }
};
```

4. Modify `onCreate()` to set up the listener:

```
final TelephonyManager telephonyManager =
        (TelephonyManager)
getSystemService(Context.TELEPHONY_SERVICE);
telephonyManager.listen(mPhoneStateListener,
PhoneStateListener.LISTEN_CALL_STATE);
```

5. Run the application on a device and initiate and/or receive phone calls. Upon returning to this app, you'll see the list of events.

How it works...

To demonstrate using the listener, we create the Telephony listener in the `onCreate()` method with this code:

```
final TelephonyManager telephonyManager =
        (TelephonyManager) getSystemService(Context.TELEPHONY_SERVICE);
```

```
telephonyManager.listen(mPhoneStateListener,
PhoneStateListener.LISTEN_CALL_STATE);
```

When a `PhoneState` event occurs, it is sent to our `PhoneStateListener` class.

There's more...

In this recipe, we are monitoring the Call State events, as indicated with this constant: `LISTEN_CALL_STATE`. The other interesting options include the following:

- `LISTEN_CALL_FORWARDING_INDICATOR`
- `LISTEN_DATA_CONNECTION_STATE`
- `LISTEN_SIGNAL_STRENGTHS`

Take a look at the `PhoneStateListener` link in *See also* for a complete list.

When we're done listening for events, call the `listen()` method and pass `LISTEN_NONE`, as shown here:

```
telephonyManager.listen(mPhoneStateListener,PhoneStateListener.LISTEN_NONE)
;
```

See also

- Developer Docs: `PhoneStateListener` at https://developer.android.com/reference/android/telephony/PhoneStateListener.html

How to send SMS (text) messages

Since you're probably already familiar with SMS (or text) messages, we won't spend time explaining what they are or why they are important. (If you're not familiar with SMS or want more information, see the link provided in the See also section of this recipe.) This recipe will demonstrate how to send an SMS message. (The next recipe will demonstrate how to receive notifications of new messages and how to read existing messages.)

Getting ready

Create a new project in Android Studio and call it SendSMS. Use the default **Phone & Tablet** options and select **Empty Activity** in the **Add an Activity** to **Mobile** dialog.

How to do it...

First, we need to add the necessary permissions for sending an SMS. Then, we'll create a layout with phone number and message fields and a Send button. When the Send button is clicked, we'll create and send the SMS. Here are the steps:

1. Open the Android Manifest and add the following permission:

```
<uses-permission android:name="android.permission.SEND_SMS"/>
```

2. Open activity_main.xml and replace the existing layout with the following XML:

```xml
<?xml version="1.0" encoding="utf-8"?>
<RelativeLayout
    xmlns:android="http://schemas.android.com/apk/res/android"
    android:layout_width="match_parent"
    android:layout_height="match_parent" >
    <EditText
        android:id="@+id/editTextNumber"
        android:layout_width="match_parent"
        android:layout_height="wrap_content"
        android:inputType="number"
        android:ems="10"
        android:layout_alignParentTop="true"
        android:layout_centerHorizontal="true"
        android:hint="Number"/>
    <EditText
        android:id="@+id/editTextMsg"
        android:layout_width="match_parent"
        android:layout_height="wrap_content"
        android:layout_below="@+id/editTextNumber"
        android:layout_centerHorizontal="true"
        android:hint="Message"/>
    <Button
        android:id="@+id/buttonSend"
        android:layout_width="wrap_content"
        android:layout_height="wrap_content"
        android:text="Send"
        android:layout_below="@+id/editTextMsg"
```

```
        android:layout_centerHorizontal="true"
        android:onClick="send"/>
</RelativeLayout>
```

3. Open `MainActivity.java` and add the following global variables:

```
final int SEND_SMS_PERMISSION_REQUEST_CODE=1;
Button mButtonSend;
```

4. Add the following code to the existing `onCreate()` callback:

```
mButtonSend = findViewById(R.id.buttonSend);
mButtonSend.setEnabled(false);

if (checkPermission(Manifest.permission.SEND_SMS)) {
    mButtonSend.setEnabled(true);
} else {
    ActivityCompat.requestPermissions(this, new
String[]{Manifest.permission.SEND_SMS},
            SEND_SMS_PERMISSION_REQUEST_CODE);
}
```

5. Add the following method to check the permissions:

```
private boolean checkPermission(String permission) {
    int permissionCheck =
ContextCompat.checkSelfPermission(this,permission);
    return (permissionCheck == PackageManager.PERMISSION_GRANTED);
}
```

6. Override `onRequestPermissionsResult()` to handle the permission request response:

```
@Override
public void onRequestPermissionsResult(int requestCode, String
permissions[], int[] grantResults) {
    switch (requestCode) {
        case SEND_SMS_PERMISSION_REQUEST_CODE: {
            if (grantResults.length > 0
                    && grantResults[0] ==
                    PackageManager.PERMISSION_GRANTED) {
                mButtonSend.setEnabled(true);
            }
            return;
        }
    }
}
```

7. And finally, add the method to actually send the SMS:

```
public void send(View view) {
    String phoneNumber =
((EditText)findViewById(R.id.editTextNumber)).getText().toString();
    String msg =
((EditText)findViewById(R.id.editTextMsg)).getText().toString();

    if (phoneNumber==null || phoneNumber.length()==0 || msg==null
|| msg.length()==0 ) {
        return;
    }

    if (checkPermission(Manifest.permission.SEND_SMS)) {
        SmsManager smsManager = SmsManager.getDefault();
        smsManager.sendTextMessage(phoneNumber, null, msg, null,
null);
    } else {
        Toast.makeText(MainActivity.this, "No Permission",
Toast.LENGTH_SHORT).show();
    }
}
```

8. You're ready to run the application on a device or emulator. (Use the emulator device number when sending to another emulator. The first emulator is 5554; the second is 5556, and it continues incrementing by two for each additional emulator.)

How it works...

The code for sending an SMS is only two lines, as shown here:

```
SmsManager smsManager = SmsManager.getDefault();
smsManager.sendTextMessage(phoneNumber, null, msg, null, null);
```

The sendTextMessage() method does the actual sending. Most of the code for this recipe is for checking and obtaining the required permissions.

There's more...

As simple as it is to send SMS messages, we still have a few more options.

Multipart messages

Although it can vary depending on the carrier, 160 is typically the maximum characters allowed per text message. You could modify the preceding code to check whether the message exceeds 160 characters, and if so, you can call the SMSManager divideMessage() method. The method returns `ArrayList`, which you can send to `sendMultipartTextMessage()`. Here's an example:

```
ArrayList<String> messages=smsManager.divideMessage(msg);
smsManager.sendMultipartTextMessage(phoneNumber, null, messages, null,
null);
```

Note that messages sent with `sendMultipartTextMessage()` may not work correctly when using an emulator, so be sure to test on a real device.

Delivery status notification

If you'd like to be notified of the status of the messages, there are two optional fields you can use. Here's the `sendTextMessage()` method as defined in the SMSManager documentation:

```
sendTextMessage(String destinationAddress, String scAddress, String text,
        PendingIntent sentIntent, PendingIntent deliveryIntent)
```

You can include a pending Intent to be notified of the send status and/or delivery status. Upon receipt of your pending Intent, it will include a result code with either Activity. RESULT_OK, if it sent successfully, or an error code as defined in the SMSManager documentation (see the following links):

- RESULT_ERROR_GENERIC_FAILURE: Generic failure cause
- RESULT_ERROR_NO_SERVICE: Failed because service is currently unavailable
- RESULT_ERROR_NULL_PDU: Failed because no PDU was provided
- RESULT_ERROR_RADIO_OFF: Failed because radio was explicitly turned off

See also

- Short Message Service on Wikipedia at
  `https://en.wikipedia.org/wiki/Short_Message_Service`
- Developer Docs: SMSManager at
  `https://developer.android.com/reference/android/telephony/SmsManager.html`

Receiving SMS messages

This recipe will demonstrate how to set up a broadcast receiver to notify you of new SMS messages. It's useful to note that your app does not need to be running to receive the SMS Intent. Android will start your service to process the SMS.

Getting ready

Create a new project in Android Studio and call it `ReceiveSMS`. Use the default **Phone & Tablet** options and select **Empty Activity** in the **Add an Activity** to **Mobile** dialog.

How to do it...

We won't be using a layout in this demonstration as all the work will be in the Broadcast Receiver. We'll use Toasts to display incoming SMS messages. Open the Android Manifest and follow these steps:

1. Add the following permission:

   ```
   <uses-permission android:name="android.permission.RECEIVE_SMS" />
   ```

2. Add the following declaration for the broadcast receiver to the application element:

   ```
   <receiver android:name=".SMSBroadcastReceiver">
       <intent-filter>
           <action
   android:name="android.provider.Telephony.SMS_RECEIVED"/>
       </intent-filter>
   </receiver>
   ```

3. Open `MainActivity.java` and add the following method:

```
private boolean checkPermission(String permission) {
    int permissionCheck = ContextCompat.checkSelfPermission(this,
permission);
    return (permissionCheck == PackageManager.PERMISSION_GRANTED);
}
```

4. Modify the existing `onCreate()` callback to check the permission:

```
if (!checkPermission(Manifest.permission.RECEIVE_SMS)) {
    ActivityCompat.requestPermissions(this, new
String[]{Manifest.permission.RECEIVE_SMS}, 0);
}
```

5. Add a new Java class to the project, called `SMSBroadcastReceiver`, using the following code:

```
public class SMSBroadcastReceiver extends BroadcastReceiver {
    final String SMS_RECEIVED =
"android.provider.Telephony.SMS_RECEIVED";

    @Override
    public void onReceive(Context context, Intent intent) {
        if (SMS_RECEIVED.equals(intent.getAction())) {
            Bundle bundle = intent.getExtras();
            if (bundle != null) {
                Object[] pdus = (Object[]) bundle.get("pdus");
                String format = bundle.getString("format");
                final SmsMessage[] messages = new
SmsMessage[pdus.length];
                for (int i = 0; i < pdus.length; i++) {
                    if (Build.VERSION.SDK_INT >=
Build.VERSION_CODES.M) {
                        messages[i] =
SmsMessage.createFromPdu((byte[]) pdus[i], format);
                    } else {
                        messages[i] =
SmsMessage.createFromPdu((byte[]) pdus[i]);
                    }
                    Toast.makeText(context,
messages[0].getMessageBody(), Toast.LENGTH_SHORT)
                            .show();
                }
            }
        }
    }
}
```

6. You're ready to run the application on a device or emulator.

How it works...

Just like in the previous recipe on sending SMS messages, we first need to check whether the app has permission. (On pre-Android 6.0 devices, the manifest declaration will automatically provide the permission, but for Marshmallow and later, we'll need to prompt the user as we do here.)

As you can see, the Broadcast receiver receives the notification of new SMS messages. We tell the system we want to receive the new SMS Received Broadcasts using this code in the Android Manifest:

```
<receiver android:name=".SMSBroadcastReceiver">
    <intent-filter>
        <action android:name="android.provider.Telephony.SMS_RECEIVED"/>
    </intent-filter>
</receiver>
```

The notification comes in through the standard `onRecieve()` callback so we check the action using this code:

```
if (SMS_RECEIVED.equals(intent.getAction())) {}
```

This is probably the most complicated line of code in this recipe:

```
messages[i] = SmsMessage.createFromPdu((byte[]) pdus[i]);
```

Basically, it calls the SmsMessage library to create an SMSMessage object from the PDU. (The PDU, short for Protocol Data Unit, is the binary data format for SMS messages.) If you're not familiar with the PDU formation, you don't need to be. The SmsMessage library will take care of it for you and return an SMSMessage object.

 If your app is not receiving SMS broadcast messages, an existing application may be blocking your app. You can try increasing the priority value in intent-filter as shown here, or disabling/uninstalling the other app(s):

```
<intent-filter    android:priority="100">
    <action android:name=
            "android.provider.Telephony.SMS_RECEIVED" />
</intent-filter>
```

There's more...

This recipe demonstrates displaying SMS messages as they are received, but what about reading existing messages?

Reading existing SMS messages

First, to read existing messages, you'll need the following permission:

```
<uses-permission android:name="android.permission.READ_SMS" />
```

Here's an example of getting a cursor using the SMS content provider:

```
Cursor cursor = getContentResolver().query(
        Uri.parse("content://sms/"), null, null, null, null);
while (cursor.moveToNext()) {
    textView.append("From :" + cursor.getString(1) + " : " +
cursor.getString(11)+"\n");
}
```

At the time of writing, the SMS content provider has over 30 columns. Here are the first 12, which are the most useful (remember, the column count starts at zero):

1. _id
2. thread_id
3. address
4. person
5. date
6. protocol
7. read
8. status
9. type
10. reply_path_present
11. subject
12. body

See also

- Developer Docs: SmsManager at
  https://developer.android.com/reference/android/telephony/SmsManager.html
- **Protocol Data Unit (PDU)** at
  https://en.wikipedia.org/wiki/Protocol_data_unit
- Developer Docs: Telephony.Sms.Intents at
  https://developer.android.com/reference/android/provider/Telephony.Sms.Intents.html

Displaying a web page in your application

When you want to show a web page, you have two choices: call the default browser or display the content in your app. If you just want to call the default browser, use an Intent as follows:

```
Uri uri = Uri.parse("https://www.packtpub.com/");
Intent intent = new Intent(Intent.ACTION_VIEW, uri);
startActivity(intent);
```

If you need to display the content in your own application, you can use `WebView`. This recipe will show how to display a web page in your application, as can be seen in this screenshot:

Getting ready

Create a new project in Android Studio and call it `WebView`. Use the default **Phone & Tablet** options and select **Empty Activity** in the **Add an Activity** to **Mobile** dialog.

How to do it...

We're going to create the WebView through code so we won't be modifying the layout. We'll start by opening the Android Manifest and following these steps:

1. Add the following permission:

    ```
    <uses-permission android:name="android.permission.INTERNET"/>
    ```

2. Modify the existing `onCreate()` to include the following code:

```
WebView webview = new WebView(this);
setContentView(webview);
webview.loadUrl("https://www.packtpub.com/");
```

3. You're ready to run the application on a device or emulator.

How it works...

We create a WebView to use as our layout and load our webpage with `loadUrl()`. The preceding code works, but, at this level, it is very basic and only displays the first page. If you click on any links, the default browser will handle the request.

There's more...

What if you want full web browsing functionality so any link the user clicks on still loads in your `WebView`? Create `WebViewClient` as shown in this code:

```
webview.setWebViewClient(new WebViewClient());
```

Controlling page navigation

If you want more control over the page navigation, you can create your own `WebViewClient` class. If you want to only allow links within your own website, override the `shouldOverrideUrlLoading()` callback as shown here:

```
private class mWebViewClient extends WebViewClient {
    @Override
    public boolean shouldOverrideUrlLoading(WebView view, String url) {
        if (Uri.parse(url).getHost().equals("www.packtpub.com")) {
            return false;  //Don't override since it's the same host
        } else {
            return true; //Stop the navigation since it's a different
            //site
        }
    }
}
```

Then, use the following code to set the client:

```
webview.setWebViewClient(new mWebViewClient());
```

How to enable JavaScript

There are many other WebView options we can customize through WebSetting. If you want to enable JavaScript, get `webSettings` from the WebView and call `setJavaScriptEnabled()`, as shown here:

```
WebSettings webSettings = webview.getSettings();
webSettings.setJavaScriptEnabled(true);
```

Enable built-in zoom

Another `webSettings` option is `setBuiltInZoomControls()`. Continuing from the preceding code, just add this:

```
webSettings.setBuiltInZoomControls(true);
```

Check the **webSettings** link in the next section for a large list of additional options.

See also

- Developer Docs: `WebView` at
  https://developer.android.com/reference/android/webkit/WebView.html
- Developer Docs: `webSettings` at
  https://developer.android.com/reference/android/webkit/WebSettings.htm
  l
- Developer Docs: `android.webkit` at
  https://developer.android.com/reference/android/webkit/package-summary
  .html

Checking online status and connection type

This is a simple recipe, but one that is very common and will probably be included in every internet application you build: checking online status. While checking online status, we can also check the connection type: `WIFI` or `MOBILE`.

Getting ready

Create a new project in Android Studio and call it `isOnline`. Use the default **Phone & Tablet** options and select **Empty Activity** in the **Add an Activity** to **Mobile** dialog.

How to do it...

First, we need to add the necessary permissions to access the network. Then, we'll create a simple layout with `Button` and `TextView`. To get started, open the Android Manifest and follow these steps:

1. Add the following permissions:

```
<uses-permission android:name="android.permission.INTERNET"/>
<uses-permission
android:name="android.permission.ACCESS_NETWORK_STATE" />
```

2. Open the `activity_main.xml` file and replace the existing layout with the following:

```
<?xml version="1.0" encoding="utf-8"?>
<RelativeLayout
    xmlns:android="http://schemas.android.com/apk/res/android"
    android:layout_width="match_parent"
    android:layout_height="match_parent" >
    <TextView
        android:id="@+id/textView"
        android:layout_width="wrap_content"
        android:layout_height="wrap_content"
        android:text="" />
    <Button
        android:layout_width="wrap_content"
        android:layout_height="wrap_content"
        android:text="Check"
        android:layout_centerInParent="true"
        android:onClick="getStatus"/>
</RelativeLayout>
```

3. Add this method to check the connection status:

```
private boolean isOnline() {
    ConnectivityManager connectivityManager = (ConnectivityManager)
                    getSystemService(Context.CONNECTIVITY_SERVICE);
    NetworkInfo networkInfo =
connectivityManager.getActiveNetworkInfo();
    return (networkInfo != null && networkInfo.isConnected());
}
```

4. Add the following method to handle the button click:

```
public void getStatus(View view) {
    TextView textView = findViewById(R.id.textView);
    if (isOnline()) {
        ConnectivityManager connectivityManager =
                (ConnectivityManager)
getSystemService(Context.CONNECTIVITY_SERVICE);
        NetworkInfo networkInfo =
connectivityManager.getActiveNetworkInfo();
        textView.setText(networkInfo.getTypeName());
    } else {
        textView.setText("Offline");
    }
}
```

5. You're ready to run the application on a device or emulator.

How it works...

We created the isOnline() method to make it easy to reuse this code.

To check the status, we get an instance of ConnectivityManager to read the NetworkInfo state. If it reports we are connected, we get the name of the active network by calling getType(), which returns one of the following constants:

- TYPE_MOBILE
- TYPE_WIFI
- TYPE_WIMAX
- TYPE_ETHERNET
- TYPE_BLUETOOTH

Also, see the ConnectivityManager link later for additional constants. For display purposes, we call getTypeName(). We could call getType() to get a numeric constant instead.

There's more...

We can also set it up so our app will be notified when the network status changes.

Monitoring network state changes

If your application needs to respond to changes in the network status, take a look at `CONNECTIVITY_ACTION` in `ConnectivityManager`. There are two ways to set up the filters to be notified of connectivity change events:

- Through the Android Manifest
- Through code

Here's an example of how to include the action in the receiver's intent filter through the Android Manifest:

```
<receiver android:name=".MyBroadcastReceiver">
    <intent-filter>
        <action android:name="android.net.conn.CONNECTIVITY_CHANGE" />
    </intent-filter>
</receiver>
```

Be careful using the Android Manifest as it will notify your app every time the network state changes, even if your app isn't being used. This can cause unnecessary drain on the battery.

 Apps targeting Android 7.0 and later will no longer receive `CONNECTIVITY_CHANGE` when declared in the Manifest. (This is to prevent unnecessary battery drain). Instead, register the Intent Filter through code as shown next.

The better solution (and required for Android 7.0 and later) is to register your intent filter through code. Here is an example:

```
registerReceiver(mReceiver, new
IntentFilter(ConnectivityManager.CONNECTIVITY_ACTION));
```

Take a look at the recipe in the file downloads for an example of logging `CONNECTIVITY_CHANGE` events.

See also

- Developer Docs: `ConnectivityManager` at https://developer.android.com/reference/android/net/ConnectivityManager.html
- Developer Docs: `NetworkInfo` at https://developer.android.com/reference/android/net/NetworkInfo.html

Phone number blocking API

A new feature introduced in Android Nougat (API 24) is the ability to handle blocking phone numbers at the OS level. This provides a consistent experience for the user across multiple devices with the following:

- Blocked Numbers block both incoming calls and text messages
- Blocked Numbers can be backed up using the Backup & Restore feature
- All apps on the device share the same Blocked Numbers list

In this recipe, we will look at the code to add a number to block, remove the number, and how to check whether the number is already blocked.

Getting ready

Create a new project in Android Studio and call it `BlockedCallList`. In the **Target Android Devices** dialog, select the **Phone & Tablet** option and choose **API 24: Android 7.0 Nougat** (or higher) for the Minimum SDK. Select **Empty Activity** in the **Add an Activity** to **Mobile** dialog.

How to do it...

We will start by creating a UI with an `EditText` to enter a phone number and three buttons: `Block`, `Unblock`, and `isBlocked`. To start, open `activity_main.xml` and follow these steps:

1. Replace the existing layout with the following XML code:

```xml
<?xml version="1.0" encoding="utf-8"?>
<RelativeLayout
    xmlns:android="http://schemas.android.com/apk/res/android"
    xmlns:app="http://schemas.android.com/apk/res-auto"
    xmlns:tools="http://schemas.android.com/tools"
    android:layout_width="match_parent"
    android:layout_height="match_parent"
    tools:context=".MainActivity">
<EditText
    android:id="@+id/editTextNumber"
    android:layout_width="wrap_content"
    android:layout_height="wrap_content"
    android:inputType="phone"
    android:ems="10"
```

```
            android:layout_alignParentTop="true"
            android:layout_centerHorizontal="true"
            android:layout_marginTop="36dp" />
        <Button
            android:id="@+id/buttonblock"
            android:layout_width="wrap_content"
            android:layout_height="wrap_content"
            android:text="Block"
            android:layout_above="@+id/buttonUnblock"
            android:layout_centerHorizontal="true"
            android:onClick="onClickBlock"/>
        <Button
            android:id="@+id/buttonUnblock"
            android:layout_width="wrap_content"
            android:layout_height="wrap_content"
            android:text="Block"
            android:layout_centerVertical="true"
            android:layout_centerHorizontal="true"
            android:onClick="onClickUnblock"/>
        <Button
            android:id="@+id/buttonIsBlocked"
            android:layout_width="wrap_content"
            android:layout_height="wrap_content"
            android:text="isBlocked"
            android:layout_below="@+id/buttonUnblock"
            android:layout_centerHorizontal="true"
            android:onClick="onClickIsBlocked"/>
    </RelativeLayout>
```

2. Open `MainActivity.java` and add the following code to the class declaration:

```
private EditText mEditTextNumber;
```

3. Add the following line of code to the end of the `onCreate()` method:

```
mEditTextNumber=findViewById(R.id.editTextNumber);
```

4. Add the three methods to handle the button clicks:

```
public void onClickBlock(View view) {
    String number = mEditTextNumber.getText().toString();
    if (number!=null && number.length()>0) {
        blockNumber(number);
    }
}
public void onClickUnblock(View view) {
    String number = mEditTextNumber.getText().toString();
    if (number!=null && number.length()>0) {
```

```
            unblockNumber(number);
        }
    }
    public void onClickIsBlocked(View view) {
        String number = mEditTextNumber.getText().toString();
        if (number!=null && number.length()>0) {
            isBlocked(number);
        }
    }
```

5. Add the following function to block the number:

```
private void blockNumber(String number) {
    if (BlockedNumberContract.canCurrentUserBlockNumbers(this)) {
        ContentValues values = new ContentValues();
values.put(BlockedNumberContract.BlockedNumbers.COLUMN_ORIGINAL_NUM
BER, number);
getContentResolver().insert(BlockedNumberContract.BlockedNumbers.CO
NTENT_URI, values);
    }
}
```

6. Add the following function to unblock the number:

```
private void unblockNumber(String number) {
    if (BlockedNumberContract.canCurrentUserBlockNumbers(this)) {
        ContentValues values = new ContentValues();
values.put(BlockedNumberContract.BlockedNumbers.COLUMN_ORIGINAL_NUM
BER, number);
        Uri uri = getContentResolver()
.insert(BlockedNumberContract.BlockedNumbers.CONTENT_URI, values);
        getContentResolver().delete(uri, null, null);
    }
}
```

7. Add the following function to check whether the number is blocked:

```
public void isBlocked(String number) {
    if (BlockedNumberContract.canCurrentUserBlockNumbers(this)) {
        boolean blocked =
BlockedNumberContract.isBlocked(this,number);
        Toast.makeText(MainActivity.this, number + "blocked: " +
blocked,
                Toast.LENGTH_SHORT).show();
    } else {
        Toast.makeText(MainActivity.this, "User cannot perform this
operation",
                Toast.LENGTH_SHORT).show();
```

```
        }
    }
```

8. You're ready to run the application on a device or emulator running at least Android 7.0.

How it works...

Before we call the `BlockedNumberContract` APIs, we check to make sure we have permission by calling `canCurrentUserBlockNumbers()`, as shown in this code:

```
if (BlockedNumberContract.canCurrentUserBlockNumbers(this)) {
```

If true, we make the actual API call.

 Important: Only the following apps can read and write to the `BlockedNumber` provider: the default SMS application, the default phone app, and carrier apps. The user can choose their default SMS and Phone app.

Adding and deleting numbers from the `BlockedNumber` list uses the standard Service Provider format.

The Update method is not supported; use the `Add` and `Delete` methods instead.

To check whether a number is already in the block list, call the `isBlocked()` method, passing in the current context and the number to check, as we do in this code:

```
boolean blocked = BlockedNumberContract.isBlocked(this,number);
```

There's more...

To get the list of all currently blocked numbers, use the following code to create a cursor with the list:

```
Cursor cursor = getContentResolver().query(
        BlockedNumberContract.BlockedNumbers.CONTENT_URI,
        new String[]{BlockedNumberContract.BlockedNumbers.COLUMN_ID,
BlockedNumberContract.BlockedNumbers.COLUMN_ORIGINAL_NUMBER,
            BlockedNumberContract.BlockedNumbers.COLUMN_E164_NUMBER},
        null, null, null);
```

See also

For more information, see the `BlockedNumberContract` reference documentation: `https://developer.android.com/reference/android/provider/BlockedNumberContract`

Location and Using Geofencing

14

In this chapter, we will cover the following topics:

- How to get the device location
- Resolving problems reported with the `GoogleApiClient` `OnConnectionFailedListener`
- Creating and monitoring a Geofence

Introduction

Location awareness offers many benefits to an app, so many in fact that even desktop apps now attempt to get the user's location. Location uses ranges from turn-by-turn directions, "find the nearest" applications, alerts based on location, and there are now even location-based games that get you out exploring with your device.

The Google APIs offer many rich features for creating location-aware applications and mapping features. Our first recipe will look at obtaining the last known location on the device along with receiving updates as the location changes. If you are requesting location updates for a proximity location, take a look at using the Geofence option instead in the *Create and monitor a Geofence* recipe.

All the recipes in this chapter use the Google Libraries. If you have not already downloaded the SDK Packages, follow the instructions from Google.

Add SDK Packages from
`http://developer.android.com/sdk/installing/adding-packages.html`.

Now that you have the location, there's a good chance you'll want to map it as well. This is another area where Google makes this very easy on Android using the Google Maps API. When working with Google Maps, take a look at the **Google Maps Activity** option when creating a new project in Android Studio. Instead of selecting **Empty Activity**, as we normally do for these recipes, choose **Google Maps Activity**, as shown in this screenshot:

How to get the device location

This first recipe will show you how to get the last known location. If you've worked with the Google Location APIs in the past, then you may notice things have changed. This recipe shows you the latest API for getting both the last location and updates as the location changes.

Getting ready

Create a new project in Android Studio and call it `GetLocation`. Use the default **Phone & Tablet** options, and select **Empty Activity** when prompted for **Activity Type**.

How to do it...

First, we'll add the necessary permissions to the Android Manifest, then we'll modify the `TextView` element to include an ID. Finally, we'll add a method to receive the last known location callback. Open the Android Manifest and follow these steps:

1. Add the following permission:

```
<uses-permission
android:name="android.permission.ACCESS_COARSE_LOCATION"/>
```

2. Under the **Gradle Scripts** section, open the **build.gradle (Module: app)** file, as shown in this screenshot:

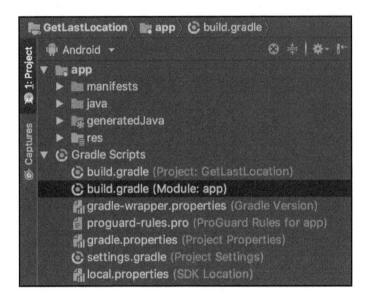

3. Add the following statement to the `dependencies` section:

```
implementation 'com.google.android.gms:play-services:12.0.1'
```

4. Open `activity_main.xml` and update the existing `TextView` with the following XML:

```
<TextView
    android:id="@+id/textView"
    android:layout_width="wrap_content"
    android:layout_height="wrap_content"
    app:layout_constraintBottom_toBottomOf="parent"
    app:layout_constraintEnd_toEndOf="parent"
    app:layout_constraintStart_toStartOf="parent"
    app:layout_constraintTop_toTopOf="parent" />
```

5. Add the following code to the existing `onCreate()` method:

```
if (ActivityCompat.checkSelfPermission(this,
ACCESS_COARSE_LOCATION)
        == PackageManager.PERMISSION_GRANTED) {
    getLocation();
} else {
    ActivityCompat.requestPermissions(this, new String[]
```

```
{ACCESS_COARSE_LOCATION},1);
}
```

6. Create the `getLocation()` method as follows:

```
private void getLocation() throws SecurityException {
LocationServices.getFusedLocationProviderClient(this).getLastLocati
on()
            .addOnSuccessListener(this, new
OnSuccessListener<Location>() {
                @Override
                public void onSuccess(Location location) {
                    final TextView textView =
findViewById(R.id.textView);
                    if (location != null) {
textView.setText(DateFormat.getTimeInstance()
                                .format(location.getTime()) + "\n"
                                + "Latitude=" +
location.getLatitude() + "\n"
                                + "Longitude=" +
location.getLongitude());
                    } else {
                        Toast.makeText(MainActivity.this, "Location
null", Toast.LENGTH_LONG)
                                .show();
                    }
                }
            });
}
```

7. You're ready to run the application on a device or emulator.

How it works...

This code example uses the latest version (12.0.1, as of this writing) of the Google Play service's `getLastLocation()` method. If you've ever used it in the past, you may notice significant changes in how this API works. It's actually much simpler now as all we have to do is call the `getFusedLocationProviderClient()` and pass our listener. Make sure we check the location in the callback to make sure it's not null. (There are several scenarios that can result in a null location, such as the device not having a location yet, the user disabled the location feature, and factory reset.)

The accuracy of the location object we receive is based on our permission setting. We used `ACCESS_COARSE_LOCATION`, but if we want higher accuracy, we can request `ACCESS_FINE_LOCATION` instead, with the following permission:

```
<uses-permission android:name="android.permission.ACCESS_FINE_LOCATION"/>
```

Make sure to check for the appropriate permission in the `checkSelfPermission()` call.

Lastly, to keep the code focused on the Location feature, we just do a simple permission check. In a production application, you should check and request permission as shown in *The Android 6.0 Runtime Permission Model* recipe in `Chapter 15`, *Getting Your App Ready for the Play Store.*

There's more...

Testing the location can be a challenge since it's difficult to actually move the device when testing and debugging. Fortunately, we have the ability to simulate GPS data with the emulator. (It is possible to create mock locations on a physical device as well, but that's not as easy.)

Mock locations

There are several ways to simulate locations with the emulator:

- Location setting through the emulator
- The `Geo` command through the ADB shell

To set a mock location in the emulator, follow these steps:

1. Click the **more** options button (the one with **...** at the bottom of the emulator control options)
2. Select the **Location** tab in the device window
3. Enter the GPS coordinates in the **Longitude** and **Latitude** boxes

Here's a screenshot showing the **Location** tab:

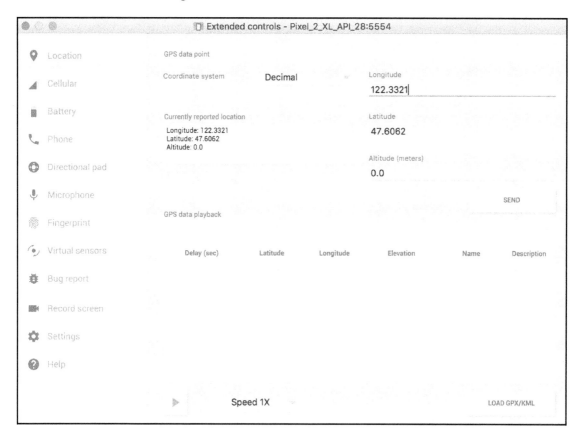

Note that simulating the location works by sending GPS data. Therefore, for your app to receive the mock location, it will need to be receiving GPS data. Testing `lastLocation()` may not send the mock GPS data since it doesn't rely solely on the GPS for determining the device location. Try the mock location with the *How to get the device location* recipe where we can request the priority. (We can't force the system to use any specific location sensor, we can only make a request. The system will choose the optimum solution to deliver the results.)

See also

- *The new Android 6.0 run-time permission model* recipe in `Chapter 15`, *Getting Your App Ready for the Play Store*
- Setting up Google Play Services: `https://developers.google.com/android/guides/setup`
- The **FusedLocationProviderClient** interface: `https://developers.google.com/android/reference/com/google/android/gms/location/FusedLocationProviderClient`

Resolving problems reported with the GoogleApiClient OnConnectionFailedListener

With the constantly changing nature of Google APIs, your users are likely to attempt to use your application, but not be able to because their files are out of date. We can use the `GoogleApiAvailability` library to display a dialog to help the user resolve the problem.

We'll continue with the previous recipe and add code to the `onConnectionFailed()` callback. We'll use the error result to display additional information to the user to resolve their problem.

Getting ready

Create a new project in Android Studio and call it `HandleGoogleAPIError`. Use the default **Phone & Tablet** options, and select **Empty Activity** when prompted for **Activity Type**. Once you've created the project, add the Google Play library reference to the project dependencies. (See the previous recipe steps.)

How to do it...

The first step for this recipe is to add the Google Play Services library to the project. From there, we'll create the classes to handle the Google Client callbacks and use toasts to give feedback. To start, open the **build.gradle (Module: app)** file and follow these steps (if you're not sure which file to open, see the screenshot in the previous recipe steps):

1. Add the following statement to the `dependencies` section:

    ```
    implementation 'com.google.android.gms:play-services:12.0.1'
    ```

2. Open `ActivityMain.java` and add the following lines to the global class variables:

    ```
    private final int REQUEST_RESOLVE_GOOGLE_CLIENT_ERROR=1;
    boolean mResolvingError;
    GoogleApiClient mGoogleApiClient;
    ```

3. Add the following two classes to handle the callbacks:

    ```
    GoogleApiClient.ConnectionCallbacks mConnectionCallbacks =
            new GoogleApiClient.ConnectionCallbacks() {
        @Override
        public void onConnected(Bundle bundle) {
            Toast.makeText(MainActivity.this, "onConnected()",
    Toast.LENGTH_LONG).show();
        }
        @Override
        public void onConnectionSuspended(int i) {}
    };

    GoogleApiClient.OnConnectionFailedListener
    mOnConnectionFailedListener =
            new GoogleApiClient.OnConnectionFailedListener() {
        @Override
        public void onConnectionFailed(ConnectionResult
    connectionResult) {
            Toast.makeText(MainActivity.this,
    connectionResult.toString(), Toast.LENGTH_LONG).show();
            if (mResolvingError) {
                return;
            } else if (connectionResult.hasResolution()) {
                mResolvingError = true;
                try {
    connectionResult.startResolutionForResult(MainActivity.this,
                        REQUEST_RESOLVE_GOOGLE_CLIENT_ERROR);
    ```

```
            } catch (IntentSender.SendIntentException e) {
                mGoogleApiClient.connect();
            }
        } else {
    showGoogleAPIErrorDialog(connectionResult.getErrorCode());
        }
    }
};
```

4. Add the following method to the MainActivity class to show the Google API error dialog:

```
private void showGoogleAPIErrorDialog(int errorCode) {
    GoogleApiAvailability googleApiAvailability =
GoogleApiAvailability.getInstance();
    Dialog errorDialog = googleApiAvailability.getErrorDialog(
            this, errorCode, REQUEST_RESOLVE_GOOGLE_CLIENT_ERROR);
    errorDialog.show();
}
```

5. Add the following code to override `onActivityResult()`:

```
@Override
protected void onActivityResult(int requestCode, int resultCode,
Intent data) {
    if (requestCode == REQUEST_RESOLVE_GOOGLE_CLIENT_ERROR) {
        mResolvingError = false;
        if (resultCode == RESULT_OK
                && !mGoogleApiClient.isConnecting()
                && !mGoogleApiClient.isConnected()) {
            mGoogleApiClient.connect();
        }
    }
}
```

6. Add the following method to set up the `GoogleApiClient`:

```
protected void setupGoogleApiClient() {
    mGoogleApiClient = new GoogleApiClient.Builder(this)
            .addConnectionCallbacks(mConnectionCallbacks)
.addOnConnectionFailedListener(mOnConnectionFailedListener)
            .addApi(LocationServices.API)
            .build();
    mGoogleApiClient.connect();
}
```

7. Finally, add this line of code to the end of the existing `onCreate()` method:

```
setupGoogleApiClient();
```

8. You're ready to run the application on a device or emulator.

How it works...

Most of the code here is standard setup for the `GoogleApiClient` with the main addition of setting up the `OnConnectionFailedListener` callback. This is where the app goes from simply failing, to actually helping the end user get it working. Fortunately for us, Google does most of the work for us by checking the conditions that are causing it to fail, as well as presenting the UI to the user. We just have to make sure to check the status Google reports back to us.

The `GoogleAPIClient` uses the `connectionResult` to indicate possible courses of action. We can call the `hasResolution()` method, as follows:

```
connectionResult.hasResolution()
```

If the response is `true`, then it's something the user can resolve, such as enabling the location service. If the response is `false`, we get an instance of the `GoogleApiAvailability` and call the `getErrorDialog()` method. When finished, our `onActivityResult()` callback is called, where we reset `mResolvingError` and, if successful, attempt to reconnect.

> If you do not have a device with an older Google API for testing, you can try testing on an emulator with an older Google API version.

There's more...

If your application is using fragments, you can get a dialog fragment instead, using this code:

```
ErrorDialogFragment errorFragment = new ErrorDialogFragment();
Bundle args = new Bundle();
args.putInt("dialog_error", errorCode);
errorFragment.setArguments(args);
errorFragment.show(getSupportFragmentManager(), "errordialog");
```

See also

- Accessing Google APIs:
  https://developers.google.com/android/guides/api-client

Creating and monitoring a Geofence

If your application needs to know when the user enters or exits a certain location, there's an alternative to continuously checking the user location: Geofencing. A Geofence is a location (latitude and longitude) along with a radius. You can create a Geofence and let the system notify you when the user enters the location proximity you specified. (Android currently allows up to 100 Geofences per user.)

Geofence properties include:

- **Location**: The longitude and latitude
- **Radius**: The size of the circle (in meters)
- Loitering delay: How long the user may remain within the radius before sending notifications
- **Expiration**: How long until the Geofence automatically expires
- **Transition type**:
  - GEOFENCE_TRANSITION_ENTER
  - GEOFENCE_TRANSITION_EXIT
  - INITIAL_TRIGGER_DWELL

This recipe will show you how to create a Geofence object and use it to create an instance of GeofencingRequest.

Getting ready

Create a new project in Android Studio and call it `Geofence`. Use the default **Phone & Tablet** options and select **Empty Activity** when prompted for **Activity Type**.

How to do it...

We won't need a layout for this recipe as we'll use Toasts and Notifications for the user interaction. We will need to create an additional Java class for `IntentService`, which handles the Geofence alerts. Open the Android Manifest and follow these steps:

1. Add the following permission:

   ```
   <uses-permission
   android:name="android.permission.ACCESS_FINE_LOCATION"/>
   ```

2. Open the `build.gradle` (`Module: app`) file and add the following statement to the `dependencies` section:

   ```
   implementation 'com.google.android.gms:play-services:12.0.1'
   ```

3. Create a new Java class called `GeofenceIntentService` and extend the `IntentService` class. The declaration will look as follows:

   ```
   public class GeofenceIntentService extends IntentService {
   ```

4. Add the following constructor:

   ```
   public GeofenceIntentService() {
       super("GeofenceIntentService");
   }
   ```

5. Add `onHandleIntent()` to receive the Geofence alert:

   ```
   @Override
   protected void onHandleIntent(Intent intent) {
       GeofencingEvent geofencingEvent =
       GeofencingEvent.fromIntent(intent);
       if (geofencingEvent.hasError()) {
           Toast.makeText(getApplicationContext(), "Geofence error
   code= "
                           + geofencingEvent.getErrorCode(),
   Toast.LENGTH_SHORT).show();
           return;
       }
   ```

```
        int geofenceTransition =
geofencingEvent.getGeofenceTransition();
    if (geofenceTransition == Geofence.GEOFENCE_TRANSITION_DWELL) {
        Toast.makeText(getApplicationContext(),
"GEOFENCE_TRANSITION_DWELL",
                Toast.LENGTH_SHORT).show();
    }
}
```

6. Open the Android manifest and add the following within the `<application>` element, at the same level as the `<activity>` element:

```
<service android:name=".GeofenceIntentService"/>
```

7. Open `MainActivity.java` and add the following global variable:

```
private final int MINIMUM_RECOMENDED_RADIUS=100;
```

8. Create a `PendingIntent` with the following method:

```
private PendingIntent createGeofencePendingIntent() {
    Intent intent = new Intent(this, GeofenceIntentService.class);
    return PendingIntent.getService(this, 0, intent,
PendingIntent.FLAG_UPDATE_CURRENT);
}
```

9. Create the Geofence item with the following method:

```
private List createGeofenceList() {
    List<Geofence> geofenceList = new ArrayList<>();
    geofenceList.add(new Geofence.Builder()
            .setRequestId("GeofenceLocation")
            .setCircularRegion(
                    47.6062,  //Latitude
                    122.3321, //Longitude
                    MINIMUM_RECOMENDED_RADIUS)
            .setLoiteringDelay(30000)
            .setExpirationDuration(Geofence.NEVER_EXPIRE)
            .setTransitionTypes(Geofence.GEOFENCE_TRANSITION_DWELL)
            .build());
    return geofenceList;
}
```

10. Create the Geofence Request with the following method:

```
private GeofencingRequest createGeofencingRequest() {
    GeofencingRequest.Builder builder = new
GeofencingRequest.Builder();
builder.setInitialTrigger(GeofencingRequest.INITIAL_TRIGGER_DWELL);
    builder.addGeofences(createGeofenceList());
    return builder.build();
}
```

11. Add the following code to the existing `onCreate()` callback:

```
if (ActivityCompat.checkSelfPermission(this,
android.Manifest.permission.ACCESS_FINE_LOCATION) ==
PackageManager.PERMISSION_GRANTED) {
    GeofencingClient geofencingClient =
LocationServices.getGeofencingClient(this);
    geofencingClient.addGeofences(createGeofencingRequest(),
createGeofencePendingIntent())
            .addOnSuccessListener(this, new
OnSuccessListener<Void>() {
                @Override
                public void onSuccess(Void aVoid) {
                    Toast.makeText(MainActivity.this,
"onSuccess()", Toast.LENGTH_SHORT).show();
                }
            })
            .addOnFailureListener(this, new OnFailureListener() {
                @Override
                public void onFailure(@NonNull Exception e) {
                    Toast.makeText(MainActivity.this,
                            "onFailure(): " + e.getMessage(),
Toast.LENGTH_SHORT).show();
                }
            });
} else {
    ActivityCompat.requestPermissions(this,
            new String[]
{android.Manifest.permission.ACCESS_FINE_LOCATION},1);
}
```

12. You're ready to run the application on a device or emulator.

How it works...

First, we add `ACCESS_FINE_LOCATION` permission as this is required for Geofencing.

Before we can call the `GeofencingApi.addGeofences()` method, we have to prepare two objects:

- Geofence Request
- Geofence Pending Intent

To create the Geofence Request, we use the `GeofencingRequest.Builder`. The builder requires the list of Geofence objects, which are created in the `createGeofenceList()` method. (Even though we are only creating a single Geofence object, the builder requires a list, so we just add our single Geofence to an `ArrayList`.) Here is where we set the Geofence properties:

```
.setRequestId("GeofenceLocation")
.setCircularRegion(
        47.6062,  //Latitude
        122.3321, //Longitude
        MINIMUM_RECOMENDED_RADIUS)
.setLoiteringDelay(30000)
.setExpirationDuration(Geofence.NEVER_EXPIRE)
.setTransitionTypes(Geofence.GEOFENCE_TRANSITION_DWELL)
```

Only the Loitering delay is optional, but we need it since we are using the `DWELL` transition. When calling `setTransitionTypes()`, we can combine multiple transition types using the `OR` operator (using the pipe character). Here's an example using `ENTER` and `EXIT` instead:

```
.setTransitionTypes(Geofence.GEOFENCE_TRANSITION_ENTER |
Geofence.GEOFENCE_TRANSITION_EXIT)
```

For this example, we used the same default latitude and longitude as the emulator. Change these values as needed.

Our call to `Geofence.Builder()` creates the Geofence object. With the Geofence list ready, we call the `GeofencingRequest.Builder` and set our initial trigger to `INITIAL_TRIGGER_DWELL`. (If you change the preceding transition types, you may want to change the initial trigger as well or the creation of our Geofence may fail.)

The second object we need is a Pending Intent, which is how the system will notify our app when the Geofence criteria are met. (Strictly speaking, the Intent service is not required and if your app will only be monitoring Geofence responses while in the foreground, you may not even need it.) Our example displays a toast in response to the Geofence trigger, but this is where you would customize the response for your app.

With both objects created, we get a reference to `GeofencingClient` after checking for the proper permission. Our example only checks for the necessary permission so you need to manually enable location permission through the app settings. A production app should prompt the user as needed. (See *The Android 6.0 Runtime Permission Model* recipe in `Chapter 15`, *Getting Your App Ready for the Play Store* for a complete example.)

There's more...

To stop receiving Geofence notifications, you can call the `removeGeofences()` method with either the `RequestID` parameter or `PendingIntent`. The following example uses the same `PendingIntent` method we used for the notification:

```
geofencingClient.removeGeofences(createGeofencePendingIntent())
        .addOnSuccessListener(this, new OnSuccessListener<Void>() {
            @Override
            public void onSuccess(Void aVoid) {
                //Success
            }
        })
        .addOnFailureListener(this, new OnFailureListener() {
            @Override
            public void onFailure(@NonNull Exception e) {
                //Failuare
            }
        });
```

See also

- The `GeofencingClient` class at: `https://developers.google.com/android/reference/com/google/android/gms/location/GeofencingClient`
- The `Geofence.Builder` class at:
  `https://developers.google.com/android/reference/com/google/android/gms/location/Geofence.Builder.html`
- The `GeofencingRequest.Builder` class at:
  `https://developers.google.com/android/reference/com/google/android/gms/location/GeofencingRequest.Builder`

15
Getting Your App Ready for the Play Store

In this chapter, we will cover the following topics:

- The Android 6.0 Runtime Permission Model
- How to schedule an alarm
- Receiving notification of device boot
- Using AsyncTask for background work
- Adding speech recognition to your app
- How to add Google sign-in to your app

Introduction

As we approach the end of this book, it's time to add the finishing touches to your application before releasing it to the Play Store. The recipes in this chapter cover the topics that can make a difference between users keeping your app or removing it.

Our first recipe, *The Android 6.0 Runtime permission model*, is certainly an important topic, possibly being the primary reason Android went from version 5.x to version 6! Changes to the Android permission model have been requested for some time, so this new model is a welcome change, at least for users.

Next, we'll take a look at alarms in *How to schedule an alarm*. One of the primary benefits of alarms is that the OS is responsible for maintaining the alarm, even when your application is not running. Since alarms do not persist after rebooting the device, we'll also look at how to detect a device reboot so you can recreate your alarms in *Receiving notification of device boot*.

Almost any serious Android application will need a way to perform potentially blocking tasks off the main thread. Otherwise, your app runs the risk of being perceived as sluggish, or worse, completely unresponsive. `AsyncTask` was designed to make it easier to create a background worker task, as we'll demonstrate in the *Using AsyncTask for background work* recipe.

If you want your app to benefit from hands-free typing or voice recognition, take a look at the *Adding speech recognition to your app* recipe, in which we'll explore the Google Speech API.

Finally, we'll end the chapter with a recipe showing how to make your app more comfortable and encourage users to log in with the *How to add Google sign-in to your app* recipe.

The Android 6.0 Runtime Permission Model

The old security model was a sore point for many in Android. It's common to see reviews commenting on the permissions an app requires. Sometimes, permissions were unrealistic (such as a Flashlight app requiring internet permission), but other times, the developer had good reasons to request certain permissions. The main problem was that it was an all-or-nothing prospect.

This finally changed with the Android 6 Marshmallow (API 23) release. The new permission model still declares permissions in the manifest as before, but users have the option of selectively accepting or denying each permission. Users can even revoke a previously granted permission.

Although this is a welcome change for many, for a developer, it has the potential to break the code that was working before. We've talked about this permission change in the previous recipes, as it has far-reaching implications. This recipe will put it all together to serve as a single point of reference when implementing this change in your own apps.

Google now requires apps to target Android 6.0 (API 23) and above to be included on the Play Store. If you haven't already updated your app, apps not updated will be removed by the end of the year (2018).

Getting ready

Create a new project in Android Studio and call it `RuntimePermission`. Use the default **Phone & Tablet** option and select **Empty Activity** when prompted for **Activity Type**.

The sample source code sets the minimum API to 23, but this is not required. If your `compileSdkVersion` is API 23 or above, the compiler will flag your code for the new security model.

How to do it...

We need to start by adding our required permission to the manifest, then we'll add a button to call our check permission code. Open the Android Manifest and follow these steps:

1. Add the following permission:

```
<uses-permission android:name="android.permission.SEND_SMS"/>
```

2. Open `activity_main.xml` and replace the existing `TextView` with this button:

```
<Button
    android:id="@+id/button"
    android:layout_width="wrap_content"
    android:layout_height="wrap_content"
    android:text="Do Something"
    android:onClick="doSomething"
    app:layout_constraintBottom_toBottomOf="parent"
    app:layout_constraintLeft_toLeftOf="parent"
    app:layout_constraintRight_toRightOf="parent"
    app:layout_constraintTop_toTopOf="parent" />
```

3. Open `MainActivity.java` and add the following constant to the class:

```
private final int REQUEST_PERMISSION_SEND_SMS=1;
```

4. Add this method for a permission check:

```
private boolean checkPermission(String permission) {
    int permissionCheck =
        ContextCompat.checkSelfPermission(
            this, permission);
    return (permissionCheck ==
        PackageManager.PERMISSION_GRANTED);
}
```

5. Add this method to request permission:

```
private void requestPermission(String permissionName, int
permissionRequestCode) {
    ActivityCompat.requestPermissions(this, new
```

```
        String[]{permissionName},
                permissionRequestCode);
    }
```

6. Add this method to show the explanation dialog:

```
    private void showExplanation(String title, String message,
                                final String permission,
                                final int permissionRequestCode) {
        AlertDialog.Builder builder = new AlertDialog.Builder(this);
        builder.setTitle(title)
                .setMessage(message)
                .setPositiveButton(android.R.string.ok,
                        new DialogInterface.OnClickListener() {
                            public void onClick(DialogInterface
                            dialog,int id)
    {
                                    requestPermission(permission,
                                    permissionRequestCode);
                            }
                        });
        builder.create().show();
    }
```

7. Add this method to handle the button click:

```
    public void doSomething(View view) {
        if (!checkPermission(Manifest.permission.SEND_SMS)) {
            if
    (ActivityCompat.shouldShowRequestPermissionRationale(this,
                    Manifest.permission.SEND_SMS)) {
                showExplanation("Permission Needed", "Rationale",
                        Manifest.permission.SEND_SMS,
    REQUEST_PERMISSION_SEND_SMS);
            } else {
                requestPermission(Manifest.permission.SEND_SMS,
                    REQUEST_PERMISSION_SEND_SMS);
            }
        } else {
            Toast.makeText(MainActivity.this, "Permission (already)
            Granted!", Toast.LENGTH_SHORT)
                    .show();
        }
    }
```

8. Override `onRequestPermissionsResult()` as follows:

```
@Override
public void onRequestPermissionsResult(int requestCode, String permissions[],
                                            int[] grantResults) {
    switch (requestCode) {
        case REQUEST_PERMISSION_SEND_SMS: {
            if (grantResults.length > 0 && grantResults[0] ==
                    PackageManager.PERMISSION_GRANTED) {
                Toast.makeText(MainActivity.this, "Granted!", Toast.LENGTH_SHORT)
                        .show();
            } else {
                Toast.makeText(MainActivity.this, "Denied!", Toast.LENGTH_SHORT)
                        .show();
            }
            return;
        }
    }
}
```

9. Now, you're ready to run the application on a device or emulator.

How it works...

Using the new Runtime Permission model involves the following:

1. Check to see whether you have the desired permissions
2. If not, check whether we should display the rationale (meaning that the request was previously denied)
3. Request the permission; only the OS can display the permission request
4. Handle the request response

Here are the corresponding methods:

- `ContextCompat.checkSelfPermission`
- `ActivityCompat.requestPermissions`
- `ActivityCompat.shouldShowRequestPermissionRationale`
- `onRequestPermissionsResult`

Even though you are requesting permissions at runtime, the desired permission must be listed in the Android Manifest. If the permission is not specified, the OS will automatically deny the request.

There's more...

You can grant/revoke permissions through the ADB with the following:

```
adb shell pm [grant|revoke] <package> <permission-name>
```

Here's an example to grant the SEND_SMS permission for our test app:

```
adb shell pm grant com.packtpub.androidcookbook.runtimepermissions
android.permission.SEND_SMS
```

See also

- System Permissions Developer Docs: https://developer.android.com/guide/topics/security/permissions.html
- See the following link on how Android 8 (API 26) modified the behavior of how permissions are granted: https://developer.android.com/about/versions/oreo/android-8.0-changes#rmp
- For a Kotlin version of this recipe, see *Runtime Permission in Kotlin* in Chapter 16, *Getting Started with Kotlin*

How to schedule an alarm

Android provides AlarmManager to create and schedule alarms. Alarms offer the following features:

- Schedule alarms for a set time or interval
- Maintained by the OS, not your application, so alarms are triggered even if your application is not running or the device is asleep

- Can be used to trigger periodic tasks (such as an hourly news update), even if your application is not running
- Your app does not use resources (such as timers or background services), since the OS manages the scheduling

Alarms are not the best solution if you need a simple delay while your application is running (such as a short delay for a UI event.) For short delays, it's easier and more efficient to use a Handler, as we've done in several previous recipes.

When using alarms, keep these best practices in mind:

- Use as infrequent an alarm timing as possible
- Avoid waking up the device
- Use as imprecise timing as possible; the more precise the timing, the more resources required
- Avoid setting alarm times based on clock time (such as 12:00); add random adjustments if possible to avoid congestion on servers (especially important when checking for new content, such as weather or news)

Alarms have three properties, as follows:

- Alarm type (see in the following list)
- Trigger time (if the time has already passed, the alarm is triggered immediately)
- Pending Intent

A repeating alarm has the same three properties, plus an Interval:

- Alarm type (see the following list)
- Trigger time (if the time has already passed, it triggers immediately)
- Interval
- Pending Intent

There are four alarm types:

- RTC (**Real Time Clock**): This is based on the wall clock time. This does not wake the device.
- RTC_WAKEUP: This is based on the wall clock time. This wakes the device if it is sleeping.

- `ELAPSED_REALTIME`: This is based on the time elapsed since the device boot. This does not wake the device.
- `ELAPSED_REALTIME_WAKEUP`: This is based on the time elapsed since the device boot. This wakes the device if it is sleeping.

Elapsed Real Time is better for time interval alarms, such as every 30 minutes.

 Alarms do not persist after device reboots. All alarms are canceled when a device shuts down, so it is your app's responsibility to reset the alarms on device boot. (See the *Receive notification of device boot* recipe for more information.)

The following recipe will demonstrate how to create alarms with `AlarmManager`.

Getting ready

Create a new project in Android Studio and call it `Alarms`. Use the default **Phone & Tablet** option and select **Empty Activity** when prompted for **Activity Type**.

How to do it...

Setting an alarm requires a Pending Intent, which Android sends when the alarm is triggered. Therefore, we need to set up a Broadcast Receiving to capture the alarm intent. Our UI will consist of just a simple button to set the alarm. To start, open the Android Manifest and follow these steps:

1. Add the following `<receiver>` to the `<application>` element at the same level as the existing `<activity>` element:

```xml
<receiver android:name=".AlarmBroadcastReceiver">
    <intent-filter>
        <action android:name="com.packtpub.alarms.ACTION_ALARM" />
    </intent-filter>
</receiver>
```

2. Open `activity_main.xml` and replace the existing TextView with the following button:

```xml
<Button
    android:id="@+id/button"
    android:layout_width="wrap_content"
    android:layout_height="wrap_content"
```

```
android:text="Set Alarm"
android:onClick="setAlarm"
app:layout_constraintBottom_toBottomOf="parent"
app:layout_constraintLeft_toLeftOf="parent"
app:layout_constraintRight_toRightOf="parent"
app:layout_constraintTop_toTopOf="parent" />
```

3. Create a new Java class called `AlarmBroadcastReceiver` using the following code:

```
public class AlarmBroadcastReceiver extends BroadcastReceiver {
    public static final String ACTION_ALARM=
"com.packtpub.alarms.ACTION_ALARM";

    @Override
    public void onReceive(Context context, Intent intent) {
        if (ACTION_ALARM.equals(intent.getAction())) {
            Toast.makeText(context, ACTION_ALARM,
Toast.LENGTH_SHORT).show();
        }
    }
}
```

4. Open `ActivityMain.java` and add the method for the button click:

```
public void setAlarm(View view) {
    Intent intentToFire = new Intent(getApplicationContext(),
AlarmBroadcastReceiver.class);
    intentToFire.setAction(AlarmBroadcastReceiver.ACTION_ALARM);
    PendingIntent alarmIntent =
PendingIntent.getBroadcast(getApplicationContext(), 0,
            intentToFire, 0);
    AlarmManager alarmManager =
(AlarmManager)getSystemService(Context.ALARM_SERVICE);
    long thirtyMinutes=SystemClock.elapsedRealtime() + 30 * 1000;
    alarmManager.set(AlarmManager.ELAPSED_REALTIME, thirtyMinutes,
alarmIntent);
}
```

5. You're ready to run the application on a device or emulator.

How it works...

Creating the alarm is done with this line of code:

```
alarmManager.set(AlarmManager.ELAPSED_REALTIME, thirtyMinutes,
    alarmIntent);
```

Here's the method signature:

```
set(AlarmType, Time, PendingIntent);
```

 Prior to Android 4.4 KitKat (API 19), this was the method to request an exact time. Android 4.4 and later will consider this as an inexact time for efficiency, but will not deliver the intent prior to the requested time. (See `setExact()` as follows if you need an exact time.)

To set the alarm, we create a Pending Intent with our previously defined alarm action:

```
public static final String ACTION_ALARM=
"com.packtpub.alarms.ACTION_ALARM";
```

This is an arbitrary string and could be anything we want, but it needs to be unique, so we prepend our package name. We check for this action in the Broadcast Receiver's `onReceive()` callback.

There's more...

If you click the **Set Alarm** button and wait for thirty minutes, you will see the Toast when the alarm triggers. If you are too impatient to wait and click the **Set Alarm** button again before the first alarm is triggered, you won't get two alarms. Instead, the OS will replace the first alarm with the new alarm, since they both use the same Pending Intent. (If you need multiple alarms, you need to create different Pending Intents, such as using different Actions.)

Cancel the alarm

If you want to cancel the alarm, call the `cancel()` method by passing the same Pending Intent you have used to create the alarm. If we continue with our recipe, this is how it would look:

```
alarmManager.cancel(alarmIntent);
```

Repeating alarm

If you want to create a repeating alarm, use the `setRepeating()` method. The Signature is similar to the `set()` method, but with an interval. This is shown as follows:

```
setRepeating(AlarmType, Time (in milliseconds), Interval, PendingIntent);
```

For the Interval, you can specify the interval time in milliseconds or use one of the predefined `AlarmManager` constants:

- `INTERVAL_DAY`
- `INTERVAL_FIFTEEN_MINUTES`
- `INTERVAL_HALF_DAY`
- `INTERVAL_HALF_HOUR`
- `INTERVAL_HOUR`

See also

- **AlarmManager** Developer
  Docs: `https://developer.android.com/reference/android/app/AlarmManager.html`

Receiving notification of device boot

Android sends out many intents during its lifetime. One of the first intents sent is `ACTION_BOOT_COMPLETED`. If your application needs to know when the device boots, you need to capture this intent.

This recipe will walk you through the steps required to be notified when the device boots.

Getting ready

Create a new project in Android Studio and call it `DeviceBoot`. Use the default **Phone & Tablet** option and select **Empty Activity** when prompted for **Activity Type**.

How to do it...

To start, open the Android Manifest and follow these steps:

1. Add the following permission:

```
<uses-permission
android:name="android.permission.RECEIVE_BOOT_COMPLETED"/>
```

2. Add the following `<receiver>` to the `<application>` element, at the same level as the existing `<activity>` element:

```
<receiver android:name=".BootBroadcastReceiver">
    <intent-filter>
        <action
android:name="android.intent.action.BOOT_COMPLETED"/>
        <category android:name="android.intent.category.DEFAULT" />
    </intent-filter>
</receiver>
```

3. Create a new Java class called `BootBroadcastReceiver` using the following code:

```
public class BootBroadcastReceiver extends BroadcastReceiver {
    @Override
    public void onReceive(Context context, Intent intent) {
        if (intent.getAction().equals(
                "android.intent.action.BOOT_COMPLETED")) {
            Toast.makeText(context, "BOOT_COMPLETED",
Toast.LENGTH_SHORT).show();
        }
    }
}
```

4. Reboot the device to see the Toast.

How it works...

When the device boots, Android will send the `BOOT_COMPLETED` intent. As long as our application has the permission to receive the intent, we will receive notifications in our Broadcast Receiver.

There are three aspects to make this work:

- A permission for RECEIVE_BOOT_COMPLETED
- Adding both BOOT_COMPLETED and DEFAULT to the receiver intent filter
- Checking for the BOOT_COMPLETED action in the Broadcast Receiver

Obviously, you'll want to replace the Toast message with your own code, such as for recreating any alarms you might need.

There's more...

If you followed the previous recipe, then you already have a Broadcast Receiver. You don't need a separate BroadcastReceiver for each action, just check for each action as needed. Here's an example if we need to handle another action:

```
@Override
public void onReceive(Context context, Intent intent) {
    if (intent.getAction().equals("android.intent.action.BOOT_COMPLETED"))
{
        Toast.makeText(context, "BOOT_COMPLETED",
Toast.LENGTH_SHORT).show();
    } else if (intent.getAction().equals("<another_action>")) {
        //handle another action
    }
}
```

See also

- **Intent** Developer
  Docs: https://developer.android.com/reference/android/content/Intent.html

Using the AsyncTask for background work

Throughout this book, we have mentioned the importance of not blocking the main thread. Performing long running operations on the main thread can cause your application to appear sluggish, or worse, hang. If your application doesn't respond within about 5 seconds, the system will likely display the **Application Not Responding** (**ANR**) dialog with the option to terminate your app. (This is something you will want to avoid as it's a good way to get your app uninstalled.)

Android applications use a single thread model with two simple rules, as follows:

- Don't block the main thread
- Perform all UI operations *on* the main thread

When Android starts your application, it automatically creates the main (or UI) thread. This is the thread from which all UI operations must be called. The first rule is "don't block the main thread." This means that you need to create a background, or a worker, thread for any long-running or potentially-blocking task. This is why all network-based tasks should be performed off the main thread.

Android offers the following options when working with background threads:

- `Activity.runOnUiThread()`
- `View.post()`
- `View.postDelayed()`
- `Handler`
- `AsyncTask`

This recipe will explore the `AsyncTask` class; since it was created previously, you won't have to use the Handler or post methods directly.

Getting ready

Create a new project in Android Studio and call it `AsyncTask`. Use the default **Phone & Tablet** option and select **Empty Activity** when prompted for **Activity Type**.

How to do it...

We only need a single button for this example. Open `activity_main.xml` and follow these steps:

1. Replace the existing TextView with the following button:

```
<Button
    android:id="@+id/buttonStart"
    android:layout_width="wrap_content"
    android:layout_height="wrap_content"
    android:text="Start"
    android:onClick="start"
    app:layout_constraintBottom_toBottomOf="parent"
    app:layout_constraintLeft_toLeftOf="parent"
    app:layout_constraintRight_toRightOf="parent"
    app:layout_constraintTop_toTopOf="parent" />
```

2. Open `MainActivity.java` and add the following global variable:

```
Button mButtonStart;
```

3. Add the `AsyncTask` class:

```
private class CountingTask extends AsyncTask<Integer, Integer,
Integer> {
    @Override
    protected Integer doInBackground(Integer... params) {
        int count = params[0];
        for (int x=0;x<count; x++){
            try {
                Thread.sleep(1000);
            } catch (InterruptedException e) {
                e.printStackTrace();
            }
        }
        return count;
    }
    @Override
    protected void onPostExecute(Integer returnVal) {
        super.onPostExecute(returnVal);
        mButtonStart.setEnabled(true);
    }
}
```

4. Add the following code to `onCreate()` to initialize the button:

```
mButtonStart=findViewById(R.id.buttonStart);
```

5. Add the method for the button click:

```
public void start(View view){
    mButtonStart.setEnabled(false);
    new CountingTask().execute(10);
}
```

6. You're ready to run the application on a device or emulator.

How it works...

This is a very simple example of an `AsyncTask` just to show it working. Technically, only `doInBackground()` is required, but usually, you want to receive notifications when it finishes, which is done via `onPostExecute()`.

An `AsyncTask` works by creating a worker thread for the `doInBackground()` method, then responds on the UI thread in the `onPostExecute()` callback. Our example uses the Thread.Sleep() method to put the thread to sleep for the specified time (1000 milliseconds in our example). Since we call CountingTask with the value 10, the background task is going to take 10 seconds. This example illustrates that in fact the task is executing in the background since otherwise, Android would display the ANR dialog after 5 seconds.

It's also important to note how we waited until `onPostExecute()` is called before we do any UI actions (such as enabling the button in our example.) If we attempt to modify the UI in the worker thread, the code would either not compile or throw a runtime exception. You should also note how we instantiated a new `CountingTask` object on each button click. This is because an `AsyncTask` can only execute once. Attempting to call execute again will also throw an exception.

There's more...

At its minimum, the `AsyncTask` can be very simple but it is still very flexible with more options available if you need them. When using an `AsyncTask` with an Activity, it's important to understand when the Activity is destroyed and recreated (such as during an orientation change), the `AsyncTask` continues to run. This can leave your `AsyncTask` orphaned and it might respond to the now destroyed activity (causing a `NullPointer` exception). For this reason, it's common to use the `AysncTask` with a Fragment (which is not destroyed on screen rotation).

Parameter types

For many people, the most confusing aspect of the `AsyncTask` is the parameters when creating their own class. If you look at our class declaration, there are three parameters for the `AsyncTask`; they are defined as follows:

```
AsyncTask<Params, Progress, Result >
```

The parameters are generic types and are used as follows:

- **Params**: This is the parameter type to call `doInBackground()`
- **Progress**: This is the parameter type to post updates
- **Result**: This is the parameter type to post results

When you declare your own class, substitute the parameters with the variable type you need.

Here's the process flow for the `AsyncTask` and how the preceding parameters are used:

- `onPreExecute()`: This is called before `doInBackground()` begins
- `doInBackground(Params)`: This executes in a background thread
- `onProgressUpdate(Progress)`: This is called (on the UI thread) in response to the calling of `publishProgress(Progress)` in the worker thread
- `onPostExecute(Result)`: This is called (on the UI thread) when the worker thread finishes

Canceling the task

To cancel the task, call the cancel method on the object as follows:

```
< AsyncTask>.cancel(true);
```

You will need to have the object instance to access the `cancel()` method. (We did not save the object in our previous example.) After setting `cancel(true)`, calling `isCancelled()` in `doInBackground()` will return `true`, allowing you to exit a loop. If cancelled, `onCancelled()` will be called instead of `onPostExecute()`.

See also

- **AsyncTask** Developer
  Docs: http://developer.android.com/reference/android/os/AsyncTask.html
- RXJava for Android is another option and gaining much traction in Android
  development: `https://github.com/ReactiveX/RxAndroid`
- Definitely take a look at the Android Architecture Components included with the
  Android JetPack: `https://developer.android.com/topic/libraries/`
  `architecture/`

Adding speech recognition to your app

Android 2.2 (API 8) introduced speech recognition in Android, and it continues to improve
with almost every new major Android release. This recipe will demonstrate how to add
speech recognition to your app using the Google Speech service.

Getting ready

Create a new project in Android Studio and call it `SpeechRecognition`. Use the default
Phone & Tablet option and select **Empty Activity** when prompted for **Activity Type**.

How to do it...

We'll start by adding a Speak Now (or microphone) button to the layout, then we'll add the
necessary code to call the speech recognizer. Open `activity_main.xml` and follow these
steps:

1. Replace the existing `TextView` with the following XML:

```
<TextView
    android:id="@+id/textView"
    android:layout_width="wrap_content"
    android:layout_height="wrap_content"
    android:text="Hello World!"
    app:layout_constraintLeft_toLeftOf="parent"
    app:layout_constraintRight_toRightOf="parent"
    app:layout_constraintTop_toTopOf="parent" />

<ImageButton
```

```
android:id="@+id/imageButton"
android:layout_width="wrap_content"
android:layout_height="wrap_content"
android:src="@android:drawable/ic_btn_speak_now"
android:onClick="speakNow"
app:layout_constraintBottom_toBottomOf="parent"
app:layout_constraintLeft_toLeftOf="parent"
app:layout_constraintRight_toRightOf="parent" />
```

2. Define the `REQUEST_SPEECH` constant:

```
private final int REQUEST_SPEECH=1;
```

3. Add the following code to the existing `onCreate()` callback:

```
PackageManager pm = getPackageManager();
List<ResolveInfo> activities = pm
        .queryIntentActivities(new
Intent(RecognizerIntent.ACTION_RECOGNIZE_SPEECH), 0);
if (activities.isEmpty()) {
    findViewById(R.id.imageButton).setEnabled(false);
    Toast.makeText(this, "Speech Recognition Not Supported",
Toast.LENGTH_LONG).show();
}
```

4. Add the button click method:

```
public void speakNow(View view) {
    Intent intent = new
Intent(RecognizerIntent.ACTION_RECOGNIZE_SPEECH);
    intent.putExtra(RecognizerIntent.EXTRA_LANGUAGE_MODEL,
            RecognizerIntent.LANGUAGE_MODEL_FREE_FORM);
    startActivityForResult(intent, REQUEST_SPEECH);
}
```

5. Add the following code to override the `onActivityResult()` callback:

```
@Override
protected void onActivityResult(int requestCode, int resultCode,
Intent data) {
    super.onActivityResult(requestCode, resultCode, data);
    if (requestCode==REQUEST_SPEECH && resultCode == RESULT_OK &&
data!=null) {
        ArrayList<String> result =
data.getStringArrayListExtra(RecognizerIntent.EXTRA_RESULTS);
        TextView textView = findViewById(R.id.textView);
        if (!result.isEmpty()){
            textView.setText("");
```

```
                    for (String item : result ) {
                        textView.append(item+"\n");
                    }
                }
            }
        }
```

6. You're ready to run the application on a device or emulator.

How it works...

The work here is done by the Google Speech Recognizer included in Android. To make sure the service is available on the device, we call `PackageManager` in `onCreate()`. If at least one activity is registered to handle the `RecognizerIntent.ACTION_RECOGNIZE_SPEECH` intent, then we know it's available. If no activities are available, we display a Toast indicating speech recognition is not available and disable the mic button.

The button click starts the recognition process by calling an intent created with `RecognizerIntent.ACTION_RECOGNIZE_SPEECH`. The `EXTRA_LANGUAGE_MODEL` parameter is required and has the following two choices:

- `LANGUAGE_MODEL_FREE_FORM`
- `LANGUAGE_MODEL_WEB_SEARCH`

We get the result back in the `onActivityResult()` callback. If the result equals `RESULT_OK`, then we should have a list of words recognized, which we can retrieve using `getStringArrayListExtra()`. The array list will be ordered starting with the highest recognition confidence.

If you want to retrieve the confidence rating, retrieve the float array using `EXTRA_CONFIDENCE_SCORES`. Here's an example:

```
float[] confidence =
data.getFloatArrayExtra(RecognizerIntent.EXTRA_CONFIDENCE_SCORES);
```

The confidence rating is optional and may not be present. A score of 1.0 indicates highest confidence, while 0.0 indicates lowest confidence.

There's more...

Using the intent is a quick and easy way to get speech recognition; however, if you would prefer not to use the default Google activity, you can call the `SpeechRecognizer` class directly. Here's an example of how to instantiate the class:

```
SpeechRecognizer speechRecognizer =
SpeechRecognizer.createSpeechRecognizer(this);
```

You will need to add the `RECORD_AUDIO` permission and implement the `RecognitionListener` class to handle the speech events. (See the following links for more information.)

See also

- **RecognizerIntent** Developer
  Docs: http://developer.android.com/reference/android/speech/Recognizer Intent.html
- **SpeechRecognizer** Developer
  Docs: http://developer.android.com/reference/android/speech/SpeechReco gnizer.html
- **RecognitionListener** Developer
  Docs: http://developer.android.com/reference/android/speech/Recognitio nListener.html

How to add Google sign-in to your app

Google sign in allows your users to sign in to your application using their Google credentials. This option offers several advantages to your user, including the following:

- Confidence because they're using Google
- Convenience since they can use their existing account

There are also several advantages for you, the developer:

- Convenience of not having to write your own authentication server
- More users logging in to your app

This recipe will walk you through the process of adding Google sign-in to your application. Here's a screenshot showing the "GoogleSignin" button in the application that we'll create in the recipe:

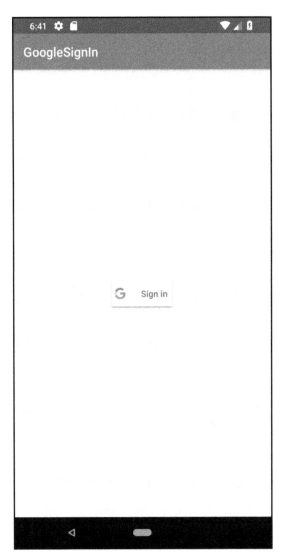

Getting ready

Create a new project in Android Studio and call it `GoogleSignIn`. Use the default **Phone & Tablet** option and select **Empty Activity** when prompted for **Activity Type**.

Google sign-in uses the Google Services plugin, which requires a Google Services Configuration file, which is available from the Google Developer Console. To create the configuration file, you will need the following information:

- Your application package name
- Your signing certificate's SHA-1 hash code (see the *Authenticating Your Client* link at the end of the recipe for more information)

When you have the information, log in to this Google link and follow the wizard to enable sign-in:

```
https://developers.google.com/identity/sign-in/android/start-integrating?
refresh=1#configure_a_console_name_project
```

 If you are downloading the source files, you will need to create a new package name when following the preceding steps, as the existing package name has already been registered.

How to do it...

After completing the preceding *Getting ready* section, follow these steps:

1. Copy the `google-services.json` file you downloaded in the *Getting ready* section to your app folder (`<project folder>\GoogleSignIn\app`)

2. Open the app module Gradle build file, `build.gradle (Module: app)`, and add the following statement to the dependencies section:

   ```
   implementation 'com.google.android.gms:play-services-auth:16.0.0'
   ```

3. Open `activity_main.xml` and replace the existing `TextView` with the following XML:

   ```
   <com.google.android.gms.common.SignInButton
       android:id="@+id/signInButton"
       android:layout_width="wrap_content"
       android:layout_height="wrap_content"
       app:layout_constraintBottom_toBottomOf="parent"
   ```

```
app:layout_constraintLeft_toLeftOf="parent"
app:layout_constraintRight_toRightOf="parent"
app:layout_constraintTop_toTopOf="parent" />
```

4. Open `MainActivity.java` and add the following global declarations:

```
private final int REQUEST_SIGN_IN=1;
GoogleSignInClient mGoogleSignInClient;
```

5. Add the following code to the existing `onCreate()`:

```
findViewById(R.id.signInButton).setOnClickListener(new
View.OnClickListener() {
    @Override
    public void onClick(View view) {
        signIn();
    }
});
GoogleSignInOptions googleSignInOptions = new GoogleSignInOptions
        .Builder(GoogleSignInOptions.DEFAULT_SIGN_IN)
        .requestEmail()
        .build();
mGoogleSignInClient = GoogleSignIn.getClient(this,
googleSignInOptions);
```

6. Add the `signIn()` method:

```
private void signIn() {
    Intent signInIntent = mGoogleSignInClient.getSignInIntent();
    startActivityForResult(signInIntent, REQUEST_SIGN_IN);
}
```

7. Create an override for the `onActivityResult()` callback as follows:

```
@Override
public void onActivityResult(int requestCode, int resultCode,
Intent data) {
    super.onActivityResult(requestCode, resultCode, data);

    if (requestCode == REQUEST_SIGN_IN) {
        Task<GoogleSignInAccount> task =
GoogleSignIn.getSignedInAccountFromIntent(data);
        try {
            GoogleSignInAccount account =
task.getResult(ApiException.class);
findViewById(R.id.signInButton).setVisibility(View.GONE);
            Toast.makeText(this, "Logged
in:"+account.getDisplayName(), Toast.LENGTH_SHORT)
```

```
                          .show();
           } catch (ApiException e) {
               e.printStackTrace();
               Toast.makeText(this, "Sign in
      failed:"+e.getLocalizedMessage(), Toast.LENGTH_SHORT)
                          .show();
           }
       }
    }
```

8. You're ready to run the application on a device or emulator.

How it works...

Google has made it relatively easy to add Google sign-in with their
GoogleSignInClient and GoogleSignInOptions APIs. First, we create a
GoogleSignInOptions object with the builder. This is where we specify the sign-in
options we want, such as requesting email ID. Then, call the GoogleSignIn.getClient()
method to get the GoogleSignInClient.

When the user clicks on the Google sign-in button (created with the
com.google.android.gms.common.SignInButton class), we send an Intent for
GoogleSignInApi to the handle. We process the result in onActivityResult(). If the
sign-in was successful, we can get the account details. In our example, we just get the email,
but additional information is available such as the following:

- getDisplayName(): This is the display name
- getEmail(): The email address
- getId(): The unique ID for the Google account
- getPhotoUrl(): The display photo
- getIdToken(): This is for backend authentication

Refer to the *GoogleSignInAccount* link in the *See also* section for a complete list.

There's more...

What if you want to check whether the user has already signed in?

```
GoogleSignInAccount account = GoogleSignIn.getLastSignedInAccount(this);
```

If the account is not null, then you have the details for the last sign-in.

See also

- Google link for authenticating your
  client: https://developers.google.com/android/guides/client-auth

- **GoogleSignInAccount** Developer
  Docs: https://developers.google.com/android/reference/com/google/andro
  id/gms/auth/api/signin/GoogleSignInAccount

Getting Started with Kotlin 16

This chapter covers the following recipes:

- How to create an Android project with Kotlin

- Creating a Toast in Kotlin

- Runtime permission in Kotlin

Introduction

Kotlin is probably the biggest change to come to Android development in the last few years, since the change from Eclipse to Android Studio anyway. Kotlin was announced by JetBrains in July 2011 and released as open source in February 2012. Version 1.0 was released in February 2016, with Google announcing first-class support for the language at Google I/O 2017. Android Studio 3.0 came with full support for Kotlin already included (and is the minimum requirement for the following recipes.)

Why Kotlin?

With so many existing languages already available, why did JetBrains create another? According to their own announcements, they were looking for an alternative to Java. Since over 70% of their existing code was already in Java, starting from scratch wasn't an option. They wanted a modern language that was compatible with Java. After comparing the many options and finding nothing that met all their needs, they decided to create Kotlin. One interesting aspect of Kotlin is that it was created by developers using the language, and not academics. Here are some of the features Kotlin brings to Android development:

- Simpler, more concise code
- Full JVM support and can be used anywhere Java is used
- Full support included in the IDE, especially since JetBrains is the creator of both the Kotlin language and Android Studio

- Safer code: Nullability built in to the language
- Rising popularity: Many big companies are adopting Kotlin
- Modern language: Offers many features found in the latest language offerings
- More enjoyable: Many surveys are finding Kotlin to have the highest satisfaction rating

Hopefully, these reasons are enough to at least take a look at Kotlin, especially since Java developers can usually follow the code without too much difficulty. As you'll see with the first recipe in this chapter, it's very easy to add Kotlin support to an Android project.

How to create an Android project with Kotlin

Developing in Kotlin couldn't be easier! As you'll see from the simple step here, full Kotlin support is already built into the Android Studio IDE.

Getting ready

Kotlin support requires Android Studio 3.0 or later, so there are no additional requirements needed for this recipe or any of the recipes in this chapter.

How to do it...

It's actually very simple to add Kotlin support to an Android project and you may have noticed the checkbox already. When creating a new project, Android Studio gives you an option. In fact, it's so obvious, you may not even notice it anymore so we'll start at the beginning and show a screenshot. To begin, launch Android Studio and click **Start a new Android project**:

1. In the **Create Android Project** dialog, click the **Include Kotlin support** checkbox, as shown here:

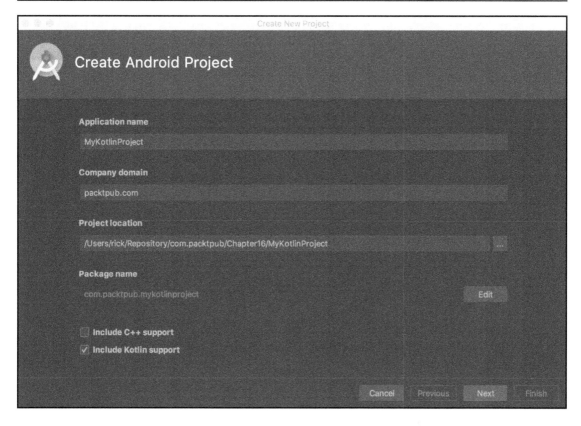

2. That's it! Click through the remaining dialogs and you'll have your first Kotlin project for Android.

How it works...

The IDE already handles everything you need to do to start developing in Kotlin. Even the first Activity is now created using Kotlin code, as you can see when you open the MainActivity.kt file:

```
class MainActivity : AppCompatActivity() {

    override fun onCreate(savedInstanceState: Bundle?) {
        super.onCreate(savedInstanceState)
        setContentView(R.layout.activity_main)
    }
}
```

As you can see, this is very similar to the Java code. Java developers will likely be able to read and at least understand Kotlin code. A few items worth mentioning if this is your first look at Kotlin include that semicolons are not needed for line termination. Another point worth noting is that variable types comes after the variable name, separated with a colon. What about that question mark after `Bundle`? That signifies the variable may be null.

There's more...

If you already have an existing project and want to add Kotlin code, this can be done with the **File** | **New** | **Kotlin File/Class** menu option, as shown here:

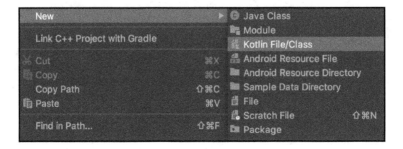

Android Studio (3.0 and above) give two options to easily convert Java code to Kotlin:

1. Open a Java file and select the **Code** | **Convert to Kotlin** menu item.
2. In Android Studio, copy your Java code to the clipboard, then paste the code into your Kotlin file. Select **Yes** when you see the following dialog asking if you want to convert the code:

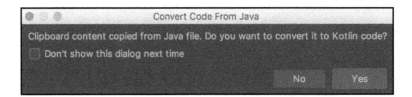

See also

Here are some resources to get you started on Kotlin development:

- The Kotlin website: `https://kotlinlang.org`
- The Kotlin GitHub repository: `https://github.com/jetbrains/kotlin`

Creating a Toast in Kotlin

Toasts are such a useful tool when developing an application, especially when learning a new language, that we're going to revisit the Toast. This recipe will show you the Kotlin way of displaying the very familiar Toast, as shown here:

Getting ready

Create a new project in Android Studio and call it KotlinToast. Use the default **Phone & Tablet** options and select **Empty Activity** when prompted for the **Activity Type.** Remember to check the **Include Kotlin support** checkbox in the **Create Android Project** dialog.

How to do it...

We'll keep this simple by using the default Toast layout and focus on the Kotlin code. Start by opening activity_main.xml and follow these steps:

1. Replace the existing <TextView> element with a <Button> as follows:

```
<Button
 android:id="@+id/button"
 android:layout_width="wrap_content"
 android:layout_height="wrap_content"
 android:text="Show Toast"
 android:onClick="showToast"
 app:layout_constraintLeft_toLeftOf="parent"
 app:layout_constraintRight_toRightOf="parent"
 app:layout_constraintTop_toTopOf="parent" />
```

2. Now, open ActivityMain.kt and add the following code to the existing onCreate() method:

```
val button = findViewById<Button>(R.id.button)
button.setOnClickListener {
    Toast.makeText(this, "First Toast in Kotlin",
Toast.LENGTH_LONG).show()
}
```

3. Run the program on a device or emulator.

How it works...

There's really only two parts to showing the Toast: creating the event listener and calling the Toast itself. We create the event listener using `setOnClickListener`. It's the same concept as in Java, just much cleaner code syntax. In the braces, we have code that will be called. In our example, it's the Toast. This basically looks the same because it's calling the exact same library, as you'll see if you check the import statement:

```
import android.widget.Toast
```

If you've used a Toast in Java, or gone through the *Creating a Toast using a custom layout* recipe in `Chapter 8`, *Alerts and Notifications*, then you'll notice this looks very similar. It is. But you'll also notice it's much simpler and cleaner code. This is one of the big appeals of Kotlin. What if you want to create a custom layout, like the earlier Java example? Basically, it's the same since the resources (the layout XML and drawables) are not Kotlin or Java specific; they are Android specific. So, use the same resources as the previous example.

See also

- *Creating a Toast using a custom layout* recipe in `Chapter 8`, Alerts and Notifications

Runtime permission in Kotlin

Even though the Runtime permission model was released back in Android 6.0 (API 23), this topic still receives many queries. Since it's basically a requirement for all future apps, you'll likely need to implement this in Kotlin as well. Take a look at the previous recipe (see links below) for information on the APIs and this recipe for the Kotlin code.

Getting ready

Create a new project in Android Studio and call it `KotlinRuntimePermission`. Use the default **Phone & Tablet** option, select **Empty Activity** when prompted for **Activity Type**, and remember to check the **Include Kotlin support** checkbox.

The sample source code sets the minimum API to 23, but this is not required. If your `compileSdkVersion` is API 23 or above, the compiler will flag your code for the new security model.

How to do it...

We need to start by adding our required permission to the manifest, then we'll add a button to call our check permission code. Open the Android Manifest and follow these steps:

1. Add the following permission:

   ```
   <uses-permission android:name="android.permission.SEND_SMS"/>
   ```

2. Open `activity_main.xml` and replace the existing `TextView` with this button:

   ```
   <Button
       android:id="@+id/button"
       android:layout_width="wrap_content"
       android:layout_height="wrap_content"
       android:text="Do Something"
       android:onClick="doSomething"
       app:layout_constraintBottom_toBottomOf="parent"
       app:layout_constraintLeft_toLeftOf="parent"
       app:layout_constraintRight_toRightOf="parent"
       app:layout_constraintTop_toTopOf="parent" />
   ```

3. Open `MainActivity.kt` and add the following constant above (outside) the MainActivity class:

   ```
   private const val REQUEST_PERMISSION = 1
   ```

4. Add this method for a permission check:

   ```
   private fun checkPermission(permission: String): Boolean {
       val permissionCheck = ContextCompat.checkSelfPermission(this,
   permission)
       return permissionCheck == PackageManager.PERMISSION_GRANTED
   }
   ```

5. Add this method to request the permission:

   ```
   private fun requestPermission(permissionName: String,
   permissionRequestCode: Int) {
       ActivityCompat.requestPermissions(this,
   arrayOf(permissionName),
               permissionRequestCode)
   }
   ```

6. Add this method to show the explanation dialog:

```
private fun showExplanation(title: String, message: String,
                            permission: String,
                            permissionRequestCode: Int) {
    val builder = AlertDialog.Builder(this)
    builder.setTitle(title)
            .setMessage(message)
            .setPositiveButton(android.R.string.ok
            ) { dialog, id -> requestPermission(permission,
permissionRequestCode) }
    builder.create().show()
}
```

7. Add this method to handle the button click:

```
fun doSomething(view: View) {
    if (!checkPermission(Manifest.permission.SEND_SMS)) {
        if
(ActivityCompat.shouldShowRequestPermissionRationale(this,
                    Manifest.permission.SEND_SMS)) {
            showExplanation("Permission Needed", "Rationale",
                    Manifest.permission.SEND_SMS,
REQUEST_PERMISSION)
        } else {
            requestPermission(Manifest.permission.SEND_SMS,
                    REQUEST_PERMISSION)
        }
    } else {
        Toast.makeText(this@MainActivity, "Permission (already)
Granted!", Toast.LENGTH_SHORT)
                    .show()
    }
}
```

8. Override `onRequestPermissionsResult()` as follows:

```
override fun onRequestPermissionsResult(requestCode: Int,
                                        permissions: Array<String>,
                                        grantResults: IntArray) {
    when (requestCode) {
        REQUEST_PERMISSION -> {
            if (grantResults.isNotEmpty() && grantResults[0] ==
                    PackageManager.PERMISSION_GRANTED) {
                Toast.makeText(this@MainActivity, "Granted!",
Toast.LENGTH_SHORT)
                        .show()
            } else {
```

```
                        Toast.makeText(this@MainActivity, "Denied!",
         Toast.LENGTH_SHORT)
                                .show()
                }
                return
            }
        }
    }
```

9. Now, you're ready to run the application on a device or emulator.

How it works...

Using the new runtime permission model involves the following:

1. Check to see whether you have the desired permissions
2. If not, check whether we should display the rationale (meaning the request was previously denied)
3. Request the permission; only the OS can display the permission request
4. Handle the request response

Here are the corresponding methods:

- `ContextCompat.checkSelfPermission`
- `ActivityCompat.requestPermissions`
- `ActivityCompat.shouldShowRequestPermissionRationale`
- `onRequestPermissionsResult`

 Even though you are requesting permissions at runtime, the desired permission must be listed in the Android Manifest. If the permission is not specified, the OS will automatically deny the request.

See also

- For the Java version, see the *The Android 6.0 Runtime Permission Model* recipe in `Chapter 15`, Getting Your App Ready for the Play Store

Other Books You May Enjoy

If you enjoyed this book, you may be interested in these other books by Packt:

Mastering Android Development with Kotlin
Miloš Vasić

ISBN: 9781788473699

- Understand the basics of Android development with Kotlin
- Get to know the key concepts in Android development
- See how to create modern mobile applications for the Android platform
- Adjust your application's look and feel
- Know how to persist and share application database
- Work with Services and other concurrency mechanisms
- Write effective tests
- Migrate an existing Java-based project to Kotlin

Learning Java by Building Android Games - Second Edition
John Horton

ISBN: 9781788839150

- Set up a game development environment in Android Studio
- Implement screen locking, screen rotation, pixel graphics, and play sound effects
- Respond to a player's touch, and program intelligent enemies who challenge the player in different ways
- Learn game development concepts, such as collision detection, animating sprite sheets, simple tracking and following, AI, parallax backgrounds, and particle explosions
- Animate objects at 60 frames per second (FPS) and manage multiple independent objects using Object-Oriented Programming (OOP)
- Understand the essentials of game programming, such as design patterns, object-oriented programming, Singleton, strategy, and entity-component patterns
- Learn how to use the Android API, including Activity lifecycle, detecting version number, SoundPool API, Paint, Canvas, and Bitmap classes
- Build a side-scrolling shooter and an open world 2D platformer using advanced OOP concepts and programming patterns

Leave a review - let other readers know what you think

Please share your thoughts on this book with others by leaving a review on the site that you bought it from. If you purchased the book from Amazon, please leave us an honest review on this book's Amazon page. This is vital so that other potential readers can see and use your unbiased opinion to make purchasing decisions, we can understand what our customers think about our products, and our authors can see your feedback on the title that they have worked with Packt to create. It will only take a few minutes of your time, but is valuable to other potential customers, our authors, and Packt. Thank you!

Index

A

Action Bar
  Search icon, adding to 151, 153, 154, 155
  setting, as overlay 160
activity
  data, passing 23, 24
  declaring 8, 11, 13, 14
  life cycle 33, 34, 36
  result, returning 25, 27
  starting, with intent object 14, 17, 18
  state, saving 27, 29, 30, 31
  switching between 18, 20, 22
alarms
  canceling 408
  repeating 409
  scheduling 404, 408
AlertDialog
  custom layout 212
  icon, adding 211
  list, using 211
  message box, displaying 209, 210, 211
Android 6.0 Runtime Permission Model 400, 401, 404
Android Manifest
  about 14
  OpenGL ES, declaring 310
Android N
  external storage, accessing with scoped directories 195, 197
Android project
  creating, with Kotlin 426, 428
Android Sensor Framework
  about 250
  events, using 254, 256
  reference link 253
animated image (GIF/WebP)
  displaying, with ImageDecoder library 298, 299, 300
animation resources
  reference link 274
app full-screen
  displaying 156, 157, 159
App Widget Design Guidelines
  reference link 150
Application Not Responding (ANR) 190, 269, 412
AsyncTask
  canceling 415
  parameter types 415
  using, for background work 412, 414
audio
  playing, with MediaPlayer 332, 334, 336
AudioManager
  used, for checking hardware type 340

B

background work
  AsyncTask, using 412
button state
  showing, with graphics 66, 67, 69

C

cache folder
  using 169
camera View
  applying, while drawing 317, 320
Camera2 API
  camera preview, setting up 352
  image, capturing 353
  used, for taking picture 345, 348, 351, 352, 353
card flip animation
  creating, with Fragment 285, 286, 289, 291
circle image
  creating, with ImageDecoder 301, 303, 305

click events
  listening for 238, 240
compass
  creating, with RotateAnimation 275, 278, 279
  creating, with sensor data 275, 278, 279
connection type
  checking 372, 374
contextual action bar (CAB) 97
contextual action mode
  enabling, for view 97, 100, 101
contextual batch mode
  using, with RecyclerView 101, 103, 106
custom component
  creating 71, 74
custom layout
  used, for creating Toast 205, 207, 209

D

data
  accessing, in background with Loader 190, 194
  passing, between Fragment 121, 124, 128, 130,
    132
  passing, to activity 23, 24
  storing 162, 164, 165, 166
default camera app
  used, for taking photo 341, 343
default video app
  calling 344
designated folders
  using, for screen-specific resources 69
device boot
  notification, receiving 409, 411
device location
  obtaining 383, 384, 386, 388
device orientation
  current device rotation, obtaining 260
  reading 258, 260
drawable animation 263

E

emulator
  used, for setting mock location 386
environment sensors 256
existing SMS messages
  reading 368

external storage
  accessing, with scoped directories in Android N
    195, 197
  available space, checking 175
  directories, working with 175
  file, deleting 175
  files, preventing from being included in galleries
    175
  public folders, obtaining 174
  text file, reading to 170, 173
  text file, writing to 170, 173

F

Flashlight
  creating, with Heads-Up Notification 227, 228,
    230, 231
floating context menu
  creating 97
Fragment back stack
  handling 132, 136, 137
Fragment
  adding, during runtime 116, 117, 120
  callbacks 114
  creating 113, 116
  data, passing between 121, 124, 128, 131, 132
  used, for creating card flip animation 285, 286,
    289, 291
  using 113, 116

G

Geofence
  creating 392, 394, 397
  monitoring 392, 394, 397
gestures
  recognizing 240, 242
GLSurfaceView.Renderer class
  creating 310
GLSurfaceView
  shapes, drawing 311, 313, 316
Google sign-in
  adding 419, 421, 424
GoogleApiClient OnConnectionFailedListener
  reported problems, resolving 388, 390, 392
graphics
  using, to show button state 66, 67, 69

GridLayout 46, 48, 51

H

hardware media controls
  responding to 337, 339
Heads-Up Notification
  Flashlight, creating 227, 228, 230, 231
Home screen widget
  creating 142, 143, 144, 146, 148, 149, 150
Home screen
  shortcut, creating on 140, 141, 142

I

ImageDecoder library
  used, for creating circle image 301, 303, 305
  used, for displaying animated image (GIF/WebP)
  298, 299, 300
images
  scaling down 265, 267, 269
Immersive Mode 156
inheritance 77
intent object
  used, for starting activity 14, 17, 18
internal storage
  text file, reading to 167, 169
  text file, writing to 167, 169

K

Kotlin
  need for 425
  runtime permission 431, 434
  Toast, creating 429, 431
  used, for creating Android project 426, 428

L

layout
  about 37
  defining 38, 40
  inflating 38, 40
  properties, changing during runtime 56, 58
  widget, inserting 61, 63, 66
limitations, Android Transition Framework
  AdapterView 271
  SurfaceView 270

TextureView 271
TextView 270
LinearLayout
  using 44, 45, 46
Loader
  used, for accessing data in background 190,
  194
long-press events
  listening for 238, 240

M

Media Player Notification
  creating 223, 226, 227
MediaPlayer
  hardware volume keys, used for controlling app's
    audio volume 337
  used, for playing audio 332, 334, 336
  used, for playing music in background 336
menu items
  grouping 92
  modifying, during runtime 93, 96
  using, to launch an activity 91
menus
  modifying, during runtime 93, 96
message box
  displaying, with AlertDialog 209, 210, 211
mock locations
  setting 386
motion sensors 257
multi-touch gestures
  used, for pinch-to-zoom 243, 244, 245
multipart messages
  sending 364

N

network state changes
  monitoring 375
Notifications
  button, adding with addAction() 219
  expanded notifications 220, 222
  lock screen notifications 222
  using, for actions 215, 216, 218, 219
  using, for lights 215, 216, 218, 219
  using, for Sound Redux 215, 216, 218, 219
  with Direct Reply 233, 235

O

online status
 checking 372, 374
Open Graphics Library for Embedded Systems
   (OpenGL ES)
 about 307
 declaring, in Android Manifest 310
 setRenderMode() option 323
OpenGL ES environment
 setting up 308, 309
OpenGL Shading Language (GLSL) 312
OpenGL SurfaceView class
 creating, by extending GLSurfaceView 310
options menu
 creating 86, 89, 91
 submenus, creating 92

P

persistent activity data
 preference file, using 32
 storing 31, 32
phone call
 events, monitoring 358, 360
 making 356, 357
phone number blocking API 376, 377, 379
photo
 taking, with default camera app 341, 343
picture
 taking, with Camera2 API 345, 348, 351, 352,
   353
pinch-to-zoom
 with multi-touch gestures 243, 244, 245
pop-up menu
 creating 108, 110
position sensors 257
progress dialog
 displaying 212, 214, 215
projection
 applying, while drawing 317, 320
property animation 263
Protocol Data Unit (PDU)
 reference link 369

R

RecyclerView
 contextual batch mode, using 101, 103, 106
 replacing, with ListView 51, 53, 56
RelativeLayout
 using 41, 43
RemoteViews
 reference 150
Request Code 27
resource files
 including, in project 176, 178, 181
RotateAnimation
 used, for creating compass 275, 278, 279

S

scenes
 defining 270, 272, 274
scoped directories
 used, for accessing external storage in Android
   N 195, 197
screen-specific resources
 designated folders, using 69
Search icon
 adding, to Action Bar 151, 153, 154, 155
sensor data
 reading 254, 256
 used, for creating compass 275, 278, 279
sensors
 environment sensors 256
 listing 249, 252
 motion sensors 257
 position sensors 257
setRenderMode() option 323
shapes
 drawing, on GLSurfaceView 311, 313, 316
shortcut
 creating, on Home screen 140, 141, 142
 removing 142
slideshow
 creating, with ViewPager 280, 282, 284
SMS messages
 delivery status notification 364
 receiving 365, 366, 368
 sending 360, 362, 363

sound effects
  playing, with SoundPool 328, 329, 332
SoundBible.com
  references 329
SoundPool
  used, for playing sound effects 328, 329, 332
speech recognition
  adding 416, 419
SQLite database
  creating 182, 184, 188
  upgrading 189
  using 182, 184, 188
Sticky Immersion 159
Storage Access Framework (SAF)
  reference link 197
style
  applying, to View 75, 77
  turning, into theme 78, 79, 80
Swipe-to-Refresh gesture 246, 247, 249
System UI
  dimming 159

T

TableLayout 46, 48, 51
tables
  creating 46, 48, 51
tap
  recognizing 240, 242
text file
  reading, to external storage 170, 173
  reading, to internal storage 167, 169
  writing, to external storage 170, 173
  writing, to internal storage 167, 169
theme
  selecting, based on Android version 80, 82, 83
Toast
  creating, with custom layout 205, 207, 209
transition animation
  applying 270, 272, 274
  used, for creating zoom animation 291, 293, 296

translucent system bars 160
triangle
  moving, with rotation 320, 322
  rotating, with user input 323, 325, 326
types, Menu API
  action bar 85
  ContextualMode 85
  options menu 85
  pop-up menu 85

U

user input
  used, for rotating triangle 323, 325, 326
users
  alerting, action used 200, 202, 204
  alerting, lights used 200, 202, 204
  alerting, Sound Redux used 200, 202, 204

V

view animation 263
View
  style, applying 75, 77
ViewPager
  used, for creating setup wizard 284
  used, for creating slideshow 280, 282, 284

W

web page
  built-in zoom, enabling 372
  displaying 369, 371
  JavaScript, enabling 372
  navigation, controlling 371
widget
  creating, at runtime 70, 71
  inserting, into layout 61, 63, 66

Z

zoom animation
  creating, with transition animation 291, 293, 296
  default duration, obtaining 297